Using Early Memories in Psychotherapy

Using Early Memories in Psychotherapy

Roadmaps to Presenting Problems and Treatment Impasses

Michael Karson

JASON ARONSON

Lanham • Boulder • New York • Toronto • Oxford

A JASON ARONSON BOOK

ROWMAN & LITTLEFIELD PUBLISHERS, INC.

Published in the United States of America
by Rowman & Littlefield Publishers, Inc.
A wholly owned subsidary of The Rowman & Littlefield Publishing Group, Inc.
4501 Forbes Boulevard, Suite 200, Lanham, Maryland 20706
www.rowmanlittlefield.com

PO Box 317
Oxford
OX2 9RU, UK

British Library Cataloguing in Publication Information Available

Library of Congress Cataloging-in-Publication Data

Karson, Michael.
  Using early memories in psychotherapy : roadmaps to presenting problems and
  treatment impasses / Michael Karson.
     p. cm.
  "A Jason Aronson book."
  Includes bibliographical references (p. 217) and index.
  ISBN-10: 0-7657-0395-5 (cloth : alk. paper)
  ISBN-13: 978-0-7657-0395-8
  ISBN-10: 0-7657-0396-3 (pbk. : alk. paper)
  ISBN-13: 978-0-7657-0396-5
  1. Early memories. 2. Recollection (Psychology). 3. Psychotherapy. I. Title.

  BF378.E17K37 2006
  616.89'14—dc22   2005033947

Printed in the United States of America

⊗™ The paper used in this publication meets the minimum requirements of American
National Standard for Information Sciences—Permanence of Paper for Printed Library
Materials, ANSI/NISO Z39.48-1992.

For Janna, redeemer of accidents

And how could I bear to be human if humans were not also creators and guessers of riddles and redeemers of accidents?

—Nietzsche, *Thus Spake Zarathustra*

Those shadowy recollections,
Which, be they what they may,
Are yet the fountain light of all our day,
Are yet a master light of all our seeing.

— Wordsworth

What has been is what will be.

— Ecclesiastes

A human life, I think, should be well rooted in some spot of a native land, where it may get the love of tender kinship for the face of earth, for the labours men go forth to, for the sounds and accents that haunt it, for whatever will give that early home a familiar unmistakable difference amidst the future widening of knowledge: a spot where the definiteness of early memories may be inwrought with affection, and kindly acquaintance with all neighbours, even to the dogs and donkeys, may spread not by sentimental effort and reflection, but as a sweet habit of the blood.

—George Eliot, *Daniel Deronda*

Contents

Contents

Preface

Every therapist needs some sort of guidance, some way to make sense of people and their problems, some way of thinking about the therapy process. Clinical theory meets this need, as do standardized treatments, generic techniques, and plain old habits. If anxiety is the feeling that accompanies not knowing what to do, then a theoretical orientation or a technical approach, at the least, can tell us what to do. The difficulty is that orientations and approaches are often selected according to the tradition in which the therapist was trained and not according to what best suits the patient and the problem. I like therapists who employ a range of treatment options and choose one according to what might work with this *particular* patient's *particular* problem.

Particularity, though, is not highly valued in contemporary psychology. Some clinical scientists advocate manualized or standardized treatments, Procrustean hospital beds that ignore individual differences. Journals reveal what amounts to a fetish for statistical significance and hypothesis testing, for abstracting behavior *from* its context as opposed to understanding behavior *in* its context. Assessment psychologists are increasingly focused on normed tests, as if typical cases are more relevant than the cases at hand, as if a comparison of patients to most people tells us more about them than understanding them in the contexts of their own lives and situations. Clinicians hear a lot more about how to treat a typical trauma survivor (or bulimic or phobic or what have you) than a particular one.

In wanting each therapy I conduct to have its own guidelines, metaphors, key terms, and goals, I have turned to material from the patient for these components. For reasons explained in chapter 1, along with two extended clinical examples reported in chapter 2, I think early memories are particularly well suited for these functions. In chapters 3 and 4, I present theoretical background for understanding memory in general and early memories in particular. My emphasis is on the implications of understanding memory, that is, remembering, as a behavior, rather than as a storehouse of events. The meaning of an act of remembering, like the meaning of any behavior, must account for the context in which it occurred. Chapter 5 reviews the work of the main contributors to the clinical use of early memories: Freud, Adler, Mayman, and Bruhn.

In chapter 6, I discuss the theoretical problems involved in inferring character from specific incidents, which underlies my situation-specific approach to their use in therapy. Chapter 7 integrates systemic, behavioral, and psychoanalytic ideas about the individual, setting the stage for my step-by-step interpretive approach, which is presented in chapters 8 and 9. In chapters 10 through 13, I consider specific therapeutic applications, including the use of early memories in enhancing the working alliance, forming a therapeutic relationship, understanding presenting problems, and resolving treatment impasses. The final chapter discusses the *use* of early memories in therapy, as opposed to merely talking about them.

My approach to theoretical orientations is integrative. Like Skinner, I interpret the behaviors of both patient and therapist in functional relation to the occasioning environment; for both parties, the most salient aspect of that environment is usually the other person. Like Bateson, I conceptualize therapy as a system, with complementary, symmetrical, and interlocking features. Like psychoanalysts, I think the relationship between patient and therapist provides the leverage needed for change.

I believe that the appropriate response to a therapist who asks, "What do I do in this kind of situation?" is "Tell me about *your* situation." Sure, some rules make good starting points if used flexibly, but in my experience, when the treatment relationship gets sticky (when the patient is not viewing us as the benign mentor we would like to be), we tend too quickly to look to the rulebook and not to what is in front of us. Rather than learn rules of conduct and apply them across the board, we should learn skills in response to specific situations and then identify similar situations for their employment.

Regarding the text, I have used *he* sometimes and *she* sometimes, rather than *he or she*, switching between the two for the sake of clarity and readability. Also for readability, I have frequently omitted *in my opinion, one way of understanding this might be*, and *a tentative formulation of what is going on might include*, where I think such sentiments are obvious or implied.

Good English is not conducive to behavioristic or systemic concepts. Good English uses active verbs, distinguishes verbs from subjects, and generally insists on a subject who initiates the action. Behaviorism, systems theory, and Darwinism all would be best expressed in a passive voice where action occurs without being initiated, and where subjects, verbs, and objects are interlinked. Our language reflects the way our species conceived of causality for its first two hundred thousand years, not the way leading theorists conceive of it now. In trying to write a readable book about ideas not well suited to readable language, I have as much as I could stand to do favored readability. For example, I have used the word *potentiation* less frequently than I might have done, in discussing how reinforcers become reinforcers and punishers punishers. Instead of saying that for a given individual certain events potentiated his mother's anger as reinforcing, I say that those events led him to experience his mother's anger as a positive occurrence. Behaviorists will recognize that the substitution emphasizes him, his experience, and the tricky word, positive, whereas the relevant action is between events and his mother's expressions of anger in his presence. Many of the ideas in this book could advantageously be translated into proper behavioristic and systemic language.

Acknowledgments

If Isaac Newton "stood on the shoulders of giants" to see farther than others, perhaps in my effort to take a closer look at therapy, I have been aided by sitting on a few laps. Martin Mayman got me interested in early memories, in the therapy relationship, and in myself. His cordial, welcoming laughter has been with me throughout this project. Edward Bordin's elfin eyes and Howard Wolowitz's prodding authenticity have also been sources of encouragement.

The psychology in this book evolved from long conversations with, among others, Janna Goodwin, Steve Bloomfield, Lyndy Pye, Debra Call, Christine Kline, and Carol Hart, not to mention one-way conversations with Skinner, Bateson, Horney, Klein, Watzlawick, Freud, Madanes, and, though I still hate to admit it, Jung. My new colleagues at the University of Denver's Graduate School of Professional Psychology have engaged my thinking about therapy individually and severally by maintaining their emotional investment in clinical work and their intellectual curiosity. Substantive dialogues reflected in this book include those with Peter Buirski, Fernand Lubuguin, John McNeill, Jonathan Shedler, and Shelly Smith-Acuña. Judy Farmer, Lavita Nadkarni, and my students at DU have helped me think about how to explain my approach to early memories. Shawn Smith read the manuscript and gave me good advice.

My mentors never made much effort to distinguish the personal from the professional, and I would feel foolish if I tried. Max, Ethan, and Tara energize my life, and Janna—colleague, crony, sweetheart—creates contexts in which that energy shines. Janna read the manuscript with her usual perspicacity and talent, offering many "notes." You can't imagine what a lucky so-and-so I am to know her.

I am grateful to the many patients and assessment subjects whose memories appear in this book. Their stories have been changed slightly by me to disguise their identities while still expressing their essences, as of course their stories were changed by them for the same purpose.

Chapter One

Why Early Memories?

What's past is prologue.

—Shakespeare, Antonio in *The Tempest*

Why, of all the things that might occur to us when we think of childhood, do we mention a few particular memories? Why, of all the things that happened to us as children, do we rehearse and remember the stories and images that we do? Why, of all the things our parents did to us and with us and for us, do we cling to certain ones?

One answer is that the memories we produce constitute a personal narrative that makes sense of our lives. Good feelings and positive events, on the one hand, can be placed in a context that makes them seem as if we deserved them and as if they help define who we are. Such a context may also include important information about how to repeat desirable experiences. If we constantly feel bad in some way, on the other hand, then it exacerbates our anxiety not to have any explanation or reason for it. A personal narrative can provide a reason for bad feelings, whether by assigning blame for them or by deriving a lesson from them. Whether accurate or wholly idiosyncratic, an explanation can reduce anxiety if it helps us to "resolve puzzlement" (Skinner, 1987).

Much of the private activity—thinking and imagining—that occupies us as we move through our lives is in the service of constructing personal narratives that both account for reality and put us in desirable roles within the account. Psychopathology can be productively thought of as an inability to strike a balance, such that the narrative is either unrealistic or the role for the self is undesirable, a sacrifice either of reasonableness or of self-sympathy. In this view, therapy helps patients construct personal narratives that are realistic *and* beneficent, largely by placing lamentable conduct in systemic, behavioral, and

1

developmental contexts. Thus, our bad memories justify and explain our bad feelings and negative self-appraisals in ways that are acceptable to us. Memories may also contain some personal lore as to when to expect good or bad outcomes and how to obtain or avoid them.

If we assume for the moment that the events narrated in our memories never happened, why would these particular stories and images occur to us when we think about our childhoods? The answer is the same. The memories of our childhoods, even if they never happened, constitute a personal narrative that makes sense of our world and of the roles we play in it. Such memories, even if they are just the invented ways we are making sense of our lives, are bound to encompass important features of any life problem significant enough to bring us in for therapy.

There are many sources of information about a person's complexes, response tendencies, role relationships, and expectations of others. Early memories are distinctively well suited to the task of acquiring this information in therapy for several reasons. One, they are likely to be personally meaningful to the patient in a way that other sources of information may not be. Their meaningfulness to the patient enhances our likelihood of using them to enter the patient's world with the patient's most durable language and symbols for understanding that world. Two, the patient is likely to want to base an understanding of the problem on real events, and the patient is likely to assume that early memories are roughly accurate, especially if the therapist keeps her doubts about accuracy to herself. Three, many of the problems that bring people to therapy are the result of power imbalances between themselves and others. Early memories tend to be filled with material about power imbalances, because they by definition depict a time of life when the person had little power. The same can be said of separation issues: these can be considered to underlie many personal problems, and early memories, almost by definition, depict the stirrings of an individuating self at a time of general dependency. Four, many of the problems that bring people to therapy are former solutions to childhood problems, solutions that have now become problematic themselves. These now-problematic coping strategies represent childish attempts to solve problems. As behaviors of similar vintage and subject to similar shaping over time, early memories can be windows into coping strategies gone bad. Five, early memories are likely to have representations of parents in them, and regardless of how our parents actually treated us, our psychological world tends to be dominated by representations of our parents. Many patients understand their problems in relation to the parenting they received, and depictions of that parenting in early memories makes them seem relevant to patients. Six, the parental relationships commonly found in early memories are analogous to the therapeutic relationship which, like parenting, is charged with guidance, personal closeness, and fiduciary responsibilities. Thus, early memories are often relevant to the patient's experience of the therapy relationship.

EARLY MEMORIES AS ROADMAPS

Patients often come to us feeling stuck. When someone is lost or paralyzed, it is often best just to get going in any direction at all, looking for a path to follow. In such a situation, *any* map will do, even a very bad map, if it suggests a direction and elicits movement. One reason tarot readings, *I Ching*, and astrology remain popular is because they provide maps to puzzling situations that, in turn, occasion movement. The problem with these maps is that they are entirely independent of the person and the problem, like pulling out a map of Tolkien's Middle Earth to get someone moving in Denver. Psychological theories also provide preexisting maps to problems, and sometimes they are relevant to the person and the situation. Good theories are analogous to using the *I Ching* not by casting coins to select one of its patterns as a guide but by reading all sixty-four patterns and choosing the one that fits the situation best. Even better, when it comes to choosing a map, is to ask the lost individual if they happened to have been following a map on their way to getting lost. One can often glean important information and, further, point out where they went wrong and how to get back on track, by examining the map they were using. In my view, early memories are just these sorts of maps.

EARLY MEMORIES AS LITERATURE

I treat early memories as literature, a term I use in a somewhat specialized way. To begin at the beginning with the purpose of words themselves, I agree with those who think that speech and language were evolutionary advantages because they enabled people to learn from each other, rather than having to discover everything for themselves. What people learned from each other through speech may have included for hunter-gatherers the location of a berry patch or the imminent presence of a snake. Modern users of language may learn from others where to park or how to ask for the car keys in a way that maximizes a parent's likelihood of yielding them.

Reading and writing allow for exposure to even more situations than does talking, since the memorialization of speech in text crosses time and space. To read nonfiction is to access information acquired by others. Information about the private world of the individual or about the relatively private world of interpersonal relations is hard to come by and hard to record, but one way around this difficulty has been the use of fiction. Fiction enables us to learn from a vastly larger number of interpersonal attempts than we could possibly be exposed to on our own. We read fiction partly because it is entertaining or enjoyable, but some fiction is read also because it provides examples of interpersonal relating. That is what I mean by literature: writing, film, or drama that, beyond entertainment, captures some truisms about human behavior, so that we can capitalize on the experiences of others and learn how the interpersonal world works.

Reading allows us to be exposed to experiments in interpersonal living without having to suffer the negative consequences of making mistakes. Instead of ruining our own lives, we can watch Tolstoy's Anna Karenina ruin hers. While it is not tailored to our specific circumstances, good literature, versus entertaining comedy or melodrama, is applicable to a large audience.

In this respect, literature functions as myths do in some cultures. Some Apaches, for example, use stories associated with specific places in the surrounding landscape to guide people through life's tangles (Basso, 1996). Religious and cultural myths are often cited by seniors as navigational guides for younger members of the society. Freud (1917c) used one specific myth—that of Oedipus—as a guide to the psychology of most boys, and Gilligan (2002) recently used the myth of Cupid and Psyche as a guide to romantic love. These myths, like literature, presumably have been retained and reshaped to fit situations that members of the culture may face from time to time.

An early memory organizes certain perceived truisms about interpersonal living in a way that, unlike literature or myth, is tailored to the situation of the individual. How this tailoring occurs is described below (see chapters 3 and 6). Early memories are narratives that do not contain timeless rules about interpersonal living that are applicable to many of us; they contain small, tentative, revised rules about one individual's interpersonal world. An early memory would be analogous to having a story like *Anna Karenina* written about oneself: The advantage is that it definitely pertains to one's situation; the disadvantage is that it will have been written by us, not by a Tolstoy. When I say that it is a disadvantage not to have memories written by Tolstoy, I do not mean merely that they are less intriguing or interesting or well crafted than a good novel. I also mean that the writer—the individual—is not as smart about human nature as Tolstoy was. Early memories are literature that is often wrong about its subject matter in some important way.

Literature that strikes one as false is often bad or outdated literature, a poor guide for navigating one's interpersonal life, a faulty text for learning from the experiences of others or from a previous self. But early memories that are wrong in their expectations of how the interpersonal world works are those that most interest clinicians. This is because the kinds of problems that bring patients to therapy are associated with mismatches between their expectations of what works in reality and what actually happens when they try these things, mismatches between the patterns or schemata through which they process their situations and the way things really are.

EARLY MEMORIES ARE NOT ARCHAEOLOGY

What I *don't* use early memories for is to try to figure out what happened a long time ago. For such uses, social science research converges with common sense to suggest that old memories are repeatedly revamped and they are unreliable indicators of what actually happened. Campbell (1998, p. 177) summarizes research on accuracy by writing, "What clients think they recall from that period amounts to a combination of client imagination and therapist suggestion." Client imagination and therapist influence ("suggestion" is too purposeful for me) are precisely what interest me about what is going on in psychotherapy. Client imagination is relevant because of what Skinner (1953, p. 215) identifies, in his discussion of the projective test he invented, as "variables in the behavior of the subject." Skinner notes, "The clinical use of the material is based upon the assumption that these variables—in the fields of reinforcement, motivation, or emotion—are probably important in interpreting other behavior of the individual." In other frameworks besides behaviorism, client imagination is a picture of the world as the client sees it, and discrepancies between the client's view and the actuality of things are bound to be important to anyone who thinks of psychopathology as related to disadvantageous conduct.

Therapist influence, in contemporary psychoanalytic thinking (e.g., Buirski & Haglund, 2001; Buirski, 2005), is not to be eradicated, but to be used. When you stop and think about it, "therapist influence" is all we have going for us. We try to influence our patients to follow our suggestions for achieving their therapeutic goals, whether those suggestions amount to approaching fears, trying out new marital behaviors, or saying whatever comes to mind. Though early memories have been grossly abused as indicators of what happened in the patient's childhood, that does not lessen their value as depictions of what is going on today. By the same token, dreams have been wildly misinterpreted as depictions of the future, but that does not lessen their value as a source of information about the patient's predilections and expectations in the present.

EARLY MEMORIES AS AUTOBIOGRAPHY

Early memories constitute the opening chapters of a person's autobiography (Adler, 1931). A strong—coherent, internally consistent, realistic, beneficent—autobiography can be beneficial in several respects, and using early memories in psychotherapy can garner these benefits. Indeed, merely retelling the story of childhood can bolster the individual's personal narrative. In the psychotherapy of seriously disturbed patients, a strong autobiography opposes the effects of their hallmark characteristic, identity diffusion (Kernberg, 1975, 1984), which may be described as an incomplete, disorganized, or overly variable sense of self. A strong autobiography can counter the effects of identity diffusion by increasing wise behavior, by enhancing self-esteem, by contextualizing emotional reactions, and by facilitating planning over impulsivity.

Autobiography and Wisdom

Seriously disturbed people are unwise. Wisdom, in my view, requires behavior that takes multiple perspectives into account. Multiple perspectives are facilitated by a well-integrated psyche, by flexible and overlapping response repertoires. Seriously disturbed people maintain a rigid, unilateral perspective partly because experiences that challenge it remain unintegrated exceptions for them. The necessary skills for integrating diverse experiences into a complex picture of reality are missing. People have to find some way of managing the kinds of bad experiences that make them seriously disturbed, and one common method is to keep them separate from good experiences. This separateness or *dissociation* is maintained by dispersing the executive functions and the sense of self that for most of us tie our experiences together. Behaviorally, most people develop a strong sense of self because on balance, more good things happen to us than bad things, and all the good things that happen do happen in the presence of the self. If all the good things that ever happened to us happened in the presence of a blanket, that blanket would become very dear to us. For most people, the self becomes dear. When enough bad things happen in the presence of the self, the self becomes aversive, and self-monitoring becomes unpleasant. The result is a weak connection between different kinds of experiences, which interferes with the ability to take multiple perspectives or to empathize with others. A strong autobiography can help the individual reconnect diverse experiences into a meaningful and benign story. The creation of such an autobiography benefits from emphasis on its opening chapters.

Seriously disturbed people are also unwise in the sense that they respond too much to short-term gratifications rather than to remote consequences. Deferral of immediate gratification requires a level of integration and organization that the seriously disturbed psyche lacks. Wise behavior is governed by an assessment of costs and benefits, both short and long term. In *U.S. v. Carroll Towing Co.* (1947), Judge Learned Hand balanced the duty of care owed to others against the expense of taking care by considering what harms are thereby prevented and the probability of those harms occurring. Included in the potential costs of any behavior in a cost-benefit analysis must be the cost of the behavior itself: the ends do justify the means as long as the cost of the means is included in an assessment of the ends. Remote or deferred benefits, reduced by their improbability of coming to fruition, weigh on the benefit side. Seriously disturbed people's ability to weigh the remote benefits of different actions they might take is hindered by their constricted time horizons. Their diffuse sense of identity lets them be defined largely by things that have happened in the last several minutes, and their objectives are often confined to things that can happen in the next few hours. Deferred consequences often, for these people, hardly seem to matter because the distant self that will accrue those benefits does not entirely seem like the same person who is weighing them. A strong autobiography can help, its availability emphasizing the continuity of the self over time and across situations.

Autobiography and Self-Esteem

Seriously disturbed children, coping with what we assume is too much environmental chaos, fail to coordinate successful response repertoires. It is hard to be successful when the environment is unpredictable, and it is hard to coordinate any success strategies that one does manage to develop when the common links between various successes are aversive. In plain English, environmental chaos produces low self-esteem and rage. By *low self-esteem*, I do not mean negative self-description; I do mean the feelings that accompany being a failure. By *failure*, I do not mean failure at love and work; I mean failure at the primary tasks of reliably garnering a smile from one's parents or reliably acquiring a hug. Because as a behaviorist I see low self-esteem as a deficiency of skills, I view as futile any efforts to build self-esteem by avoiding pass-fail scenarios. For example, certain school districts have recently banned the game of tag because the current loser has to be *it*; some little leagues refuse to keep score; and teachers are admonished not to correct papers with red ink because it is experienced by students as criticism. These efforts to avoid contingencies of failure cannot improve self-esteem. Self-esteem is improved by teaching skills: skills require reinforcement, and reinforcement requires the possibility of not being reinforced. Strategies that focus only on building positive self-description founder as soon as the student enters a situation (read *the real world*) that *does* involve failure and success.

People with low self-esteem are often stuck with autobiographies that make sense of their pervasive feelings of failure. They see the world as a pointless or as a threatening place; they see themselves only vaguely, for self-monitoring is no fun when the self that is monitored is so unappealing. Reworking their personal narratives with a therapist cannot improve self-esteem directly, although learning how to do so (a skill) might, and the interpersonal skills acquired in the therapy relationship can also improve self-esteem. What a stronger autobiography can also do for a seriously disturbed person's self-esteem is to change the conditioned reaction to self-monitoring. After repeated experiences that make self-awareness aversive, the therapeutic development of a sympathetic autobiography leads to a more positive view of the self and detoxifies self-monitoring. This process is validated in every death penalty defense. Regardless of the legal standard employed, the true strategy in these cases is to lay out the defendant's biography in front of the jury. The more detailed a biography, and the more coherently it is told, the less animosity we bear toward its main character. In therapy, a more positive view of the self allows for readier application of newly learned skills to new situations, since the common element from one situation to the next is the self. Early memories can play a key role in the development of a more sympathetic autobiography.

Autobiography and the Contextualization of Emotional Reactions

Environmental chaos produces rage in children, secondary to frustrating their attempts to garner nurturance and comfort. *Rage* is one of those psychoanalytic code words for serious disturbance, where *anger* would be used for a healthier person. Rage may be thought of as anger that occurs in a context relatively devoid of alternative responses. *Anger* suggests that some part of the person, a part that cares about social approval or that intends to remain related to the object of the anger, is also operating; *rage* suggests that the angry response is relatively pure. The younger a person is when frustrated, the fewer alternative or contextualizing repertoires there are. I think it is a fair summary of Kernberg's (1975) position to say that it is hard to build an integrated self when one of the figures that must be included is enraged, just as it is hard to develop a good dinner conversation when one of the guests is angry.

Infantile rage produces identity diffusion because of this difficulty of including a significant aspect of the self in a coherent identity. Behaviorally, as noted above, most people experience positive stimuli that transcend most situations and which therefore occasion various private behaviors described as having a core sense of self. Such stimuli include those associated with early caregivers. When these stimuli have become conditioned punishers, the child loses the basis for connecting one situation with another. A strong autobiography produces exposure to these stimuli in mild enough form to make them tolerable (that is, they are being talked about and evoked metaphorically rather than directly experienced) and their conditioned effects can be extinguished. A strong autobiography can also do for the subject's parents what it can do for the subject: put them in a more realistic, and therefore more sympathetic, light.

When something disappointing happens to most of us, we absorb that disappointment into the larger sense of who we are. It becomes a feature of our autobiography, an episode. When the larger sense of who we are is missing, that is, when the identity is diffuse, then recent events do more than affect the individual, they define him. Instead of an autobiography with a variety of events happening to the main character, the character of the autobiographer gets defined according to recent events. When a borderline patient's wife disobeyed him, he would not merely feel impotent and enraged, which implies a separate part of him doing the feeling. He would *become* enraged impotence. A strong autobiography can put feelings into a narrative context.

Autobiography and Planning

If I plan to make you dinner, I want to know something about you, including your dietary restrictions and your culinary preferences. If all I know about you is that you have severe restrictions and strong preferences, but I do not know their specific nature, then I will not bother to plan. Instead, we can pick a restaurant at the last minute. Planning is hampered by not knowing much about the person for whom one is making plans. Identity diffusion produces impulsivity partly because the person doing the planning lacks knowledge about the person being planned for, even though they are the same person. Lacking a solid sense of the people, themselves, for whom they would be planning, seriously disturbed people respond by not making plans. A strong autobiography can teach the person about the person, so that planning can proceed sensibly.

Autobiography and Performance Theory

Performance theory supports the proposition that autobiography, or personal narrative, is restorative. Park-Fuller (2000) notes that "personal narrative has been celebrated for its potential to . . . enable a re-appropriation of voice and reconstitution of self" (p. 21). She emphasizes in particular the value of articulating an autobiography as a way to cope with disease (p. 24). Goodwin (2005) summarizes the utility of arts programs in general, and writing and performing autobiography in particular, for disenfranchised and marginalized people, as follows:

> Applied, expressive and contemplative arts were introduced into corrections well over thirty years ago, the therapeutic effects of artistic engagement having been established through empirical evidence, obvious to advocates and practitioners without statistical confirmation of improved mental health, for example, or reduced recidivism. Within the past decade, numerous studies have clearly demonstrated that participation in the arts contributes to individuals' competencies in many areas; to their sense of "self" as constituted by their art activities, and to their proactive and conscientious involvement in the processes of community-building, maintenance and health (Murfee, 1995; Hillman, 2001; The Commission on Children At Risk, 2003; Van Erven, 2001; Wali, Severson, & Mario, 2002).
>
> At the same time, scholars and practitioners of theatre and dance have shown how knowledge and transformation come through embodied practices of expressive forms, specifically through explorations of physical relationships, movement, the production and interpretation of imagery; through reflection, and through dialogue about the experience of participation in such activities (Boal, 1979; Johnstone, 1981; Shapiro & Shapiro, 2002). Performance theorists have argued, too, that performance subverts authoritative texts, a source of power where power may be in short supply (Conquergood, 1998; Corey, 1998; Langellier, 1998; Park-Fuller, 2000).

The implication is that marginalization or disempowerment, whether political or familial, can be treated by strengthening the voice or the ability to speak one's truth. That ability is further strengthened by a strong sense of self and a justified existence. Early memories can be used to help the patient develop a sense of autobiography and therefore a stronger sense of self and the right to speak directly rather than symptomatically.

Autobiography and Self-Love

In *Thus Spake Zarathustra*, Nietzsche (1891) presents several ideas relevant to the salubrious influence of autobiography. Essentially, he adapts his belief that exercise of the will is a sign of health to Darwin's assault on will as a force in human nature. He outlines a way to use will within the constraints of determinism to better oneself. In this book, more than in any other, Nietzsche writes metaphorically, so much of what follows is my translation of his ideas into contemporary psychology. Thus, instead of *health*, Nietzsche is concerned with becoming godlike, but by *godlike* he means what many of us would mean by psychologically healthy: proactive, unparalyzed by doubt, considerate, and truthful.

What is missing from the Darwinian account, Nietzsche thought, was an opportunity to express one's godliness. His solution was the doctrine of *amor fati* ("embrace your fate"). Nietzsche thought that the will, puzzled by science and doubt, could free itself first by understanding one's past, its forecast of the present, and its trajectory into the future, and then by willing this trajectory to be just as it was, is, and will be. By willing what *is*, rather than what one might *want*, the power of the will is restored, and people assume the position of a god (for whom what is and what is wanted are by definition identical). Santayana (1910) made a similar point about transcendence: "Let a man once overcome his selfish terror at his own finitude, and his finitude is, in one sense, overcome." Dale Carnegie (supposedly) said, more simply, "Success is getting what you want; happiness is wanting what you get."

In the otherwise forgettable movie *Mary Reilly* (TriStar Pictures 1996), Dr. Jekyll suggests that his housemaid, while discussing her abusive childhood, must very much regret the things that happened to her. She replies that she regrets nothing, because all that happened made her into who she is, so she cannot regret her past without regretting herself. This is the essence of *amor fati*: more than an acceptance of the past and of the course of one's autobiography, it is an embrace of these. Logically, perhaps it is unnecessary to point out, disownership of or displeasure with significant features of one's past makes no sense. To believe that I would be happier now if X had not happened (whether X is losing the lottery, being abused by a parent, or being born when I was born) is to believe that the *I* making the statement would remain even if the event had occurred differently. This fantasy of an *I* that transcends its own life is the fantasy of immortality, the preservation of which often keeps people from optimal behavior, since optimal behavior requires accepting the situation as it is rather than wishing it away. As Shakespeare put it, "The dread of something after death . . . puzzles the will, and makes us rather bear those ills we have than fly to others that we know not of." Strong, benevolent autobiographies can help people inhabit their own lives, therein to take effective action, rather than merely wish their lives to be different.

I am not suggesting, of course, that therapy should primarily entail the development of an autobiography, or even that a therapist's stance should be one of inviting the patient to embrace her past. I am suggesting that articulation of an autobiography can be a healthy side effect of any therapy, and I am further suggesting that such an articulation will naturally lead to acceptance and ultimately an embrace. The better we know complex situations, the more natural and even inevitable they seem. A detailed personal narrative leads to sympathy, toward others as well as toward ourselves. Inquiry about early memories and discussion of them can assist in this process, as they are the first chapter in every autobiography.

HOW EARLY IS EARLY?

I raise this topic merely not to avoid it, but there is really no good answer. The question itself presupposes a way of thinking about memory as a storehouse of actual events, whereas my thesis emphasizes memory as a behavior and as a communication. A good answer might be that early memories are those that the individual believes occurred earliest. Another good answer is Mayman's (personal communication, 1972) terse "seven or younger."

Chapter Two

Early Memories as
Guides to Presenting
Problems and Treatment Impasses

When to the sessions of silent thought
I summon up remembrance of things past,
I sigh the lack of many a thing I sought

—Shakespeare, Sonnet 30

CASE EXAMPLE: MAKING BREAKFAST

Sue, a twenty-eight-year-old white woman, was one of the smartest people I have ever met. I do not know whether she was much good at arithmetic or brainteasers, but she had an almost uncanny access to her own intuition. For example, despite my belief that I hardly ever self-disclose as a therapist, she walked in for her session one day after three or four months of treatment and said, "Happy Birthday." I was nonplussed, because in fact my birthday had come only two days before. "How on earth . . . ?" I spluttered. She shrugged and said, "You're wearing new pants that you would never buy."

Her intelligence, she had said at the outset, was half her problem. The other half was what she identified as her "fear of success." She had been reading Matina Horner's research on women—she was the type of person who *read* Matina Horner's research on women—and she realized that she was "only" a third-grade teacher because she was afraid of doing better. Her mother and her sister were highly educated professionals; her father was a college professor at an extremely competitive school. When she announced her intention to major in elementary education, her family had assumed that this was a preface to doing research on how children learn. She reported that they were shocked when she accepted a job teaching in a public school. At the time, she thought she was putting social change ahead of intellectual pretensions, but after five years of reminding eight-year-olds to stow their mittens, she was wondering why she had settled for this.

We had probably covered enough ground to justify starting treatment: Sue had come for help with her dissatisfaction at work, and she had indicated her sense that this was a psychological problem somehow related to her family of origin. I am always hesitant, though, about embarking on a generic therapy. The patient has a psychological problem and the proposed solution is psychological treatment, but how the treatment is supposed to solve the problem is often left unclear. I remember in graduate school, I was interviewing a new patient with my supervisor. He was there to watch or to help, depending, and I intended to run the interview without his input, the better to demonstrate my readiness to fly solo. The session went pretty well until I recommended therapy and the patient asked me how that would help. Against my conscious will, my head swiveled in my supervisor's direction. Maybe *he* could explain to her how therapy helps; *I* was just there to do it.

Later, I would tell my own supervisees that nobody would agree to pay a mechanic if all she recommended was "car repair." "Bring your car around to the shop twice a week until it works." "How will 'car repair' help?" customers might ask. I do not think the mechanic is going to make a very good living if her only answer is, "You said yourself the vehicle isn't working properly. Obviously, it needs repair." And yet this is as good a rationale as most therapy patients get.

To avoid generic treatments, we therapists like to get a specific example of the problem behavior. "But what actually *happened*?" is as central to our ability to help as is "What else have you tried?" Specific examples do not just provide us with more information. They also provide us with a problem that is treatable. Abstractions are not treatable; traits are not treatable; behaviors embedded in situations *are* treatable. Just as Alcoholics Anonymous does not try to keep a member from drinking ever again, but only until tomorrow, we are often better off trying to help a bulimic, say, with her last and her next bout of purging than with her much more daunting purging history.

Sue, though, could not give me much in the way of a specific example of fearing success, largely because she had inferred this fear from her reading and her professional station and had never actually felt afraid of doing well. In fact, she had been an excellent student, and she liked showing off her inferential powers with me and with others. I fell back on the old standby of asking her when she had first gotten the idea of seeking therapy, but she described a scene involving herself and a book on the psychology of women. Discussing her love life, she said that she had been in three relationships of about a year each, but when commitment loomed, she felt the good men were not smart enough and the smart man was not good enough. She denied that any of them had ever felt threatened by her intellect or her potential, acknowledging that this did not fit the profile of "fear of success": this would have implied relationships with men where she felt intimidating or, to avoid feeling intimidating, subdued. Instead, in all of her relationships, men had admired her intelligence and were disappointed when she left.

I was casting around for specifics, for situations in which this supposed fear of success emerged, or for some other way of understanding her professional dissatisfaction. I asked about her memories of early childhood.

I did not just spring this topic on her, perhaps needless to say. I first echoed her reflections on her family members' accomplishments and their reactions to her own vocational choice. I noted her parents' importance to her on the issue of what she was supposed to make of her intellect. And then I asked about old patterns of expectation, specifying my interest in her earliest memories of childhood. Someone as well read as Sue probably did not need any of the dots connected, but I like to connect them anyway. Not connecting the dots—leaps of faith and leaps of insight—can lead to admiration from patients, but admiration just makes me feel queasy. I do not want my patients to admire me. My ideal fantasy testimonial from a patient would be that she found me to be honest, practical, and curious, and *herself* to be brilliant, intuitive, and brave. Sometimes, though, as Sue was soon to discover, I just cannot keep myself from showing off.

Sue said her earliest memory of childhood was "making breakfast" for her little sister. Sue had gotten up early, opened a box of cereal, and was watching the snow fall from the kitchen window while munching handfuls of cereal from the box. When her little sister toddled in, Sue invited her to sit beside her and then gave cereal to her a handful at a time. They talked about making snow angels.

Her next earliest memory was of sitting on the arm of her father's easy chair, reading the newspaper to him. She was proud of this accomplishment and felt very close to him. Her little sister got jealous, and she clamored and whined for attention. Her father told Sue it was important to ignore the whining, so her sister would learn not to interfere.

Several interpretations of these memories present themselves. In this context, *interpretation* can be defined operationally as a restatement of the memory in language that preserves much of the original but which is general enough to make the pattern in the memory applicable to a new situation (Bruhn, 1985; Langs, 1978).The idea is not to pick the *correct* interpretation, but to pick one that is plausibly linked to the matter at hand and that suggests something that can be done about it (Watzlawick, Weakland, & Fisch, 1974). Because the practical emphasis is on usefulness, rather than on stating an abstract truth about what the memories mean, there is nothing wrong with letting our knowledge of the referral question affect our interpretation of the memories, the better to tailor these interpretations to the needs of the therapy.

The first memory might be summarized as follows: when notable achievement is not reached for ("making breakfast" turns out to be digging into a cereal box, not shirring eggs), infantile needs are met (the sister is fed as well), the personal scene seems comfortable and cozy, and a world that could be construed as cold and unwelcoming seems instead to be beautiful and playful. Conversely, when infantile needs are met, there is no need to strive for notable achievement, the personal scene seems comfortable and cozy, and the world seems inviting. In this respect, I treat early memories as a family interchange is treated in family therapy, and a systemic view of such an interchange will punctuate it from various starting points. I will not spell out all the permutations, but because of the potential relevance to therapy, I will note one last one: when the personal scene is comfortable and cozy, infantile needs are met, there is no need to strive for notable achievement, and the world seems inviting. This is relevant to therapy because more than any other element in the system, the comfort and coziness of the personal scene is under my control as a therapist.

The second memory might be summarized as follows: when Sue is in her father's world, she is intellectually capable, excited, and esteemed, but there are infantile needs not being met elsewhere in the system. Conversely, when there are infantile needs not being met, a part of her feels intellectually engaged, and she feels embraced by her father. Or, punctuating the system yet again differently, when she senses a divide between her intellectual needs and her infantile needs, she experiences a father figure who firmly sides with the intellectual needs, and closeness with this figure depends on her agreeing with his priorities. These interpretations of Sue's early memories accept the little sister and the father as aspects of Sue, a treatment that I address more fully in chapter 7.

Together, Sue and I used these memories as roadmaps to understand the lay of the land in which she found herself when wrestling with the presenting problem. We hypothesized that she likes her job, even putting boots on eight-year-olds, when she is not thinking about whether it is a good enough job for her. These periods are like being in the kitchen with her sister, where warmth and nurturance are simple and enjoyable, and there is no parental voice asking whether she has amounted to anything. When something happens to make her take stock of her situation though, the part of her taking stock is like the father in the second memory, with clear priorities dictating that accomplishment is more important than nurturance. The "something" that happens to make her take stock might be Sue reading an article about education and getting into a complex about why she is reading these articles and not writing them. Or it might be realizing that she has developed a clever method of teaching that would be suitable for publication. Once she thinks about publishing, it puts her on the arm of her father's chair, as it were, and she is both excited by the prospect of recognition and troubled by her sense that infantile needs are not being met. Sue suggested that this sense of being troubled sometimes takes the form of thinking about how much she would miss the kids if she stopped teaching, and sometimes takes the form of thinking that she would somehow be exploiting them if she wrote about them. In either case, the fantasy of paternal approval is shadowed by an image of child neglect (i.e., she connects writing about them with leaving them or exploiting them).

One way to divide all therapies is into those that use the therapy relationship itself as the leverage for change and those that do not. Should the therapy Sue and I were starting become a relationship that would change her, or should it be a source of guidance that she could apply to her problems in living? I am all for advice, generic solutions, and confrontation. When I was running a psychoanalytically oriented clinic, I told my staff that my great fear was that one day someone would knock on the door and ask how to get downtown, and we would put him in therapy for two years to find the *downtown* within. But the problem is that advice and generic solutions often do not work, largely because they have already been tried. Before seeking therapy, most patients have gotten plenty of advice. Sue's father, for example, integrating her desire to teach elementary school with his desire to have her publish articles, suggested she write about the kids. "After all, Piaget did it," he told her. The trouble, of course, is that this suggestion merely tells her not to have the complex that she is trying to resolve. His advice was the equivalent of telling her to "get over it," or, as Mel Brooks in a comedy routine told a man whose symptom was that he tore paper, "Don't tear paper." Other advice is not so blunt, but still it often ignores both the power of the pattern and the patient's investment in it (what analysts call resistance, what Jungians call the wisdom of the symptom, what systems theorists call homeostasis, and what behaviorists call idiosyncratic reinforcement). Sigmund Freud would not have had to invent psychoanalysis if patients took good advice.

Good advice is often given to a part of the person not available in the problematic situation. The question was not what Sue, the capable, intelligent, independent woman, could do when she was worrying about her career. The question was what Sue, the proud, distressed little girl on the arm of her Dad's chair, could do. If the mature woman were on the scene, I doubt there would be a problem in the first place.

Relationship-based therapy is often indicated, in my experience, when good advice is refused because the complex governing the problem does not

have a figure in it who will take good advice. Therapy then consists of replicating the complex's scenario in the therapy, casting the therapist in the role
of one of the figures (usually, a parent figure), and in that guise behaving differently enough from the original to change the situation, but not so differently that the only thing that changes is the therapy. Thus, good advice directed at Sue's father can be taken by *me* when I am in his role. Of course, it's
no good to point all this out to the patient. If we do, her response tendencies
will change in the therapy but will not generalize to the situation that concerns her. It is perfectly acceptable for a therapist to tell his *wife*, "I'm not
your father; don't treat me as if I were." But to help a patient change more
than the way she relates to the therapist, we must communicate, in effect, "I
may or may not be your father." Then, new tendencies learned with the therapist may be expressed in situations where she is again essentially confused
about where she is. This all adds up to some time-honored (Freud,
1911–1915) features of therapeutic effectiveness, namely, neutrality,
anonymity, and transference resolution, but casts them in terms that are more
easily translated from narrative material into new situations.

In nonpsychoanalytic terms, neutrality means that the therapist does not have
an agenda beyond that which is expressed in the therapy contract. Neutrality is
essential to entering the patient's complex and addressing it on its own terms.
Neutrality also avoids the inevitable systemic, homeostatic, resistant response
to pressure from the therapist to conform to the therapist's agenda. Anonymity
means that the therapist does not reveal anything beyond what cannot be
helped; it heightens response generalization, since self-disclosure makes the
therapy relationship so specific that what is learned there, stays there. One patient told me, about a previous self-disclosing therapist, "I started therapy thinking nobody likes me, and now I think one person likes me." Transference resolution means that the therapist capitalizes on the moments when those variables
that drive problems are also operating in the therapy office.

I told Sue that she could use therapy to let the patterns in her memories play
out in my office, so as to find new ways to organize them or sort them out.
The goal of therapy, expressed in the terms of the memory, would be to find
a way for her father to enter the kitchen without ruining the girls' pleasant
breakfast, and to find a way for her to sit on the arm of her father's chair without excluding the little sister. The best way to let inner, old dynamics play out
in therapy, I said, was to say whatever comes to mind while in my office,
holding nothing back. Letting her inner world run free was bound to produce
moments when we would have her complexes right in the room to work on,
rather than merely talking about them.

Meanwhile, as a guide to my own conduct, I was thinking about ways in
which the father in her memories might act differently. If I could imagine a

realistic (in the memory's own terms), successful behavior on his part, I could translate it into an equivalent behavior on my part when the situation arose. In the first memory, I thought the father might slip into the kitchen and make an effort not to disrupt the girls' closeness, not to take over the space between them. How might I, as Sue's therapist, avoid taking over the space between the competent girl and the needy girl? Perhaps when she would sit with feelings, I could resist my tendency to relate them to me. Or if she were lost in her imagination in my office, perhaps I could avoid asking her to tell me about her thoughts.

In the second memory, I thought the father might find a way to include the little sister while still encouraging and admiring the big sister's accomplishment. For example, he could have asked Sue to read a story for her sister, or at least he could have cuddled the sister on the other arm of the chair while they admired Sue's reading together. In therapy, this might mean giving Sue her due for her intellectual fireworks in the sessions, while still pursuing attunement with what it felt like for her. (In those days, of course, I didn't think of it as attunement. In those days, *attunement* was something that happened when people smoked marijuana, not something that happened in intersubjective therapy.)

After a few weeks, while we were still settling into the process of revelation, exposure, and acceptance that is central to all therapies, Sue told me of an incident that had happened that week. An old boyfriend, now happily married, called her and asked her if she would read his first novel in manuscript form, to make suggestions and offer feedback before he sent it to agents. There was, he said, nobody whose opinion he valued more. She spent the whole weekend on it. As she told me this story, I was wondering if I might be like an old boyfriend (now sexually safe as her therapist instead of sexually safe as happily married) getting her invested in therapy (instead of a novel) at some hidden cost to her own enjoyment. I worried that the therapy was becoming my novel instead of her novel or our novel. However, warned by the kitchen memory not to appropriate her associations and link them all to me, I stuck with the manifest content and wondered aloud what she might have done over the weekend if she had not read the novel. This led Sue to connect the novel to the newspaper she read to her father and the missed weekend activities to her little sister's being ignored. She mulled over how quickly she had given up her time because she felt proud to be asked to read the novel.

Eventually, Sue's intelligence began to make me self-conscious. Once, she was telling me a story and I asked an innocuous question about it. She said, "I just had a fantasy the phone was going to ring. I guess I experienced your question as an interruption." She thus provided me with her free associations and the very interpretations I would have made of them. Her heightened awareness made me even more abstemious than usual. I stopped talking except for the occasional summarizing of a story, which I did only to let her know I was following along. Eventually, not wanting to intrude, I desisted even in this sort of summarizing speech. I ran the ground rules of the therapy like clockwork. For several sessions, I did not speak at all, a fact I smugly reported to my colleagues, since in our little therapy culture, we interpreted utter silence as an accomplishment. Sue felt she was doing terrific work, drawing connections, understanding herself. I thought I was being excluded from the kitchen, but I couldn't see how to get myself into her monologue without disrupting her obvious pleasure in self-exploration. Perhaps predictably, with speech on my part connoted as a failure in attaining a psychoanalytic ideal and further connoted as an intrusion on her imagination, I stopped speaking, and a good way to refrain from speaking, of course, is to refrain from listening. Instead of listening, I would remind myself how special these silent sessions were. Instead of playing the role of her father, I had become possessed by him, lost to emotional connection in a haze of narcissism.

During this phase, Sue told me about an insight she had had, when she was in the sixth grade, about her mother. Her mother would frequently bake brownies for the girls, from scratch, and nothing tasted better than her mother's brownies. One day, as she was about to take a big bite out of one, she noticed that the crushed walnuts embedded in the frosting were in a symmetrical pattern. "At that moment," she said, "I realized that my mother wasn't making the brownies for *us*; she was making them for herself."

"That's great," I blurted out.

"What's great?" she said.

I told her I thought the brownie story was an insightful interpretation of the way I was running the therapy. I thought she had uncovered a preciousness to my silence and my carefulness about the time boundaries that revealed that I was just trying to be a really good therapist instead of trying to help *her*.

"And that's 'great'?" she said.

"I meant, it's a great analogy."

Consciously, I think she felt like I had pulled the rug out from under her. She liked to be in control of her own interpretations, and my springing this idea on her made her feel embarrassed. This was especially so because I had not waited for her to mention even some minor aspect of my technique that would allow me to draw the connection between the brownies and me. Unconsciously, I think that my excitement about understanding the brownie story put me on the arm of my own chair, as it were, and put her in the position of the excluded little sister.

We tried to sort out what had happened. Here, I think having the two memories as guides helped us accomplish this, although I can also acknowledge that her general mental health and my general honesty probably would have got things worked out even without the memories, if not as elegantly. Instead of surprising her with another full-blown interpretation of what had occurred, I merely wondered if the memories might help us. We came to understand that while I was feeling like a father who could not get into the kitchen, I was actually very much in the kitchen, and the therapy was going excellently even as I was worried that nothing was being done to generalize her comfort with self-exploration to other situations in her life. In other words, I had felt excluded from her meditations, but she had been very aware of, and appreciative of, my presence.

Thus, we had been on the road to fixing her complex around accomplishments versus childish needs by introducing the father figure to the kitchen scene without disrupting it, just as I had planned. However, like a real father "just being there" while his girls watch the snow, I was bored. An old lawyer's adage says that if you fall asleep in a trial, when you do wake up, shout, "I object." When therapists fall asleep, or when we do the psychological equivalent and drift off in boredom, we snap out of it by saying, "But what's going on between *us*?" Boredom, as a father, was an old friend of mine (at least until my own boys were old enough to converse), but I had never knowingly been bored before during a productive therapy session: boredom in therapy had always been to me a sign of disconnection with my patients. With Sue, I had converted my boredom into pride: I was not doing merely adequate work and allowing her to shine, I was brilliantly and heroically achieving a monastic silence. Somehow, she had sensed this pride, maybe in the way I looked after a session in which I had said nothing at all. My pride had reminded her of her mother's pride in making perfect brownies.

My feeling bored by just being there for her came as much from Sue as from me. Even though it is the patient's contribution to such relational problems that constitutes the proper grist for the therapy mill, the question arises as to how to approach the patient's part of it. When the therapist focuses on the patient's contribution to relationship problems, the focus typically makes the patient defensive; in systemic terms, initial focus on the patient can awaken a homeostatic, balancing response that makes her want to focus on someone else. As in a good romantic partnership, therapy often works best if each person takes responsibility for his or her own contribution to problems. When I discuss what I have done wrong, I do not merely model how to do so, I also, I hope, invite the patient to look inward in the context of not having to fear being blamed for her part of things. Thus, after I spoke about my awkwardness and pride, Sue volunteered that it was probably not just coincidence that we had slipped from her primal kitchen scene to her primal easy chair scene. Since these scenes that emerged between us looked so much like her early memories, they probably had a lot to do with her own psychology.

Using the memory as a template, Sue's reaction of feeling disheartened by my exclamation seemed less like something I had done to her and more like her getting a load of what the little sister role was like. I do think this change of perspective from interpersonal (between her and me) back to intrapsychic (within her) was facilitated by my not insisting that her reaction was disproportionate to my small mistake. My patients, like most people, are usually willing to step up and look at their own contributions to what goes wrong if I step up and look at mine. Only the truly narcissistically impaired patients seize on my apologies in triumph.

Psychotherapy seems at times to be a process of making and cleaning up interpersonal messes. The patients, one hopes, learn to avoid them or to clean them up more gracefully than they used to do. The minor mess between us produced a couple of valuable lessons for Sue. She became aware of her tendency to make the father figure feel excluded in the kitchen scene, which then made him assert his presence in a way that pushed the family into the easy chair scene. The girl in the memory might offer the father a handful of cereal; Sue might have let me know how much she was appreciating the therapy. Yes, it would be even better to have a father figure who did not need this kind of reassurance, but here was something she could do about it when he did. This idea might be practically applied when she was teaching in a new or clever way. Her exclusion of the part of her that might want to write something made that part of her assert itself in a way that became an intellectual tyrant instead of a wise commentator. Not to exclude him might look like jotting down ideas during or after class, tape recording certain lessons for later analysis, or starting a peer supervision group to discuss pedagogy. What Sue actually did was to raise the issue of mentoring with her administration, and she accepted a request to mentor newer, younger teachers as they came into the school. As many of us who have done supervision know, this produced a friendly, intellectual conversation that focused her thinking while she was doing her own work. She did not take on the full freight of trying to publish ideas, but she did find a way to integrate teaching and thinking about teaching that appealed to her. In the terms of the memory, when she was interacting warmly with the children, she could acknowledge her father's presence in a way that did not disrupt the warmth, where "acknowledge her father's presence" meant she could think about how she might use the classroom example in her mentoring conversation.

The second lesson Sue learned from our little mess, after I accidentally and maladroitly put her in the position of her little sister, was that she found out that it was not as horrible a role as she had imagined. I want to stress that, in my opinion, even though some good came of my mistake, and even though in the grand scheme of things, it was a pretty minor mistake, minimizing mistakes typically puts the patient in the position of emphasizing them, while emphasizing mistakes tends to put the patient in the position of moving on. Anyway, Sue began to look for situations where she was the little sister, and to detoxify them. The worst of these occurred when a Pulitzer Prize–winning writer started a book about an elementary school teacher in a nearby town. Sue naturally felt the book should have been about her (now she has to settle for my book, just as she had to settle for my attention then). In exploring her feelings about this writer (whom she had never met), Sue felt dejected and insignificant, but notably not devastated.

Sue's investment in teaching reminded me of the closing lines of *Middlemarch*, the main character of which is celebrated for her small effects on others rather than for greatness. These might be watchwords for anyone, any therapist, trying to do good in small ways: "[T]he effect of her being on those around her was incalculably diffusive: for the growing good of the world is partly dependent on unhistoric acts; and that things are not so ill with you and me as they might have been, is half owing to the number who lived faithfully a hidden life, and rest in unvisited tombs" (Eliot, 1871, p. 838). Sue had begun to underline and cherish the plain, private moments of her life without letting them be overshadowed by the intellectual pretensions she associated with her parents.

With respect to Sue's romantic frustrations, I took the liberty of advising her how to evaluate a man. I suggested that she focus not on his intellect or his kindness, but on how she felt when she was with him. When the therapy ended, she was engaged and planning her wedding. I had hoped that one day she would spontaneously reveal that the cereal she and her sister had eaten that day was Sugar Pops (which would have meant to me that her father figure was there all the time providing playful nurturance), but you can't have everything.

CASE EXAMPLE: UNZIPPING THE SKIN

David was referred to me for insomnia by the employee assistance program at the elite private college where he taught. He lay awake in bed, seemingly all night, obsessing about the fact that he had gotten the coveted job, selected above the other four hundred applicants. He was a new assistant professor in the biology department, unable to believe his good fortune. His classmates were either still working on their dissertations or they were cobbling together temporary staff positions and adjunct teaching assignments. David had "survivor's guilt," as he called it.

David's ruminations circled around the thought that getting the job was too good to be true. It was as if his mind could not process his good luck. This seemed peculiar since he did not see himself as someone who had ever questioned his good fortune before. Getting into the good college, getting into the good graduate school, and obtaining his doctorate had all come naturally to him. He kept thinking about all the people who did not get the job, which is why he called it survivor guilt, but in fact, his friends and fellow students did not seem to begrudge him the position at all. There was some envy, of course, but of the direct and understandable sort, nothing ugly or festering.

A friendly black man, David had grown up in a working-class neighborhood in New York City. Both parents worked for the city, his father on the subway and his mother as a paralegal for one of the city's law offices. His family was happy that he was only three hours away, having faced the prospect of a nationwide job search. His two little brothers were still in college. David had dated his high school girlfriend through college. They had lived together for a year and then had parted amicably when she felt they had become friends rather than lovers. In graduate school, he was involved in a torrid and inflammatory relationship with a woman he met on the first day of school. He eventually broke it off because he just could not see settling down with her. He avoided involvements for the last year of school, recognizing that he was willing to move just about anywhere for an academic job and not wanting to compromise for a relationship.

I mentioned that when I had first moved to western Massachusetts, I had gone to a public swimming pool and there, with everyone almost undressed, it was visually shocking to see how white the population was. I said this partly to open the door to our discussing, sooner or later, the fact that I was white; partly to communicate my willingness to talk about race in general; and partly to imply that his insomnia might be related to his feeling like a fish out of water. As to the last, David said he was of course aware of how few black people he saw, but he also noted that when he walked into a diner, he was peered at with curiosity rather than with suspicion. He thought that if he had to live in a place where there was no real black community, it might actually be better to have almost no black people at all. Earlier in the first session, I had said to him point blank, "I'm white; you're black." He said, "I'm glad you said that, but I have no idea what to make of it." I said, "Me neither, but let's keep our ears open."

David reported early memories that sounded like Norman Rockwell paintings: Christmas with his little brothers, a Mets game with his Dad, the first time he saw snow, and his mother joking with him about what a mess he had made of himself after licking the beaters. For a "worst or unhappiest" memory, he mentioned a few childhood injuries, but they did not have much psychological meaning to me. I asked him his most surprising or unusual memory of early childhood, and he said, "Well, once I thought my Dad might be replaced by an alien." He was about five years old and the new baby was riding beside him in the back seat of the car his mother and father had borrowed to take him to the zoo. He was staring at the hairs in the back of his father's neck, trying to memorize the pattern. He had recently seen a cartoon where either Bugs Bunny unzips his body suit and turns out to be an old lady, or an old lady unzips a body suit and turns out to be Bugs Bunny. Either way, it occurred to him that someone might put on a body suit to pass as his father, but that it was unlikely an impostor would get every hair on his neck right. So he was preparing for a future identification.

In chapter 8, I will discuss nonreductionism, or as I call it, "why this and not that." For now, suffice it to say that I was curious about some of the details he had provided, including especially the fact that the car was borrowed and that the destination was the zoo. Like Jung, I am perfectly happy to supply my own associations to some of the images in early memories (for example, the zoo may be where impulses are caged); like Freud, though, I prefer finding out, if possible, what the images mean to the patient.

David said the zoo meant the trip was all about him. His career in biology had started even before he could walk, according to family stories, with his fascination with animals. Then, when other boys were playing with GI Joe and Superman, he was playing with plastic and ceramic animal figures. Later, when the others were idolizing Willie Mays, Walt Frazier, and Earl Monroe, he was idolizing George Washington Carver and a few scientists I had never heard of. Even when very young, he was constantly defending himself against overt and implied criticism of his interest in animals. Male family members would try to engage him in sports and age-mates would call him a sissy. Later, "sissy" turned into "Oreo cookie," the implication being that pure science was not a proper focus for a black man. David said he shrugged off most of this criticism, because his parents and his close friends were totally supportive of him. David could remember his father advising him that he would have a better life if he found people who liked him as he was than if he tried to get people to like him. Indeed, the trip to the zoo, with all the effort involved given the new baby, symbolized his family's support.

David had few associations to the borrowed car. He thought it was just a practical matter to borrow a car, given how long the train ride would be with an infant. He assumed he remembered that detail only because a car ride was such an unusual event in his life. To me, a borrowed car might mean a situation where your father is not on his home turf.

The memory might be summarized as saying that when things are going his way, without adversity, he becomes unsure of his father's support, and he relies on obsessive-compulsive defenses (memorizing the hairs, ruminating at night) to rekindle that support. This formulation casts his presenting problem in a new light, I think. One can imagine parents who were reliable and attuned when he was struggling, as he almost constantly seemed to be, whether because he was a nerd or because he was black. I have no idea, of course, what his actual parents were like; I am talking about the parents he has inside him. When his little brother was born, I can see them in my mind's eye deciding to do something extra special for David, resulting in the trip to the zoo. When things were going well, though, they may have been either too busy to be there for him in the same way, or at a loss as to what to do. "Too busy" because they had two jobs and eventually two younger children, and the squeaky wheel gets the grease. "At a loss" because while they may have been experts at the emotional aspects of raising children and experts at being black in America, rather soon in David's development they may have found themselves unable to follow him into his field of dreams. Again in my mind's eye, I see them playfully engaged as he describes the hunting habits of Bengalese tigers, and then I see them glazed over and stifling yawns as he explains the maternal determination of mitochondria.

When David got the academic job, he was going to the zoo. The little brothers (the other applicants) might be in his awareness, but they were not his responsibility. His parents' support of his interests and his education were coming to fruition. He was a good-looking, good-hearted man reasonably expecting to be attractive to women in his new location. Gravy, as far as the eye could see. In David's psychology, though, the pillars of his identity did not always seem to function for him when there was nothing to complain about. This left him anxious or, more accurately, somewhat depersonalized. If he could suffer enough with insomnia, he could count once again on parental support, we agreed. And maybe some other fly in the ointment would arise, to spare him further sleeplessness.

"With any luck," I said, "you'll discover the town's underlying racism before your health suffers."

David laughed heartily at that. "Maybe I'll call my Dad and tell him I can't sleep and all the therapists are white."

Even though he was joking, I thought it was a good idea to engage his parents. He was alone in New England. Even though he had taught quite a bit as a graduate student, he had to adjust to the new expectations at his school, the new environment, and the new kind of student he was encountering. Thus, on top of everything else, his days were filled with learning new skills rather than with relying on old skills, meaning that he was not retiring at night with feelings of competence and self-esteem. He resisted calling his parents for help, though, saying he did not want them to worry.

I suggested that instead of calling them for help with his insomnia and loneliness, he call them for help with his teaching. My idea was that the boy in the memory could engage his father in a meaningful conversation about the zoo, instead of merely being grateful for going there. This might relieve the boy of his anxiety about alien replacement, as the connection between them might be cemented relationally, rather than by memorizing how his hairs looked. I suggested he tell his parents that he had to learn how to communicate complex ideas to undergraduates, and that his parents could help him with this by being his guinea pigs. David asked his parents to spend the weekend with him, going over his dissertation page by page. The overt agenda was that if David could explain his dissertation to his parents, he would learn how to explain things to college students. The covert agenda was that his parents would be with him, psychologically, even in his inner temple, his holy of holies.

It is hard to say why David's insomnia disappeared so quickly. Perhaps our formulation based on his early memory was "correct," and the right solution was just as prescribed. More likely, I think, I helped David find a graceful way out, in Erickson's (Haley, 1973) felicitous phrasing. He may simply have been conflicted about asking for help in light of his new status as an adult, a Ph.D., and a college professor. He may have created a symptom that required some assistance, and I helped him find a way to reconnect with his family without the symptom.

When he reported a quick cure, I thought we were done with therapy. But David felt that our conversation had raised some questions about his identity as a black man that he wanted to explore. *Was* he an Oreo cookie? *Should* his research have more political implications? Was there something weird about admiring Charles Darwin more than Magic Johnson?

I felt honored and vaguely queasy about being invited into this relationship. In my worldview, there could be few higher compliments than being trusted by a black man to engage in an honest conversation about race. The queasiness, though, came from the fact that for much of the time I did not have the faintest idea what David was talking about. As the months went by, I repeatedly found myself on the horns of dilemma. He would mention a famous black person I had never heard of, and I could either somewhat deceptively let him think I knew who he meant or I could intrude on his fantasy of being understood by inquiring. He would discuss a situation and I could tell he thought we had a shared understanding of it, and again I could either dispel the illusion that he seemed to be thriving on or I could feel like I was passively lying to him by letting the illusion persist.

During a recent performance, Wanda Sykes, the black comedienne, told a story about going into a convenience store with a friend on a hot day, walking to the cooler in the back to get a couple of sodas, and watching as her friend opened her soda and started drinking it on the way to the cash register. Sykes said, "Now at this point, the white people in the audience are like, 'Yeah, so what?' while the black people in the audience feel like this is the beginning of a Stephen King story." In those days when I was seeing David, I might not have known what she was talking about (i.e., that black people expect to be accused of theft, and white people might not even realize it was a possibility).

You can probably see where this was headed. David felt he was on the way to the therapeutic equivalent of the zoo, enjoying a safe place where he could work out the complexity of his identity. I never really grasped the problem, frankly; almost all of the examples he gave of nonstandard identifications were still of black people, like Leontyne Price and Paul Robeson and George Washington Carver and other scientists whose names I still do not recognize. So I was driving him to this zoo in a vehicle that felt strangely not my own, alien to his concerns. He used the word *privilege* in discussing a situation that had come up at work, and in my reply I inadvertently made it clear that I thought he meant confidentiality (as in *privileged communication*). I had never heard of *white privilege*. (I mean, I had never heard the term, even though the principle was not new to me; my own father often commented on situations that would have gone differently if one of the parties had been black.) It was as if I had just unzipped my skin and revealed, not Norman Rockwell, but something closer to American Nazi Party leader George Lincoln Rockwell.

Was it an error to tip my hand, to let him see that I was not understanding him? Certainly, some would say that the only error, if any, was letting it go on so long. But I believe we were doing genuinely good work during these sessions when I felt white and befuddled. In retrospect, I do not think my mistake was letting him believe I was attuned to him around race. Indeed, Jung says somewhere that children create the parents they need (as long, I would add, as the parents supply enough raw material and do not interfere too much), and I think to a large extent patients create the therapists *they* need, too (with the same proviso). I think my mistake was not trusting enough in my attunement to his emotions and his psychology, letting myself think that getting the details right on race were more important than getting the relationship right on revelation, exploration, and acceptance. If I had not questioned the value or authenticity of the relationship, I might not have tried to prove to him that I *did* understand what he meant by privilege. I might not have showed him what is always true in every therapy and in every parent-child relationship, namely, it is never as empathic as the patient or child thinks it is. I wonder, in fact, if David's father had stumbled on the same problem, letting his anxiety about not understanding biology interfere with his ability to be with David even when things were going smoothly.

It is complicated to apologize to a patient for an attunement error. If I say I should have known what he meant, it implies that it is possible for me to be perfectly attuned. If I say I should not have revealed my lack of attunement, it implies I prefer to hide stuff. So even though some sort of acceptance of responsibility is called for after an attunement error, an apology does not quite work. Instead, I commented on how alarmed he looked when he realized I did not know what he meant by privilege, and I kept the resolution to myself to be better attuned in the future.

David acknowledged that it was a rude awakening when I misunderstood him. There is an old *New Yorker* cartoon that shows a patient saying, "I never meet any interesting people," while the therapist is thinking, "What am I, chopped liver?" I would prefer a therapist who says this out loud. So, what I said to David was, "It was like I unzipped my skin and there was somebody you didn't recognize." The unzipping image brought the memory into our discussion. As with Sue in the preceding case example, David and I probably would have worked things out between us anyway, but I do think having the memory to refer to helped. We were able to reconstruct the parallels between what happened in the therapy and what happened in the memory. This enabled David to view my breach of empathy as something that it made sense to process for his own growth, not just to put aside as a mistake on my part. Also as with Sue, I saw my job as taking responsibility for my error and letting *him* then draw the connections to his own psychology. Relying on the memory as a guide, we were soon piecing together his experience of what had happened between us, piecing it together, together.

The breach in empathy had been fairly minor. It is not as if he had stumbled on a part of me that was overtly racist. Rather, he stumbled on a part of me that was ignorant about his experience of the world, and this can happen in any therapy. Using the memory to repair the breach, though, made it clear that our relationship could also be reparative with respect to the complex in the memory. We established a new working alliance that led to questions and answers about his experience of race, consciously mimicking the relationship with his father that he wished he could have had around science. Even though I could never really know what it was like to be black (even though his father would very likely never know what it was like to be an academic or a scientist), we could maintain a close relationship while on the topic and help give him a sense that he need not be alone in such matters when they are going well.

As a coda to this story, as we were terminating during his second year of therapy, David decided to move back to New York, taking a job at a less prestigious college. He said that in western Massachusetts, the "main thing" about

him was that he was black, the second thing about him was that he was a biology professor, and the third thing about him was that he was "David." In
New York, he said, the main thing about him, usually at least, was that he was
"David," then that he was a biology professor, then that he was black. The organization of his identity in New York fit him better, he felt, as he had never
seen being black as the main thing about him, albeit an important aspect of
his sense of self. I am always tempted to see therapy outcomes in the best possible light, but even allowing for that, I do think this was a good decision for
him, and I may have helped him make it by helping him feel like his supportive father was now available to him even when things were going well.

THERAPEUTIC PRIVILEGE

In my view, a key aspect of *white privilege* is the power to decide when and
when not to be identified with one's race, when and when not to be put into
one's skin. The great psychological privilege, in addition to the social and political privileges, is this power to define oneself. When black people mistrust
white people, in my experience it makes many white people angry because
we do not like being put into our skins unexpectedly or without our consent
any more than black people do. In this respect, unzipping the skin was a
metaphor not only for revealing something, but also for controlling something, and the retention of the memory would accord with Bruhn's (1985)
conception of early memories as unfinished business. In the aftermath of my
stumble, as David and I discussed privilege, my contributions to that discussion focused on what might be called *therapeutic privilege* (although in truth,
we both referred to the phenomenon as a "power differential," as the word
privilege symbolized our breach of attunement).

Therapeutic privilege takes many forms. Like white privilege, perhaps the
greatest benefit conferred on those in power is the freedom not to think about
such things as disenfranchisement, social injustice, and abuse of power, in
other words, to assume that all is well, or to assume that what is not well is a
reflection on those who are suffering rather than on the system in which they
suffer. Next comes the freedom to take only as much responsibility for things
going badly as one chooses to take. Any dismissal of responsibility usually
comes in the form of characterizing the complainer as whining or lazy, or as
obsessed with race, gender, status, or envy. In therapy, we have a special form
of dismissing patients, namely, we diagnose them ("throw the book at him,"
I say). There are only two kinds of therapists, it might be said: those who,
when things go wrong, try something else and those who, when things go
wrong, up the diagnosis. Finally, therapeutic privilege takes the form of be-

ing put in one's childishness, one's imperfection, only when one chooses. Our mantra is the Wizard of Oz's "Pay no attention to that man behind the curtain." Much energy in society is exerted in the service of maintaining a social façade or what Goffman (1959) calls face work, and we like to choose when to acknowledge that our childish selves are still operating. Patients abandon this freedom at the door, as we repeatedly put them in the position of losing face, being transparent, and not managing their definition of themselves. We generally do this for their own good, of course, but often we do it to avoid having it done to us. Thus, though I say it myself, I think I managed my breach with David in a way that did not capitalize on my therapeutic privilege, that did not overly pathologize or infantilize him. It seems likely that my relinquishing of therapeutic privilege substituted for or enhanced my relinquishing of white privilege, and allowed us to talk openly about his racial identity. Instead of getting huffy, as many white people do in my experience, about a black man's distrust for no better reason than the color of my skin, I got curious. Instead of accusing him of falsely generalizing his experience of other white people to me, I wondered what if anything I might do to distinguish myself from other white people, to make our space together comfortable enough to talk about race. Admittedly, I was able to do this partly or even largely because in my own office, and while being paid to do it, it is relatively easy for me to accept my own skin as a metaphor, rather than to feel genuinely and dreadfully at risk.

Chapter Three

Memory Is Something We Do, Not Something We Have

Like one who, having into truth by telling of it, made such a sinner of his memory to credit his own lie.

—Shakespeare, Prospero in *The Tempest*

I have done that, says my memory. I cannot have done that, says my pride, and remains adamant. Eventually, memory yields.

—Nietzsche, *Beyond Good and Evil* (1886, aphorism 68)

In the next three chapters, I explore the theory of early memories, largely by bringing behavioristic and systemic ideas to bear on the occurrence and the reporting of remembering. Along the way, I also take a behavioristic and systemic look at what happens in good psychoanalytic therapy. I touch on the so-called false memory debate, which has become so prominent because of legal cases, but which has implications for any therapy in which the patient reports an historical event and the therapist treats the event as if it happened. Finally, I review the work of four major contributors to the understanding of early memories.

Choosing between different theoretical approaches in psychology reminds me of an old joke: A shipwreck survivor was marooned on a tropical island for twenty years. When he was finally rescued, the captain of the rescue ship asked for a tour of the island. He was impressed. The man had built an aqueduct system for indoor plumbing, a series of traps for food, a lovely three-room home, and most impressive of all, a temple with carved pews, inlaid parquet floors, and stained-glass windows. Continuing the tour, the man showed the captain another temple, equally beautiful, with carved pews, inlaid parquet floors, and stained-glass windows. The captain said, "Excuse my asking, but you've been alone on this island for twenty years. Why two temples?" The man replied, "Well, this is the temple I worship in, and the other is the temple I wouldn't be caught dead in."

Both are necessary for the true zealot.

All too often, in my experience, it is not enough to be psychoanalytic; one must also despise behaviorism. It is not enough to be systemic, one must also reject the psychoanalytic. Legion are those who sniff at Skinner and have never read *Science and Human Behavior*, or whose understanding of systems theory amounts to, as one famous psychoanalyst said, having a social worker see the parents. Behaviorists are equally guilty, hailing discoveries of such phenomena as transference and resistance (by appropriately behavioristic names) as if they had never been discussed before by clinicians.

Early memories have been the province of psychodynamic practitioners, but there is much to learn about them, in my opinion, from behaviorism and from systems theory and in other temples that, in my youth, I would not be caught dead in.

MEMORY IS SOMETHING WE DO

Memory is something we do, not something we have. It certainly *seems* like something we have, a closet or filing cabinet in which we can rummage for lost treasures. As long as there have been methods for improving memory with devices, these devices have been used as metaphors for memory (Skinner, 1985). Such devices involved recording, storing, and retrieving information; memory is typically and incorrectly considered to be a system of recording, storing, and retrieving. Thus, early on in the development of writing, text was inscribed on tablets, and in Aeschylus' *The Suppliants Part IV*, one character bids others to "hoard my words, inscribing them on memory's tablets." And consider Proverbs 3:1–3: "My son, do not forget my teaching, but let your heart keep my commandments . . . write them on the tablet of your heart." And when Hamlet's father's ghost leaves him with the words, "Remember me," Hamlet soliloquizes, "Yea, from the table [tablet] of my memory I'll wipe away all . . . that youth and observation copied there, and thy commandment all alone shall live within the book and volume of my brain, unmix'd with baser matter." Recent metaphors for memory center on video cameras and computers, our latest storage devices.

Scientists now recognize that there is no copy of past events in the brain, but they still cannot seem to free themselves from the storage metaphor. Thus, a leading memory researcher writes, "We do not record our experiences the way a camera records them. Our memories work differently. We extract key elements from our experiences and store them. We then recreate and reconstruct our experiences rather than retrieve copies of them" (Schachter, 2001, p. 9). In other words, to account for the fact that remembering is affected by all sorts of personal and environmental variables, the current mainstream view is that we only store *parts* of experiences. The problem is that the storage bin or medium or receptacle has never been found.

Treating memory as something we do, as the behavior of remembering, instead of treating it as a system for storing and retrieving information, resolves this problem. It is not immediately obvious how remembering is like other behaviors, and a full appreciation of this approach to memory may require at least a brief review of behavior theory.

Behaviors can be public, observable by other people, or private, observable only by the person emitting the behavior. Usually, when we think of behavior, we think of something public or overt, like throwing a ball, disobeying a parent, or blinking. Indeed, much criticism was leveled at early behaviorists for ignoring behaviors that were not visible to other people. Such behaviors, like thinking, remembering, fantasizing, and dreaming, were hard to study, but ignoring them was a lot like the well-worn story of the fellow who looks for his keys under the street lamp where the light is better rather than by the porch where he dropped them. Overt behavior is easier to study than private behavior, but it would be foolish to deny the existence or importance of private behavior.

Having studied publicly observable, gross motor behaviors of animals closely enough to articulate some laws of behavior, psychologists then applied these laws to covert or private behaviors, including those behaviors of most interest to therapists. In this, as in so much else, behaviorists followed Darwin, who first discovered natural selection by studying animals (Darwin, 1859) and then applied the scheme to humans (Darwin, 1871). People predictably objected that the laws articulated via the observation of pigeons would not apply to humans, and that the laws derived from the observation of public behaviors would not apply to private behaviors. Like-minded critics had argued, a century earlier, that a theory derived from finches and dogs could not be applied to humans. To behaviorists, this objection sounded like the first objections to Galileo's observations of the planets: people insisted that there was one physics applicable on earth and another, separate set of laws applicable in the heavens (Feyerabend, 1975). Behaviorists even saw the same motives behind the objections, namely, the desire to preserve a sense of immortality, a sense of significance. Copernicus demolished people's sense of centrality in the universe. Darwin destroyed the belief that we were created all at once in God's image. (God may have created us in his image, but he seems to have done it by setting certain forces in motion at the outset of the universe, not all at once like Athena springing from Zeus's head.) Freud thought he had dealt a similar blow to humans' narcissism, by showing that we were not in control of ourselves. But to Skinner, Freud merely pushed control farther back into the head, into the *unconscious*. Skinner's view places control outside the person altogether.

Skinner called his behaviorism "radical behaviorism" because it rejected the prior agnosticism about private events. What was radical was the assumption that the laws of behavior applied equally well to private events as to public events, just as physical laws apply equally well to observable events and those that are not (whether they are unobservable either because they are microscopic or because they are far away). What was especially radical about radical behaviorism was the assertion that the laws of behavior apply as validly to the scientist as to the lab rat, and that a scientific treatment of reality must account for the behavior of the scientist, not just the behavior that the scientist observes.

Skinner's behaviorism is, quite self-consciously, an almost exact analogy to Darwinism. Darwin believed that random variations in genes were favored or disfavored according to their consequences under contingencies of survival and contingencies of reproductive success. Skinner believed that random variations in behaviors were made more probable or less probable according to their consequences under contingencies of reinforcement and operational success. Genetically based behaviors (instincts and reflexes) are those that have had a history of success under contingencies of survival and were then preserved in the next generation. Through a poor choice of words, Darwin called this process natural selection; *selection* is a poor choice because it forms a verb, select, that needs a subject, whereas Darwin's new kind of causality happened without a subject making it happen. Genes that work survive; genes that do not work become extinct. In contrast to genetically based behaviors, *operants*—so-called because they operate on the environment—survive if they are successful, not by being passed down to the next generation, but by becoming more probable under similar circumstances. In other words, Skinner took the new kind of causality discovered by Darwin—selection by consequences—and applied it to behavior.

Skinner identified three kinds of consequences that can affect the probability of an operant being repeated. A consequence that is positive (and complicated animals like people can have extremely complicated definitions of what is positive) increases the probability of, or reinforces, or strengthens a behavior. A consequence that is negative or aversive is called *punishment*, and reduces the probability of emitting the behavior, if only in the presence of the punisher. Consequences that are neutral have varying effects in the short run, depending on such things as the ratio and timing of prior reinforcement, but in the long run, neutral consequences will cause a behavior to go extinct, to extinguish.

Behaviorism does not exclude psychoanalytic theory; it contextualizes it. Almost everything Skinner had to say about Freud was positive, his only complaint being the same complaint he had about all prebehavioral thinking, namely, that it was mentalistic (see below). Psychoanalysis answers (in its own language) such crucial behavioristic questions as the following: How does an apparently aversive event (such as cutting the wrist or banging the head or being rejected) become a reinforcer? How are we to understand metaphors and symbols? How are conflicting contingencies managed by the person? As a matter of fact, Skinner was friendly enough to psychoanalytic thinking that he developed his own projective test, which he called the verbal summator. He played recordings of indistinct speech that were actually an actor reading only vowel sounds and omitting all consonants. Then he asked the subject what was said, and used the results to draw inferences about the individual's response tendencies. Skinner also agreed with Freud about dream interpretation. Skinner saw dreams and fantasies as behavior that, being private, escaped punishing consequences that the same or similar behavior, if public, would occasion. To call such behavior *wishes* is to say that these are the things the person would do if aversive consequences were out of the question. In my view, psychoanalysis is to engineering as behaviorism is to physics. Cathedrals did not crash to the ground when Newton discovered gravity, but enhanced knowledge of gravity could be used by engineers and architects. Psychoanalytic technique did not fold its tent with the discovery that behavior is selected by consequences, but psychoanalytic therapists can use this enhanced knowledge of behavior.

In behavioral terms, remembering is the act of seeing (or hearing, tasting, etc.) something that is not there. It is one of many kinds of behavior that typically occur under one set of circumstances and can occur, to different effect, when that set of circumstances do not obtain. For example, if my car is going too fast, I step on the brake. I recently *stepped on the brake* while watching a movie, an animated picture, no less (meaning that it was obviously not real even beyond the usual movie). I did this as the Polar Express lost control going over a roller coaster-like crest. The behavior of stepping on the brake, learned in response to the presence of certain external stimuli, was emitted in the absence of an automobile, road, or brake pedal. Analogously, we learn to visualize what *is* there. We then emit visualizing behavior (called remembering) when the thing is not there.

Erroneous and unnecessarily complicated, the metaphor of storage and retrieval suggests that I stored *stepping on the brake* as a memory and retrieved it in response to the visual image on the screen. What actually happened was that thirty-six years of driving changed me in some way, the interior details of which are of interest only to brain surgeons and neuropsychologists. Thus changed, I became someone in whom certain visual images affect the right foot. Presumably, repeated exposures to the movie under circumstances that demonstrate no relationship between my right foot and the visual image would change me further, such that I could be said to have learned to discriminate between the theater and my car. The behavior of stepping on the brake is not inside me any more than the light, in Skinner's metaphor, is in the tungsten filament of the light bulb. Instead, the tungsten's properties (how it was changed by nature over eons) and its shape (how it was changed by circumstance) and the electrical system in which it found itself combine to emit light when the switch is thrown. Subatomic physicists care about those changes, but you and I do not, and neither did Edison. All Edison cared about was whether it worked.

The reason, incidentally, that we do not care about the interior changes in the person is that there is nothing we can do about those interior neurochemical states to help a person or to improve a situation. Certain medications may have broad effects on impulsivity or on general sadness, but to fix a specific problem we cannot intervene directly on neurology. Even if we *could* intervene directly on neurology, or if we were just intellectually curious about those interior changes, there would still be no storage bin, no attic filled with copies of experiences or pieces of experiences.

Remembering—seeing in the absence of the thing seen—is like stepping on the brake in a movie theater. To fully appreciate this position, one must understand the analogy between seeing or hearing something in the first place and stepping on the brake in the first place (i.e., in a car). I step on the brake in a car because of natural selection, experience (learning history), and circumstances. Natural selection has made me capable of seeing what is ahead of me and reacting by moving my foot to the brake. (If not, the car would be designed differently to take advantage of what nature did make me capable of. More properly, the behavior of designing cars that people are not equipped to drive meets with little success.) I had experiences that changed me in such a way that a link was established between my stepping on the brake and slowing down the approach of objects in the windshield. (Also, the kinesthetics of braking add to the experience of slowing down when the brake is pressed.) Finally, I sometimes find myself in circumstances (i.e., driving a car with things approaching swiftly) where braking works, which strengthens the behavior when things approach swiftly. Incidentally, most of us have learned to brake *only* when driving the car less than perfectly, and we emit braking behavior even in the passenger seat. The discrimination between driving and being a passenger is difficult to learn, since braking in the passenger seat is almost as reliably followed by a slowing of the car as is braking in the driver's seat, because the driver is usually braking at about the same time the passenger is. (My partner is especially bad at telling the difference. Since her braking behavior in the passenger seat does not always produce slowing of the car, she has learned to yell while braking, and *this* invariably works.)

Seeing and hearing are also behaviors. When confronted with an apple, I see an apple, because of natural selection, experience (learning history), and circumstance. Natural selection has endowed me with the ability to be responsive to light waves in the visible spectrum, which are reflected by the apple. Experience has taught me to attend to things that look like apples, especially when I am hungry, and to see them when they are there, so I can eat them. Circumstances have placed an apple before me. *Seeing an apple* in front of an apple is like *stepping on the brake* while driving a car, except that seeing what is in front of me took less training than did stepping on the brake. Seeing an apple as I write this, with no apple in front of me, is like stepping on the brake at the theater, with no car to slow down.

It seems as though seeing and hearing are more automatic than are behaviors like stepping on the brake. Surely, they are behaviors that are more natural or hard-wired or evolution-based than is the behavior of stepping on the brake. In that respect, perhaps a better analogy than stepping on the brake would have been blinking. Blinking seems to be, like seeing and hearing, a behavior selected by contingencies of survival. Animals that had a gene that produced blinking when the eye's surface was touched were more likely to live long enough to produce and raise offspring than animals who did not have the gene. Those offspring also had the gene, and passed it on to their own offspring. Seeing an apple when an apple is present has analogous survival advantages. Seeing and hearing are behaviors that we are evolutionarily equipped to do, but these are behaviors that can, like blinking, also be emitted in the absence of the kind of circumstances that selected them.

There is survival value in having as many hard-wired behaviors as possible become adaptable to circumstances, releasing them from hard-wired stimuli and allowing their linkage to changing conditions. Beyond the general advantages of flexibility, the liberation of seeing and hearing from reflexive reaction to the immediate environment also produced all the benefits derived from having an imagination. Most notable of these from a survival standpoint is the opportunity afforded by imagination to try out behaviors in fantasy to discover how they might do in reality, before taking actual risks. The general advantages of operant control would not hold true for a behavior like heart-beating. If the heartbeat came under operant control, experimenting children would kill themselves by playing with it. A gene that allowed for the operant control of the heartbeat would not propagate. But even breathing, which is nearly as basic as the heartbeat, has come under operant control (presumably for swimming), although the gene that allows for it has the fail-safe of making the person pass out before dying. Operant control of so-called instinctive behaviors, and the implied sensitivity to changing environmental conditions, requires an ability to experience pleasure and pain (else environmental consequences would be ineffective) plus a complicated neural network that can change in response to different environmental effects. Enhanced pleasure and pain and enhanced neural networking imply a relatively big brain. Our big brains are an evolutionary investment in adaptability to changing circumstances.

When we see or hear (or taste, feel, or smell) something that is not there, we are remembering it. We are emitting roughly the same behavior we emitted when it was there (the seeing of it, the hearing of it), but now we are emitting this behavior in its absence.

Critics say it is more complicated than that. They say that what people do is too rich, too exquisite to be an aggregation of response repertoires. Critics of Darwin also say that life is too complex to be a jury-rigged aggregation of adaptations (*McLean v. Arkansas*, 1982). They invoke *intelligent design* to explain what they believe are organisms too complex to be constructed via natural selection. Critics of Skinner invoke *will* or *mind* or the *human spirit* or something equivalent to explain what they believe are behaviors too complex to be constructed via conditioning. Much of Skinner's writing is devoted not to explaining his position, which is simple to understand, but to defending it against accusations of simplicity. He covers everything from trying to remember a name to creating music to deciding on a chess move. His writing on these topics is directly analogous to the long discussions in zoological writing as to why pandas have pseudothumbs and how the eye evolved. Nobody really cares how the eye evolved; Dawkins (1996, pp. 138–197) explains it at such length because so many people have claimed that the eyeball is too complicated to be jury-rigged by the process of natural selection. Thus, I do not intend to answer every conceivable objection about the behavioristic view of memory (one can read Skinner and other behaviorists for that). My purpose here is to explore what can be learned from it as a therapist.

Perhaps though, it is worth a detour into the main reason that behaviorism is derided: there is just no getting around the fact that Skinner does not believe in the mind. In a behavioristic account, there is the body and there is behavior and there is nothing left over to ascribe to a mind. I do not think we need to accept this belief to benefit from viewing memory as a behavior, but if we follow the path far enough, we find ourselves in a world where mind does not exist. Put simply, the only evidence we have of a mind is the seeing of images that are not in front of us, hearing ourselves think, and feeling, tasting, and smelling things that are not there. The fact that every bit of evidence that we have of minds comes from our five bodily senses I find a bit suspicious. The fact that the mind is said to be the part of us that is immortal I find even more suspicious. We believe in an entity of which we have no evidence and the existence of which would allay our deepest fears. Descartes said, "I think, therefore I am," claiming that the existence of his mind was the one thing he was certain of. A behavioristic reply might be: I hear words when nobody is speaking them, and even though I call this thinking, all it proves is that I have ears and I have heard people speak.

The behavioristic notion of not having a mind analogizes people to rats and pigeons. Even biologists who are utterly committed intellectually to our descent from other animals balk at this analogy. They think there must be something in the complexity and size of the human brain that produces consciousness, and they believe that this consciousness distinguishes us from other animals (Wilson, 1998). As noted, though, there is nothing in what is called consciousness that is different from what we hear, see, and so on. Behaviorists think that people are certainly more complicated than pigeons, because our bigger brains make us more responsive to deferred consequences, conflictual contingencies, and peculiar reinforcers. However, behaviorists do not see us as fundamentally different from pigeons. Objections to behaviorism include statements like "pigeons roost on statues of people, not the other way around." These arguments are designed to appeal to our pride, not to our reason. Skinner (1971) answered these arguments in his book *Beyond Freedom and Dignity*, and I will not rehash his rebuttal here, except to note his use of the word *dignity*. A behavioristic account of humanity is an undignified account; it is therefore a humble account, and it is not surprising that many behaviorists are drawn to similarly humble accounts of humanity, such as Taoism and Buddhism (Hayes, Follette, & Linehan, 2004; Baer, 2003).

REPRESSION

A behavioristic account of repression may illustrate how behaviorism can help us think about memory more sensibly. Freud (1915) used the term to conceptualize the reasons that verbal expressions of forbidden impulses relieved hysterical symptoms. He wondered what happens when a fight-flight threat occurs within the self, in the form of a memory or an unacceptable impulse. He posited repression as a method for managing such impulses midway between the overt fight-flight response we use for external threats and the moral condemnation we eventually use as civilized persons. "The essence of repression lies simply in turning something away, and keeping it at a distance, from the conscious" (p. 147).

People are sometimes unable to remember things, but then different cues or prompts produce the memory. When the inability to remember was substantially a function of the unpleasantness of remembering, we call it repression. This concept has fallen into disrepute as putative victims of sexual abuse have used it to explain why they could not recall the abuse until their therapists dug it out of them (Loftus & Ketcham, 1994; Campbell, 1998). The light shed on repression by a behavioristic account also, I think, demystifies the sudden recollection (i.e., the sudden visualizing) of abuse.

Repression means motivated forgetting. Having conceived of remembering as a behavior, we can define forgetting as the failure to emit the behavior of remembering under circumstances where the behavior is expected. This again makes it like any other behavior. If we think a child has never learned to play chess, and she sets up the pieces incorrectly, we say she does not know how to play chess. But if we expect correct setting up, because, for example, she was able to do it last week, then we say she has *forgotten* how to play chess. Forgetting means the behavior is expected, not produced, currently or formerly within the individual's repertoire, and, importantly, not emitted covertly. In other words, the person has not forgotten if she can visualize the correct arrangement of pieces. If she can visualize the correct arrangement, we think she may be feigning ignorance, pulling our leg, or trying to be annoying, but we do not say that she forgot. The rub is in the necessity that the behavior not be emitted covertly, because we do not have access to her private world to determine if she has forgotten or if she is faking, playing, or annoying.

We do have access to our own private worlds, however, so even though we cannot be entirely certain that someone else has forgotten something, we know that forgetting is possible and what it looks like up close. In other words, we are familiar with situations where we expect ourselves to emit a certain behavior (a geography question may be such a situation) and where we can observe that we not only do not do it overtly, we also cannot do it covertly. Again, by *covertly*, I mean that we do not visualize the answer or hear (think) it. Such failures to respond as expected can occur either because too much time has expired for the situation to occasion the response (simple forgetting; we knew the capital of Chad in the fourth grade, but not now), or because something about the situation motivates the person to forget. These latter situations are what are meant by repression.

To get a sense of repression, let's first consider what happens when a person remembers or fantasizes about something exceedingly pleasant. In these circumstances, the behavior of, say, visualizing oneself having sex with a favorite movie star is reinforced (i.e., strengthened, made more probable) by the images thereby produced. The seeing and the result of the seeing are so closely linked that it might even be said that pleasant fantasies are self-reinforcing, but an account that separates them as behavior and consequence squares better with behaviorism and is easier to follow. Pleasant images (sounds, words, smells, feelings, tastes) reinforce the behavior of imaging, or imagining, them. Conversely, then, unpleasant images punish the behavior of imagining them. Other things being equal, a person will imagine good things and not bad things. Of course, other things are never equal, and mitigating the tendency not to think of unpleasant things are the benefits of doing so. These advantages include solving problems, mastering unpleasantness by repeated exposure to make it less unpleasant, learning from mistakes by trying out different alternatives in one's imagination, and, especially, all the benefits that accrue from maintaining a reasonably accurate view of reality (remembering the scary dog is less aversive than forgetting it and walking by it again). More likely than wholesale forgetting, then, is making the remembering more pleasant by changing details to a more gratifying version. It is more gratifying to see oneself behaving effectively than passively, so people tend to be more effective in memory than in action.

Thus, remembering something unpleasant is punished by what is remembered, just as looking at something unpleasant can be punished by the thing seen. The person looking may look away, with the averting of the eyes being reinforced by the disappearance of the unpleasant sight. The person remembering may *look away* by thinking of something else, with the thinking-of-something-else being reinforced by the disappearance of the unpleasant memory. Eventually, stimuli associated with an unpleasant memory may also be ignored or looked away from, to avoid the punishing effects of the unpleasant memory.

Repression is also influenced by extrinsic factors. These relate to the effects of what the person will do as a result of remembering, what the person will do that *is* visible to other people. If remembering some unpleasantness with her father makes a girl look at him with fear, and if he responds to such looks with anger, the girl must learn to tolerate his anger, hide her reactions, or not remember unpleasantness. Hiding reactions is difficult for some people. It is no coincidence that repression, in clinical theory, is linked to the hysterical end of the hysterical-obsessive continuum. Obsessive-compulsives are much better than hysterics at detaching overt behavior from private behavior. As Hamlet put it, excessive thinking—the hallmark of obsessive-compulsives— can cause "enterprises of great pitch and moment [to] lose the name of action." Given the hysteric's propensity to act broadly and overtly in response to private stimulation, the hysteric must choose between learning to tolerate anger (unlikely, given his or her sensitivity to emotional cues) and learning not to remember.

If remembering an appointment means I have to go to a meeting that I find aversive, then the immediate behaviors of visualizing the meeting or of hearing myself think the words "You're busy at noon" would operate under contingencies of punishment (i.e., they would lead me to attend, an aversive outcome). Conversely, the meeting might be neutral to me, but remembering could mean discontinuing an activity that is rewarding, and again the algebra of the situation might lead me to forget the meeting (especially if I have been trained not to feel good about blowing off meetings on purpose).

Every act of remembering is a compromise between the advantages of accuracy and other factors, which include the intrinsic pleasantness or unpleasantness of what is remembered, the effect of remembering on the person and on the people and circumstances around the person, and the pleasantness or unpleasantness of seeing oneself doing certain things. One can see from this analysis why a memory of a distant event cannot be recovered wholesale and accurately, as if being unlocked from a vault. There is no memory to unlock; there is only remembering, and remembering, like any behavior, is affected by history and circumstances.

THE REPRESSED MEMORY DEBATE

A slew of cases have emerged over the last few decades in which people recall being abused as children after years of not having any memory of the abuse. A contentious debate has emerged between those who, on the one side, think such memories must be taken seriously (to protect the person who recalls them or to seek justice against the perpetrators in the memories) and those who, on the other, think such memories are unreliable guides to what really happened (APA Working Group, 1998). Researchers have struggled with understanding how it might be possible to recall a memory after years of not having access to it, and forensic psychologists have struggled with the potential injustice of depriving someone of freedom on the sole basis of decades-old eyewitness testimony, when even immediate eyewitness testimony is unreliable (Loftus, 1979).

Understanding memory as something we do, rather than as something we have, clarifies many of the issues involved. It is not the case that (a) some memories are accurate and (b) some memories are colored by personality or the situation of recall and (c) some memories are pseudomemories that never happened at all. Instead, *all* remembering, like all other behaving, has communicative aspects that vary with circumstance and *all* remembering reflects a learning history associated with current stimuli and expectations of reinforcement and punishment. Remembering is a subset of seeing because it is a form of seeing (or hearing, tasting, etc.) in which the objects seen are not immediately present; remembering, when it leads to a report of what was covertly seen, is also a form of communication. Like seeing (of which it is a subset), remembering is evolutionarily and environmentally useful when it is accurate, but, like communication (of which it is also often a subset), remembering is also evolutionarily and environmentally useful when it meets with the approval of others.

Since there is no storage closet in the brain, no videotape to go to, there can be no locking away and then retrieving a memory. What there *may* be, instead, is a behavior of remembering not emitted for a long time, either because the necessary prompt had not been presented or because the aversive consequences of remembering were too great. Evaluation of a memory for accuracy needs to examine the occasioning stimuli, the current contingencies of reinforcement or punishment, and the interpersonal meanings of the memory report. The more the remembering or its report was expectably rewarded by the communicative context in which it occurred, the more suspect is its accuracy. Relevant rewards can include, among others, pleasing a therapist by fulfilling his expectations regarding the source of symptoms, finding an explanation for one's dissatisfactions in life, developing a sense of oneself as a tragic hero, exacting revenge on imperfect parents, and pleasing a therapist by contrasting his parenting efforts with those of parents who did harm. Eyewitness unreliability suggests that memories are better used by therapists for their communicative and personal meanings than for accuracy; accuracy is better determined by corroborating evidence.

Attribution error is the term used when a person cannot distinguish a memory from a real event. Attribution error, in the behavioristic/systemic view, is not a problem with some memories; it is a fundamental characteristic of all remembering. In theory and in practice, the behavior of remembering something that happened should be a lot like remembering something that never happened. Both involve the emission of visual behaviors under the control of environmental stimuli. The distinction, like all internal knowledge, is learned in response to queries from the verbal community. Parents and others ask us questions about ourselves, and the answers to these questions are described as self-awareness or self-knowledge (Skinner, 1974). Parents cannot ask sufficiently careful questions to teach us to discriminate fine details of remembering, because they cannot see what we are recalling. Neither can parents accurately reward correct answers about the details of remembering when the remembering concerns something they did not personally witness. Indeed, in celebrating the developing increase in dominion over our bodies and our things, we as children cherish our ability to disguise our private experiences from our parents. Lying and fantasizing can never be brought under perfect control, partly because the verbal community cannot make the necessary distinctions required to train the child to avoid all attribution error, and partly because, even if this were possible, the child would find it aversive and decline the training. Thus, I cannot recall whether I was first told how or shown how to throw a ball, deal cards, or dice carrots. If I was shown, then my first visualization of these activities was of an external event; if I was told, then my first visualization was constructed internally. I prefer to think I was shown rather than told because the showing suggests more hands-on parenting and makes me feel good, but such attribution errors are fundamentally unavoidable.

SOME PSYCHOANALYTIC
IMPLICATIONS OF BEHAVIOR THEORY

Some of the implications of a behavioristic approach to motivated forgetting or repression are surprisingly (to me, at least) psychoanalytic.

One of the grand truisms about psychotherapy, I think, is that many of the kinds of problems that bring people to treatment are related to the effects of punishment. (Another grand truism is that many such problems unfold in misused power imbalances, such as that between parents and children, a subject I take up in chapter 4.) Recall that *punishment*, in a behavioral account, simply means encounters with aversive consequences, and not a specific form of discipline administered by an authority. Thus, trauma, disaster, abuse, neglect, and bad luck all come under the rubric of punishment. Punishment produces anxiety; anxiety is what people feel when they do not know what to do, and the potential for aversive consequences puts people in a position where they would like to know what to do to keep them from occurring. Punishment also produces depression, in the sense that a set of aversive contingencies will teach the person to do nothing, will teach the person that any move toward a goal is likely to produce pain. Anxiety and depression, it goes without saying, are two of the major subjective experiences that lead to therapy referrals.

Parenthetically, many behavior therapies, in my experience, are not behavioristic, in the sense that they do not comply with the following suggestions. By the same token, many so-called psychoanalytic therapies do not focus on the therapist-patient relationship, and many systemic therapies ignore the therapy system. All of these therapies, as practiced, are susceptible to the tendency to apply psychology to the patient's life and not to the therapist's office. Skinner developed radical behaviorism to address the problem of psychologists who were behavioristic about rats but not about themselves; there are also long traditions that might be called radical psychoanalysis and radical systems theory that apply to the therapist and the therapy as well as to the patient.

A behavioristic therapy, then, should have several features. Anything the patient remembers during the session can only be understood by first understanding its functional relationship to the environment in which it was remembered. Whether that necessarily translates to an unconscious comment by the patient about the therapy (Langs, 1978) is debatable, but surely the therapist should locate every memory in the immediate environment in which it was produced. This means that the memory should not be taken by the therapist as a literal representation of a past event, but as a current behavior in response to current events

The therapist should allow the effects of punishment to extinguish by occasioning similar behaviors to the ones that were punished and reacting to them neutrally. This would mean a stance of analytic neutrality (which I define as not having any agenda other than that specified in the therapy contract, and therefore not passing personal judgment on the patient's memories or statements about them). Neutrality is necessary partly because it is hard to guess which behaviors were previously punished, so the best stance is to punish none of them. Also, the therapist should avoid being perceived as a potential source of punishment.

Therapists should encourage an active and accurate imagination in patients. An active and accurate imagination helps a person solve problems in living, because to the extent that one's imagination is active and accurate, one can try out solutions to problems without the aversive consequences of trial and error. This means that the therapist should encourage the patient to talk freely and not punish (react aversively to) what is said. One problem with reacting *positively* when patients say things is that it creates an expectation of positive reactions that makes a nonreaction aversive. For all these reasons, neutrality and acceptance are the best behavioristic practice.

A behavioral account of memory, or remembering, can help us avoid the erroneous and misleading metaphor of storage and retrieval. It should alert us to the effect of the immediate environment on the memory, such that we always consider the circumstances of the remembering, not just or even primarily the circumstances in which the original events did or did not take place. A behavioral account should also alert us to reinforcers and punishers affecting the remembering, including the general reinforcement history for accuracy and the general reinforcement history for spinning the memory to make oneself look better. At least in therapies that are organized around discussing the problem (as is typical of office-based, individual therapy) and not around intervening directly in the problematic situation, a behavioral approach to memory implies some of the cornerstones of psychoanalytic technique, including neutrality, free association, and understanding the connection between a memory and the therapy.

Behavior theory also implies that case conceptualizations should not depend entirely on histories or on reports of incidents. The therapist is advised to observe the behavior-environment relations in front of her, and to emphasize these in her formulation of the patient's problem. It is only when she can observe a problematic response within its occasioning environment that a therapist can fully appreciate its function. Such *derivative behaviors*, derived from the same factors that produce problems in living, not only give the therapist a chance to observe them in action, they also give her a way of measuring her progress. For example, a patient may come for help with his distance from others, and this may be reframed as a need to change his domineering behaviors. The therapist is advised to identify derivative behaviors in the therapy relationship, namely, the patient's efforts to dominate (or to be overly submissive to) the therapist. Absence of such behaviors should make the therapist question the utility of the formulation as to the basis of the patient's distance from others.

A behavioristic view of training is that supervisors should help the trainee experience certain signs from the patient that the trainee did something right as reinforcing, so that the trainee/therapist will continue to do such things (Karson & Dougher, 1980). A typical example would be the patient who complains about a therapist's firm boundaries but then reports success at work managing a disagreeable customer: supervisors should help the trainee experience the patient's overt complaints as irrelevant and the patient's story as reinforcing. Conversely, supervisors should teach the student to experience as irrelevant certain signs from the patient that most therapists enjoy but which are not actually signs of having done right. Among the latter are overt expressions of gratitude and overt praise. If the therapist tries something that the patient praises, the therapist does not know whether the intervention was useful or whether it induced praise for some other reason. Praise, gratitude, gifts, and new information are all suspect as reinforcing consequences of therapist behaviors, because they are all the kinds of things that people do in subordinate positions in an effort to appease people with power. One of the greatest appeals of therapeutic privilege is not having to worry about what the effects are of our technique on the patient, as people in power rarely have to worry about the effects of policy on those without a political voice. Good training identifies reliable indicators that therapists can use as guides to their own behavior.

Ideally, therapist behaviors are reinforced by subtle signs from the patient that the problem is being resolved. These include the diminishment of derivative behaviors, that is, of behaviors derived from the same response tendencies that the therapy is about. If a narcissistic patient's narcissistic behavior in the sessions diminishes, it is a good sign—as long as it has never been called to the patient's attention as an example of narcissism. If it has been called to the patient's attention, there is too great a chance that the patient is desisting as a result of the punishing effect of this attention, and not because the variables responsible for his narcissism have changed.

Another subtle sign of progress is the appearance of new skills. If a patient with poor metacommunication skills responds to an intervention by discussing the situation, it is a sign that something has been learned, and use of that type of intervention should be strengthened under similar circumstances. Other relevant skills might include solving a problem in the therapy room, as when an autocratic patient responds flexibly to a conflict with the therapist around what was said in a previous session. Such flexible responding should reinforce the therapist behavior that occasioned it. Since many of the problems that bring people to therapy involve interpersonal skill deficits, the emergence of relationship skills in the therapy is often a good sign that should reinforce what the therapist did to elicit them.

Finally, therapists should find it reinforcing when patients report stories that are metaphorical representations of help occurring. Bateson, Jackson, Haley, and Weakland (1956) suggest, as noted in the next chapter, that it is a bad sign if the therapist is late for a session, apologizes, and then the patient tells a story about a friend who missed a boat that almost sank. Such a story should, in behavioristic terms, be potentiated as an aversive consequence and should punish the therapist's behavior of starting late and apologizing lamely. If, however, the therapist's apology had been effective—not merely an "I'm sorry" designed to deflect criticism but a thorough taking of responsibility for being late and for its effects on the patient—then the patient might tell a story about the nice crewman who rushed his baggage through the terminal so he could make his ferry. These kinds of positive metaphors should be made into reinforcers by the people responsible for training therapists, which would reinforce the therapist behavior of taking full responsibility for coming late. Making different patient behaviors reinforcing, punishing, or irrelevant to trainees depends on supervisors who can recognize and highlight different patient reactions for the benefit of the trainee (Karson & Dougher, 1980). Overall, supervisors should use their power to direct trainees' attention to the effects of their interventions on patients and away from whether the supervisor liked the intervention.

Chapter Four

Systems Theory, Psychotherapy, and Reporting Memories

Though it be honest, it is never good to bring bad news.

—Shakespeare, Cleopatra in *Antony and Cleopatra*

Systems theory is best known to many clinicians by way of the concept of the *identified patient*. The term implies that the person brought to therapy or seeking therapy has been identified by self or others as having the problem, but often the problem is really in the system, and the system's problem is manifesting itself in one of its members. The real patient, as it were, is the family, the couple, or the organization in which the patient is functioning. A trivial, but true, example is the seven-year-old boy referred for enuresis at school. After examining him for anxiety, defiance, and impulsivity, and after starting him in play therapy, the problem was eventually solved by consulting with his teacher. She then changed her rule that the bathroom could only be used in the last ten minutes of every hour, a rule that this boy could not accommodate.

A more typical systemic resolution might emerge in an examination not of the little boy or the teacher's rules, but in an examination of the effects of his enuresis on the relevant systems. A fundamental tenet of systems theory, then, is that the meaning or purpose of a symptom can only be understood by stepping back and looking at the larger picture, just as the purpose of a gear can only be understood by looking at the machine of which it is a part. Likewise, a problem can only be understood by appreciating the larger context. So, if a gear has a broken tooth, before blithely replacing it with a new part, the systemically minded mechanic wonders if some idiosyncrasy in the machine is manifesting itself in the broken gear. For example, a design flaw in the exhaust system may be overheating the gear

51

and weakening it, or an inadequately trained driver may be shifting gears before fully depressing the clutch pedal.

For a little boy, the relevant systems (the machines of which his enuresis is a part) are likely to be either the classroom (where the behavior occurs) or his immediate family (whose reactions are highly relevant to him). For example, his classmates might jeer at him when he wets his pants, and jeering may be a reinforcer because it allays anxiety by casting him in a familiar role or because it makes him feel in control of social rejection which otherwise sneaks up on him. Regarding his family system, enuresis may make it impossible for his mother to continue her education, an education that the boy associates with her crippling feelings of self-doubt. Enuresis forces her to return to the mothering role, in which the boy senses her feelings of competence and self-assurance.

This aspect of systems theory—locating symptoms in their systemic contexts for the purpose of understanding them and directing interventions at the system rather than at the symptom—will be taken up in chapter 7. Indeed, my approach to interpreting early memories can be summarized as viewing the characters in the memory as aspects of the self that operate in a system analogous to a family system. In chapter 6, I will use systems theory to explore the meaning of the memory itself; for now, I am using it to explore the *reporting* of a memory. In that context, the memory report is like a symptom in the sense that it is a metaphorical communication within a system. In a confidential, individual therapy, it is hard to see what other system than the therapy relationship can be relevant to the patient, since the only recipient of the communication is the therapist. To understand the report of a memory, we must consider the effects of the report on the therapy relationship.

REPORTS AND COMMANDS

An important element of systems theory treats all communication as having a *report* function and a *command* function (Watzlawick, Bavelas, & Jackson, 1967). Essentially, the former is the message per se and the latter is the way the communication of the message affects the definition of the relationship between sender and receiver. For example, a newspaper editor announced at the outset of a high-level meeting that journalists have an obligation to get the story right. The report function of this communication was trivial, in that everyone there already endorsed it; the command function was controversial, as the editor tried to define her relationship with others as her being the keeper of the flame and their needing instruction on journalism.

The report and command functions are somewhat analogous to Skinner's (1957) delineation of *tacts* and *mands*, where tacts (from *contact*) are verbal behaviors whose utility is in the conveyance of information ("We're out of butter") and mands (from *command*) are verbal behaviors whose utility is in their direct effect on the listener ("Duck!"). A fascinating aspect of Skinner's approach is the extent to which verbal behaviors that sound like tacts on their face are actually mands: simple reports of information are often maintained not by the potential use made of the conveyance of information but by the effect on the listener. For example, *we're out of butter* may impel the listener to apologize, to defend himself, or even to go buy some.

The report/command distinction of systems theory can also be described as content and position, where content is the information conveyed and position is the role relationship implicit in the fact of its conveyance and in the manner in which it was conveyed. A fundamental tenet of systems theory is that the essential unit of concern is not a particle or bit of energy, but the relationship between things. Thus, people are constantly in the business of defining their relationships to each other, and every communication carries information about how the communicator would like to define that relationship. An arrogant graduate student approached the professor after the first day of class and told her that she had given a really good lecture, that she had done a nice job. The content was that the lecture was good; the positional relationship attempted by praising the professor with a compliment, and not just a compliment but an evaluation, was one of supervisor-teacher rather than student-teacher.

PARADOXICAL COMMUNICATION

Paradoxical communications risk symptom formation, according to systems theorists (Watzlawick et al., 1974). One form of paradox is an irreconcilable contrast between the content and the positioning of a communication. "Throw me a birthday party" is an order, but the content is a request to be treated as a child. "Throw me a *surprise* party" compounds the paradox by requiring that the listener be obedient and surprising at once. "Take a shower" is consistent between content and position if the speaker is a parent and the listener is child of eight. If the listener is an adolescent, the positional element becomes paradoxical. Unless the child has some way to step outside the communicative field, she cannot comply with the content without accepting the positional statement that the parent is still her boss. The lose-lose options of the listener can cause her to resort to symptomatic communication, such as taking a shower and making a mess, or taking a shower and expressing contempt for the parent. Thus, therapists are well advised to keep the tasks they ask patients to complete within the parameters of the patient role, and to keep the asking within the parameters of the therapist role.

The report of an early memory in therapy typically affirms the patient-therapist relationship, at least superficially, and by its very nature does not induce symptomatic functioning. It is the patient's job to be vulnerable, to show the man behind the curtain, to be less powerful than the therapist, and the report of an early memory is consistent with that positioning. Even if the report is in response to a direct query, it implicitly accepts the therapist's role of asking about the patient's childhood. When the report of a childhood memory is not a response to a direct query, it proactively invites the relationship to be defined as parental, as the patient voluntarily assumes a childlike, vulnerable position.

Examples of tasks that therapists ask of patients that do induce symptomatic functioning are not hard to find. When a patient calls the therapist's office for help, only questions designed to protect both parties from a total waste of time should be asked. For example, a therapist who does not see substance abusers might inquire if this is an issue. Extra questions are likely to position the patient in a role (while answering the questions) not suitable for psychotherapy, whose practitioners usually want patients to self-disclose in a trusting context. For example, one clinic asked patients on the phone about their sexual orientation, presumably in an effort not to communicate an assumption of heterosexuality. The question itself, though, required patients to abandon aspects of the role of patient, notably, the position of revealing information when relevant, when comfortable, and in the context of a confidential and caring relationship. The question also forced the patient to accept a generic label (e.g., heterosexual, homosexual, or bisexual), when therapy usually encourages unique self-definitions. Similarly, excessive questioning, even in person, creates a role-relationship in which the patient is bound to become focused on the therapist's agenda, rather than balancing awareness of the therapist with attention to her own agenda and her own imagination.

THERAPY AS A SYSTEM

Systemic therapists often intervene directly in the problematic system, whether by bringing a whole family into the therapy office or by entering an organization or classroom or home. Behaviorists also like to see the problem directly; they are more likely than psychoanalytic therapists to assess a problem in its environment and to intervene there as well. As noted in the previous chapter, when therapy consists of discussing a problem in a therapist's office, behavior therapists are not always as behavioristic as they might be about the behaviors emitted in the office; they do not always interpret patient's (or therapist's) behavior in functional relation to the environment that occasioned them (the therapist's office). Analogously, when systemically oriented therapists help people in the therapy office, they do not always think systemically about the therapy system.

A systemic look at the therapy relationship supports certain approaches to individual treatment. Systems theorists have written about the importance of metacommunication (talking about talking, talking about what is going on) as a means of conflict resolution (Watzlawick et al., 1967). They note that the big problems in life have usually been exacerbated by an inability to metacommunicate when necessary. This difficulty often occurs because a genuine invitation to metacommunicate typically involves a positioning statement of equality, regardless of the content of the conflict, and people with a power advantage, or who think they have a power advantage, are often unwilling to relinquish it in the service of metacommunication. Systems theorists note that couple and family therapy often teaches people who are important to each other to metacommunicate, and individual therapy often teaches this skill through discussions of conflicts in the patient's life. The psychoanalytic twist on this would be that metacommunication skills are best taught to individual therapy patients by metacommunicating about conflicts that arise in the therapy relationship itself.

If humans are constantly trying to define their relationships to each other, then one way to look at individual therapy is as an opportunity to resolve conflicts between the patient's and the therapist's definitions of their relationship. Ideally, the therapist defines the relationship as a helping relationship with certain boundaries and structures, while the patient attempts to define it in some problematic way that is also very familiar to his sense of self. Metacommunication on this topic would equate to transference interpretation. Early memories can guide these interpretations when they are used as roadmaps to the patient's primary expectations of the world and as roadmaps to treatment impasses, as explored below, especially in chapters 6 and 13. Here, though, I want to discuss how the reports of early memories can also set the therapy relationship back on course when it is the therapist rather than the patient who is defining the relationship in some idiosyncratic way.

POWER IMBALANCE IN THERAPY

One way to summarize the majority of patients is to say that they have been, typically as children, exposed to power imbalances where the difference in power was exploited or misused to their detriment. The cure, if you will, for such misuse of power is not to invite them into a relationship in which the power imbalance is dispersed; the cure is to invite them into a relationship with an intense power imbalance and then to manage that imbalance caringly and judiciously. This is arranged in individual therapy by disguising the fact that the therapist has been hired to work for the patient, by deemphasizing the payments and emphasizing the therapist's maturity and expertise and the patient's emotionality and dependence. Similarly, the structural authority of parents is ideally arranged by emphasizing the parents' strengths and the children's dependence, and deemphasizing the parents' emotional dependence on the children.

For better or worse, though, we are only human. As humans, we are subject to certain facts about the way we use power. The point has been made many times, and I like James Madison's (1788) version; he wrote, "The accumulation of all powers, legislative, executive, and judiciary, in the same hands, whether of one, a few, or many, and whether hereditary, selfappointed [*sic*], or elective, may justly be pronounced the very definition of tyranny" (p. 322). His point is that absolute power does not run the *risk* of becoming tyrannical; it is the *definition* of tyranny, because human nature is such that possession of such power is bound to be exploited; power corrupts. Now, individual therapists do not have *absolute* power over patients, but it can seem that way to patients during sessions. The fact that therapists may have to answer to licensing boards and legal standards is usually no more present in the day-to-day business of running a session than is the fact that parents may have to answer to child protective services. Indeed, the less power the therapist has within the therapy office, the less curative the relationship will be, if one accepts the idea that the patient typically needs a relationship with an intense power imbalance where the power is managed well.

The therapist's justifiable desire to increase her power in the therapy combines with her all-too-human propensity to abuse her power. Because of this propensity, a power imbalance created for the purpose of disconfirming the patient's expectations can instead become one that confirms them. In this context, the patient's early memories can be used as a guide not only to his expectations of how power will be mismanaged, but also to how it *is* being mismanaged.

In a seminal article, Bateson et al. (1956) describe the crazy-making *double bind* that, they hypothesize, produces schizophrenic communication. They note that the double bind also occurs in psychotherapy, and that therapy patients typically respond to it with metaphorical speech. The double bind has three components, namely, an intensely important power-imbalanced relationship, a mixed message from the person with greater power, and the impossibility of metacommunicating about the problem. As mentioned at the end of chapter 3, Bateson et al. give the example of a therapist who comes late for a session and apologizes. The individual therapy relationship is, ideally, intensely important enough (else, there will not be sufficient leverage for change) to meet the first requirement for a double-bind. Coming late communicates not caring, but apologizing communicates caring, a mixed message. Apologizing right away communicates a desire on the part of the therapist not to discuss the matter further. Bateson et al. suggest that the patient is likely to respond with a story, say, about a friend who missed a boat that almost sank. The story serves both as an invitation to metacommunicate about being late, and also as protection from the consequences of accusing the therapist of imperfection if the therapist declines the invitation and treats the story as only about the friend and not about the therapy.

Reports of early memories in therapy, then, may be instances of metaphorical speech designed to comment on the therapist's behavior, but with a protective coating of metaphor, just as theater in a dictatorship may be an attempt to comment on politics without engaging the wrath of the government. Dictatorships have been much more alert to this aspect of metaphorical theater than one might expect, perhaps even more alert than many therapists. The Nazis shut down Renoir's film *Rules of the Game*, which was ostensibly a screwball comedy about a social gathering at a hunting lodge that made fun of the French, and the Elizabethan government routinely censored and even executed playwrights for writing plays "perceived to have 'application to the times'" (Wood, 2003, p. 155). Similar concern may have contributed to Jesus' preference for parables under threat of punishment for heresy (Asimov, 1969). In therapy, if the therapist accepts the metaphor, the metacommunication can proceed. If the therapist ignores the metaphor, the patient feels protected from recrimination because it is likely that the therapist did not hear the embedded evaluation and will not retaliate by blaming the patient.

Case Example: The Bath

An example occurred when I was working with an attractive woman, Nancy, about my own age (I am heterosexual). Normally, sexual tension with patients in my experience dissipates after a session or two, as the therapeutic relationship cultivates the pained, childlike aspects of the patient's personality. I see her as a child, and this role relationship for me and for many therapists I know is inconsistent with a sexual response. Once my own sexuality is out of the question, the patient rarely in my experience sexualizes the relationship, but even when she does, I can manage the sexualization without conflict, just as I would if a little girl expressed sexual interest in me. Nancy was different,

though, because the therapeutic relationship was from the outset almost social. She was seeking therapy for what amounted to vocational counseling,
trying to choose between two job offers. Our conversation certainly covered
private matters, but no more so than one might have covered at a dinner party
with a friend of a friend. There was never any risk of my breaching professional boundaries, but when she flirted with me, I think I deflected it the way
I would from any woman, communicating in effect that I was not available,
rather than the way I typically would from a patient, that is, by trying to explore it. Nothing was ever said about flirting or about sex. She would look at
me or smile at me in a certain way and I would ignore it, or at least not comment on it, just as I would do if a social friend flirted with me.

In the context of our discussing what her various family members would
say if she chose one job over the other, Nancy said that her mother would prefer whichever job made Nancy seem like she was being a "good girl,"
whichever one her mother thought was more suitable for a woman. Nancy's
description of her mother's agenda reminded her of an early memory of her
mother scrubbing her "down there" while giving her a bath, to the point that
it hurt somewhat. I took the report of the memory as a metaphorical response
to the situation. I was in a position of power with Nancy, telling her to be self-
disclosing and emotionally close to me, but at the same time not to feel or discuss sexuality.

When I heard the memory, I did not immediately get the connection to
how I was deflecting her flirting. I did, however, get the connection to a
parental, intimate scene, and I was willing to explore what it might have to
say about me. This comports with my general approach to therapy as a series of making messes and trying to sort them out. Eventually, I interpreted
the memory as a commentary on how she felt her sexuality was being treated
by me, as something I would like, impossibly, to obliterate. I do think in general that no matter how cognitive a brief treatment attempts to be, after six
or seven sessions, the parental and personally close aspects of the relationship become more prominent. This is probably the reason that therapists doing even programmed, manualized therapies are more successful if they de-
part from the manual and attend to the relationship (Ablon and Jones, 1999;
Jones, 2000).

Homeostasis

The way I managed this interpretation of Nancy's early memory relates to the
systemic concept of homeostasis. Homeostasis refers to the tendency of systems to sustain themselves by countering a push to change with a push to remain the same. Systems without this feature tend to dissipate or change un-

recognizably, so by definition a system that has become a pattern probably has homeostatic elements. Some family therapies are organized entirely around this concept. For example, the reflecting team tries not to push and thereby avoids the pushing back. Strategic therapies go even further, attempting to push in the direction of stasis, hoping to induce a push for change in the therapy. Put more simply, homeostasis is familiar to anyone who has ever commented on a friend's annoying romantic partner. If you say he is irritatingly arrogant and you do not understand why she is with him, your friend will tell you how he comes through on her birthday. If you applaud the fact that he always comes through on her birthday, your friend will tell you that this is scant compensation for his irritating arrogance.

I was tempted to describe myself as having made the slightest imaginable technical mistake in ignoring Nancy's flirtation, and to describe her reaction to me as a pathological construction of the world that led her to experience me as trying to obliterate her sexuality under cover of caregiving. However, even though I believe the image of a parent figure scrubbing Nancy's genitals was an unfair metaphor for what I had done, I think we got further with the memory because I took full responsibility for the characterization, leaving it up to her to take full responsibility for her reaction.

I told Nancy, after leading her up to it with observations about similarities between the memory and the therapy, and after some brief discussion of her harmless efforts to flirt with me, "That image of a parent trying to obliterate your sexuality was a picture of me ignoring your flirtation and making you feel like you were dirty." My style is not to ask if I am right, or to couch my interpretation in speculative terms, but rather to communicate that this is what I think and if I am wrong, so be it. I do this because, as noted above, I do not want to democratize the relationship. This left Nancy free, after digesting this interpretation, to discuss her own contribution, namely, her preparedness to view herself as sexually dirty and to have her sexuality greeted with hostility. Nancy's and my new level of intimacy and honesty enhanced the topic of job choice, which then broadened into a discussion of her ability to make gratifying decisions in other areas of her life. The therapy, now relationship-based, lasted for about a year. Many things besides the reporting of an early memory might have led to this deepening of our relationship, but in my opinion the early memory served especially well. Because it was an early memory, it likely seemed more intrinsic to her sense of self than might a dream or an incidental story from her daily life. This quality facilitated her ability to use the memory as a guide to her own complexes about feeling accepted versus feeling dirty.

As an epilogue to this story, I think Nancy's termination dream is worth reporting. The night before our last session, she dreamed that she was driving on a country road, and her car just stopped running. She coasted to a farm-house, where she knocked and was greeted by a man in overalls. She asked if she could use his phone, but when she got inside, she was distracted by his remodeling project. He was sheet rocking and painting the living room, and she became engaged in helping him. She also helped him make some design decisions, and by the time she left after a satisfying day's work, she forgot she had wanted to use the phone. She went back to her car, and it started right up.

I think this dream captures something essential about the process of many therapies. The patient has some problem (her car will not run), and comes to therapy. Once in therapy, the original problem is barely mentioned. Instead, the therapist and patient work together on improving their space, with each taking part in design and construction. Changed by the experience of work-ing with the therapist, the problem resolves (presumably in real life not by magic but because of its no longer fitting the changed patient).

CHARACTER VERSUS ROLE

A systemic view of behavior often finds people acting according to their roles, rather than according to their character. When the boss gets frustrated that paperwork is not completed, she is not a domineering, impatient person; she is merely the boss. When a police officer is gruff and reserved with a cit-izen, he is just acting like a cop. I leave aside, for now, the question of whether there is any room for character left over at all once the various roles are accounted for, whether there is anything to us besides the roles we play.

Two good examples of people playing roles include *King Lear* and the Stanford prison experiment (Haney, Banks, & Zimbardo, 1973). In *Lear*, the King thinks the way he has been treated—with deference, obedience, and declarations of adoration—is the result of his character rather than the result of the role he is in. When he gives up the role, he is tragically surprised to find that he is no longer treated the same way. Ironically, those who treated him with love for his person even when he was King did not act as deferent, obe-dient, or adoring as the others at court, and he banished them. In the Stanford prison experiment, students for a long weekend were divided randomly into prisoners and guards. Before long, the guards were treating the prisoners sadistically. The way actual guards act in prison—all too often derogating the prisoners—may reflect more on the role relationship than on the character of the guards. Truth to tell, though, some people ill suited for the role of guard would just quit.

THE NEED TO BE ONESELF

I want to mention the happiness that results when the roles that life offers are the ones we are suited to, the ones we are good at. I think one of the most powerful human motives is the need to be oneself. Like the powerful need for oxygen, however, it is a motive rarely observed. The drive for oxygen is only visible when a person is deprived of it, and the drive to be oneself is visible only when the person is not in a role suitable to her. However, people almost always have plenty of oxygen, and people are almost always in situations that suit their self-definitions. The latter is true because people drift toward situations that are familiar, and they influence other situations to become more familiar.

The tendency to find ourselves in suitable situations—the need to be oneself—is related to reinforcement because we generally like being ourselves. Even when we fantasize about being someone else, we don't really imagine being *them*; we imagine being *us* being them. One reason we like being ourselves is because, as noted in chapter 1, everything good that has ever happened to us has happened in the presence of ourselves. If everything good that ever happened to us happened in the presence of the ocean, we would like the ocean. Of course, everything bad that ever happened to us also happened in the presence of ourselves, so we are not unambivalent about being ourselves. On balance, though, many more good things than bad have typically happened. When this is not the case, it is not surprising to find such people not wanting to be themselves, which takes various pathological forms depending on the details.

PROJECTIVE IDENTIFICATION

We also find ourselves drawn to familiar situations, or making new situations look like old, familiar ones, through a communicative process that looks a lot like projective identification. Projective identification is a defensive process in which unacceptable features of the self are exported by acting in a way that causes other people to embody those features. It is different from pure projection in that pure projection exports unacceptable features of the self only by *imagining* that other people embody them. In pure projection, the person who needs to export anger imagines that others are persecuting him. In projective identification, the person behaves in such a way as to get other people actually angry with him. He may drive slowly in the left lane, forget appointments, or accidentally insult people when he thinks he is just providing them with useful information.

The term projective identification is often used clinically to describe relatively pathological defensive operations, because healthy people tend to have few features of the self that they find unacceptable. (That statement may be tautological; psychological health may mean only that few features of the self are disowned.) I am using the concept of *acting in such a way as to influence others to act in conformity* to describe a normal mode of systemic interaction between people. Trivial examples include acting friendly to induce friendliness in others, acting important to induce respect in others, and acting reliable to induce trust in others. More interesting examples involve acting out one of the roles in a systemic pattern and inducing others to adopt complementary roles. For instance, Nancy's version of feeling ashamed about her sexuality may have carried communicative messages and interpersonal pressures that induced others to be harshly obliterating. *Projective identification* describes the same interpersonal dynamic as does the positional or command aspect of communication: the imposition of a role relationship.

Again, I do not think it would have been wise to tell Nancy that her pattern of expectations made me ignore her flirtations, because that disownership of responsibility, even if true, is likely to have induced a homeostatic reaction in which she would have been thinking about *my* contribution to what happened instead of her own. And truly, I do think therapists are making mistakes, however understandably, when they succumb to patients' inducements to play complementary roles rather than to comment on such inducements. Still, the early memory can be used as a guide to treatment impasses or problems that arise in the relationship because it constitutes a map of the system that is likely to be re-created by the patient, and because more than other maps (free associations, dreams, theoretical complexes), it is likely to be accepted by the patient as hers.

When patients use projective identification in therapy, they cast the therapist in a role from an operative pattern. If the role is aversive, like an abuser or an abandoned child, the therapist may not like the casting decision. Therapists, being people, naturally reject such roles. A therapist told a patient, "You are perceiving me as abusive because that is how your father treated you." Translated, the therapist is saying, "I can't handle the image of abuse any better than you can. Let's join together and agree that this is all your father's fault." A second natural reaction to projective identifications is to enact them. If someone drives slowly in front of us to export anger, it is natural to get angry. And if a patient fails to pay for a session and then tells the therapist he spent all his funds on cigarettes, the therapist may get angry as well. Berating the patient merely reenacts the complex, however, solidifying the patient's commitment to that particular road map. (Berating by therapists usually takes the form of diagnosing the patient's behavior as deviant and pathological.) Instead, therapists are advised to metabolize or contain projective identifications (Ogden, 1981). This is generally accomplished by retaining the therapeutic stance while neither rejecting nor enacting the role. Specifically, the therapist can comment on the process, often by suggesting that the patient is showing the therapist something important. For example, "I think you are showing me what it is like to be caught in an abusive relationship," or "You are showing me what it is like to feel uninformed and powerless."

THERAPY AS A SYSTEM: THE EXAMPLE OF BOREDOM

Psychoanalysts have written from the start about their own reactions and using them as a basis for understanding the patient. However, it is not always clear how the information thus obtained is to be used in the treatment. Often, psychoanalytic therapists are reduced to the ineffective stance of using their reactions merely to describe the patient, and stating these descriptions aloud is considered to be an interpretation of the transaction. Considering the therapy as a system can clarify the therapist's use of self-monitoring.

As an application of systems theory to the therapy dyad, let's take the example of being bored by a patient. The therapist is often in the position of treating her own boredom either as a sign that she needs to work out some countertransference problem or as a sign that the patient is too cut off from his affect. The analogy would be a couple that comes for therapy because the husband does not listen to the wife. A couple's therapist is unlikely to treat the husband for being afraid of intimacy or the wife for being a drone. The couple's therapist, at least if she is thinking systemically, is more likely to wonder about the role that not-listening plays in the marriage, what function it serves. She then might try to change the marriage (rather than either participant) or to fulfill the function that is being served by the not-listening in some other manner. For example, if she thinks the marriage is not good at regulating intimacy, and that the marriage relies on the husband's boredom for this purpose, she might introduce a different method for doing so that is not as upsetting as not-listening. The therapist might get the couple to agree to set a kitchen timer for thirty minutes once a day for conversations, so that it becomes the therapist and the kitchen timer that regulate intimacy, rather than the husband's boredom. (The therapist would be well advised to invent some plausible alternative reason for the use of the timer, so that the couple can solve their problem without having to admit they cannot regulate intimacy well.)

When a therapist is bored, a systemic view of the therapy relationship invites her to treat the patient and the therapist as a couple. Rather than trying to fix herself or diagnose the patient, the boredom can be addressed either by changing the relationship or by discerning its function and fulfilling it in some other way. Changing the relationship, in this context, often means changing its setting. For example, boredom in a therapist may be a symptom of a therapy set-up in which privacy is so impaired that the patient dare not speak of anything that is genuinely personal. Instead of diagnosing the patient with isolation of affect, and instead of berating herself for not listening intently, the therapist can examine ways to enhance the confidentiality of the treatment.

An example of gleaning the function of boredom and fulfilling that function more constructively is provided by the all-too-common example of the beginner who talks as much as the patient. She may not subjectively experience boredom, but boredom can be inferred from her not listening carefully to the content of the patient's speech, and from her tendency to proceed with the next item on her own agenda almost regardless of what the patient says. The function of the boredom, and of its talkative disguise, is to hide the distressing fact that the therapist does not know how to help the patient. A supervisor can replace this function by taking the onus of failure on herself. The supervisor might suggest that the therapist's job, at this point in her training, is just to tell the supervisor what happened in the therapy, and the supervisor will be responsible for helping the therapist design successful interventions. If, in addition, the supervisor requires detailed process notes, written immediately after the session, as the method by which the therapist is to report on the session, this task will interfere with the therapist's talkativeness (since it is hard to memorize speech while speaking) and will also interfere with boredom (since it gives the therapist something to do that she *can* do, and since memorization requires careful listening).

The intersubjective model views such issues as therapist boredom as arising from the relationship rather than from either party. It is no coincidence that it is often called intersubjective *systems* theory. I share the assumption that viewing therapist boredom as mutually created is a good starting point both for resolving it and for enhancing the relatedness of therapist and patient. I am saying that early memories can provide a more specific guide to the problem than a general interest in mutuality and collaboration.

Case Example: Sleeping on the Job

One patient, Tom, had pronounced schizoid tendencies and came for therapy because he was aware that other people had emotional connections that he lacked. Specifically, he did not have trouble meeting women, but his relationships petered out after a few weeks. Invariably, the woman complained that he was not emotionally responsive. He was white, young, attractive, and intelligent. During the first session, I very nearly fell asleep, and I had to resort to pinching myself surreptitiously to stay awake.

Tom's earliest memory was of trying on his mother's high heels while she was taking a nap and he was supposed to be playing quietly by himself. Most uses of memories are not this literal, but it would seem that in his psychology, playfulness, at least of the sort that revealed the self, was connected with a sleeping audience. When women became interested in him, their vitality and self-expression led him to fall asleep psychologically, by shutting down his emotional responsiveness. In therapy, something about the way he revealed himself induced sleepiness in me. The child in the memory needed to learn how to play even when the parent was awake, and the parent needed to learn how to be awake even when the child was playing.

This simple formulation, I think, helped me see the connection between what might be called our intersubjective space and Tom's psychology. All too often, students who identify with the intersubjective approach understand that they are supposed to be attuned to their patients, and that this somehow fixes symptoms associated with their patients' parents not having been sufficiently attuned when the patients were children. However, they are not able to spell out how this helps, any more than they might be able to articulate how it helps to kiss a boo-boo. In Tom's world, fearful expectations of playful interaction were regulated by sleepiness (whether literal or psychological). If we could fix the sleepiness between us, it would open the door to finding a better way to manage his fearfulness, for example, by detoxifying or extinguishing his fearful reactions to play.

I could not find a way to bring up the topic based on my own sleepiness that did not sound insulting. "Let's explore why I can't stay awake when I'm with you" did not sound particularly therapeutic to me. This may be entirely because I was too angry with him to say it caringly rather than because the content was intrinsically impossible to discuss. Instead, I kept the room ten degrees cooler than usual, drank extra coffee, and sat in an uncomfortable position. These precautions were of no avail, as it happened, and as soon as Tom sat down, sleepiness would wash over me like a fairy spell.

I fought back. I resolved to present the situation to a colleague for guidance. At the time, this meant I had to write detailed process notes and read them to my friend, and this in turn meant that I had to memorize the session as it was unfolding. Such a posture of memorization usually blunted the emotionality in a therapy session, but in Tom's and my case, memorization operated slightly in the same manner as the kitchen timer. It created a distance between us that made my sleepiness less necessary. More importantly, perhaps, memorization interfered with sleep. Perhaps even most importantly,

I graduated from coffee to a caffeine pill, which I swallowed shortly before our session started. By the time he came in, I was cortically operating on all cylinders, wide awake.

Tom talked as usual for about ten minutes, while I memorized not only the gist of what he was saying, as was my custom in preparation for consultation, but long patches verbatim. Suddenly, as if he had been injected with narcotics, he fell asleep. This gave me almost forty minutes to reflect on roles, patterns, and projective identification, and to consider whether to wake him up. With a few minutes left in the session, he woke up. He expressed surprise that he had fallen asleep, and left. The next session, I connected his having fallen asleep with his early memory. Now I could mention my own sleepiness without it sounding so insulting, relating it instead to the possibility that one of us needed to be asleep. We even drew the analogy to his psychological sleepiness in relation to women. The therapy seemed to be making progress for a while, at least in the sense that we both managed to stay awake for the sessions. However, when his own train of thought led him to consider the meaning of wearing high heels, he feel asleep again. This time, I wakened him right away, but then he started missing sessions, presumably as a new and lamentable method of regulating closeness, and eventually I lost him.

WHAT KIND OF SYSTEM?

If the therapy dyad is a system, it means the parties are interconnected. This often comes as a surprise to the patient, who may have imagined that the relationship would be more like a doctor-patient relationship than a social or familial relationship. It also comes as a surprise to quite a few therapists, who often expect the real relationship to be one of helpfulness from the therapist and gratitude from the patient, rather than the gritty reality that unfolds when two people get close. As noted above, even therapies designed specifically not to involve the relationship end up doing so, as several hours together discussing intimate concerns inevitably leads to an intermingling of expectations and patterns of relating.

What kind of system is it? I have considered the metaphor of couple's therapy, where the therapist is both a member of the couple and the couple's therapist. But couples are intrinsically sexual in a way that makes the metaphor suspect. Couples are also, ideally, equals in power and status, whereas in my view much of the restorative power of individual therapy derives from making good use of the power imbalance. The parent-child relationship has also been used as a metaphor for psychotherapy. This has much to recommend it, as the therapy relationship is growth-oriented, cherishing, and bounded by a structural hierarchy, just as parenting is. The parenting analogy, though, overstates the importance of the patient to the therapist and, usually at least, the importance of the therapist to the patient. The parenting analogy also ossifies the therapist's metaphorical responsibility for what transpires in the therapy relationship. In other words, the therapist usefully acts as if she has cocreated the roadblocks that emerge in the therapy, and usually this is true. But my children and I really have cocreated our relationships in a way that I don't think is quite true of my patients and me, owing largely to the unity and irreplaceability of my relationships with my children. And it is also true that sometimes the cocreation of roadblocks in therapy is lopsided on one side or the other, and this is a distinction that I am not at all sure can be applied to a reasonably healthy parent-child relationship. My children and I may have cocreated some difficulties, but especially in their infancy and school years, it does not seem valid to say they were ever *primarily* responsible for any difficulties (except Max).

Thus, I am currently thinking of therapy as a foster parent–foster child relationship. This metaphor appeals to me because it includes all the parental overtones mentioned above. It also contains some recognition that many of the patient's problems and many of the therapist's modes of relating are not cocreated, even if they are treated as such. It's also a metaphor that addresses the monetary aspect of the relationship. Few therapists are primarily in it for the money, as is also true of foster parents; both patients and foster children, though, often wonder whether the money is more important than it typically is.

I have not shared this fostering metaphor with many patients. Like actual foster children, I think they are generally fantasizing about the patient equivalent of being a natural child or being adopted, and confronting them with their being foster children might be more hurtful than elucidating. Still, the analogy is useful to me in examining my cocreation of sticking points in the relationship. When a foster child has a problem, I wonder whether it is a functional response to the foster home system, and I consider whether the problem was thus cocreated by the foster parents. But I am nowhere near as likely to lean in that direction as I am with a natural child's family system. Similarly, when a problem arises in therapy, I look first at my own contribution to it, but I am open to the idea that I am more likely to be part of the solution.

Chapter Five

Critical Review of the Literature: Freud, Adler, Mayman, and Bruhn

Those who cannot remember the past are condemned to repeat it.

—Santayana, *Reason and Common Sense* (1905, p. 284)

In this chapter, I critically review the four main approaches to early memories, which may be summarized under the names of Freud, Adler, Mayman, and Bruhn. Each approach is embedded in a particular psychology, and each has certain implications for treatment. Each successive writer had the advantage of capitalizing on the others, and Bruhn (1990), in particular, writing most recently of the four, was able to benefit from developments in the fields of perception, cognition, and memory.

Freud, Adler, Mayman, and Bruhn are all, judging from their published examples, inspirational in their abilities to translate a subject's early memories into pertinent clinical formulations. Only Bruhn provides a systematic approach to interpretation. Freud, Adler, and Bruhn, but not Mayman, have an endpoint in mind as to what kind of thing the memory is about, which is a desirable practice only if the underlying theory is correct for all people and all problems. All four theorists mention, but do not fully explore, the communicative aspects of early memory reports, by which I mean their connection to the circumstances that elicit them. All four tend to interpret the narration of a memory from the subject's point of view, rather than systemically as a pattern of interaction that could have cast the subject in one of the other roles. None, as far as I know, mention the nonhuman characters as part of the cast. None write, at least at any length, about the uses of early memories in psychotherapy, beyond the presumed indirect benefits of enhancing the therapist's general understanding of the patient or the advantages of acquiring information about the patient's childhood.

FREUD

Writing before behaviorism developed to the point where it could sensibly account for complex human behavior and before information theory had been articulated, Freud's psychology is as susceptible to ridicule as is Aristotle's physics. Contemporary psychoanalysis (e.g., Buirski & Haglund, 2001; McWilliams, 1999) bears scant resemblance to Freud's drive theory. Still, certain aspects of human nature do not change, and one may find great psychological insight in the writings of people whose concept of the physical world was even more primitive than Freud's (e.g., Chuang-Tzu and Ecclesiastes).

Unfortunately for Freud's reputation, there is a tendency in contemporary psychology to take his insights for granted and to attribute to him only that which is cockamamie, such as the pervasive phallic symbol and his confusion about women. In explaining what he thought about early memories, and what was wrong with his thinking, I do not intend to diminish his crucial contributions. These might be summarized as the belief in the relevance of philosophy to current problems in living (Bettelheim, 1982); in the limitations of self-knowledge; in the pervasiveness of dark, animalistic human motivations; in the centrality of childhood and the importance of parents in creating response tendencies; and in the viability of helping people in anguish by forming relationships with them. In many ways, we are all Freudians now. If you slip a towel around your waist upon leaving the shower before tending to your three-year-old, you may be a Freudian. If you think the sixth-grader who argued with you about everything was really sweet on you, you may be a Freudian. And if your lover cries out someone else's name in bed and you take umbrage, you may be a Freudian.

Freud believed that it was good for people to take as much ownership as possible of themselves, and this ownership was reflected in their speech when they used the pronoun, *I*, rather than the pronoun, *it*. *I did that* is healthier than *it came over me*. Unfortunately, many aspects of the self are embarrassing or otherwise troubling, so we are motivated to disown many things we do. A summary of Freud's position on symptoms, dreams, and early memories might be called a compromise between what we would like to do and what we can accept about ourselves. The unacceptable is disguised as metaphor, precisely as Bateson et al. (1956, p. 209) describe the weak individual disguising communication among the powerful as metaphor. Freud's view of health led him to conclude that the treatment for such compromises was to unearth or reveal the unacceptable element of symptoms, dreams, and early memories. Such revelation would allow the person to accept the unacceptable, and the compromise would no longer be necessary.

Freud (1915) used the word *repression* to describe the tendency to ignore what is unacceptable in the self. Repression protects the individual's definition of herself, but it comes with certain costs in adaptability and functionality. Like many psychological difficulties, the current problem was once a solution (Watzlawick et al., 1974). Since repression is a kind of forgetting, the cure for its unfortunate effects in Freud's view is to remember. Freud (1898) wrote, "Thus the function of memory, which we like to regard as an archive open to anyone who is curious, is in this way subjected to restriction by a trend of the will, just as is any part of our activity directed to the external world" (p. 296). In other words, Freud asserted that motivation affects remembering and forgetting. He continued, "Half the secret of hysterical amnesia is uncovered when we say that hysterical people do not know what they do not *want* to know; and psycho-analytic treatment, which endeavors to fill up such gaps of memory in the course of its work, leads us to the discovery that the bringing back of those lost memories is opposed by a certain resistance" (p. 296). In other words, forgetting is the problem and remembering is the cure. Forgetting keeps us from embracing ourselves and remembering allows us to do so.

Freud (1898) analogized his forgetting a name with his losing a piece of paper with an address written on it, their common attribute being the rewards involved in not having the information available. The name he forgot reminded him of sexuality and death and therefore, by forgetting the name, he need not think unpleasantly of a patient who killed himself; by losing the slip of paper with the address on it, he need not take time out from a vacation to make an obligatory social call. Unfortunately, like every other prebehaviorist, he thought that losing the piece of paper was a metaphor for forgetting something, rather than the other way around. Freud's dependence on the metaphor of storing information on paper was evident when he wrote, in "Screen Memories," "No one calls in question the fact that the experiences of the earliest years of our childhood leave ineradicable traces in the depths of our minds" (1899, p. 303). This, as noted in chapter 3, is precisely what is called into question about the storage metaphor for memory. Freud's view that childhood experiences are ineradicable led inevitably to his trying to solve adult problems by unearthing those experiences. It also led to his conceptualization of innocuous memories as *screens* that disguised upsetting memories.

Freud (1899) wondered why ineradicable childhood experiences are not accessible to us as adults. He dismissed the idea that their disappearance is a simple function of the child's immature mental activities, noting that children perform quite complex mental operations. He did not consider, of course, the behavioral view that it is not the child who is too immature to develop a narrative autobiography, but the relationship between the child and the verbal community. People simply do not ask very young children the kinds of questions that produce a narrative accounting of themselves, because children need a couple of years of speaking before progressing to the point of answering such difficult questions. The behaviors of remembering and narrating a coherent account are not learned until the conversation with parents reaches this level of complexity. Freud's premise, like the premise of those who argue for the lockbox metaphor for trauma, was simply wrong: There are no "ineradicable traces in the depths of our minds." However, viewing memory as something we have rather than as something we do naturally led Freud to be suspicious about the relative dearth of memories of early childhood. Instead of attributing this dearth to a lack of training, as one might attribute a dearth, say, of reading in children to a lack of training, he attributed it to amnesia and repression. That is, he analogized the dearth of childhood memories to hysterical repression and assumed that the failure of recollection was not a function of the behavior never having been learned in the first place but a function of the aversiveness of remembering. Children, then, were like hysterics, and benefited from forgetting that which they could not own comfortably.

Hysterics compromise between what is unacceptable and what is desired by expressing the desired in a weaker, disguised form. This concept conforms neatly with both behaviorism and systems theory. Where Freud parts company with these theories is in his analogy to childhood. Freud (1899) assumed that childhood memories were also compromises between the unacceptable and the desired. Thus, he interpreted early memories as palimpsests. A palimpsest is reusable parchment, and sometimes under the latest writing, an earlier writing can still be discerned. In Freud's view of the human condition, that which is forgotten must be unacceptable, so he concluded that childhood memories concealed bad things that happened to the child or that the child did. He based this conclusion in part on the notion that children, like adults, ought to recall that which is extraordinary or emotion laden, so that when they do not, their commonplace recollections must conceal the extraordinary and emotion laden. "[P]recisely what is important is suppressed and what is indifferent retained" (p. 306).

When, as Freud reported, a subject could not recall his grandmother's death but could recall an unremarkable occasion from the same period of life when the table was set with nothing but a basin of ice, it seems reasonable to infer that the ice was a symbolic representation of his grandmother's corpse. But that does not necessarily imply that the subject needs to recall the funeral, or even that the subject *can* recall the funeral. After all, the behavior of seeing the funeral has not been rehearsed for decades, and the images from the funeral are no more likely to be reproducible by the subject than directions on how to get to the funeral home. In my view, what the recollection of the basin of ice could be used for in therapy is for information about the family inter-actions in its presence. The basin of ice and the events surrounding it may have been rehearsed and strengthened all these years because that narrative or depiction proved useful to the subject in its own right, say, as a navigational guide to certain kinds of situations, rather than as a disguise for some other memory.

Freud measured the utility of an interpretation of a memory by what else is recalled, because he believed that airing out the contents of the mental appa-ratus was the best way to acquire their power and to take ownership of them. He was not naïve as to the problem of validating reports of memories for ac-curacy, but he simply felt he could tell when he was hearing a true story. Of course, today, largely because of Freud's influence in the area of claims re-garding self-knowledge, we are skeptical of this supposed ability. When we read an assertion by Freud that a patient recalled something that confirmed his theory of the case, we are likely to wonder whether his desire to validate the theory influenced the patient's satisfying response.

Freud did, from early on, understand the difference between a memory and its report, even if he called his (1900) magnum opus "The Interpretation of Dreams" and not "The Interpretation of Dream Reports." For example, in in-terpreting (1899) what he supposed was a screen memory of himself and a boy cousin taking flowers from a girl cousin, he saw the key to unlocking the mystery as the situation in which the memory had recurred to him: as a late adolescent returning to the countryside and falling in love. In the memory, the girl runs home and is given fresh bread, so the boys follow her, tossing away the flowers, and they too are rewarded with fresh bread. The recollection oc-curred when Freud was seventeen and torn between his teenage romance, his father's desire that he settle down with the girl cousin in the memory as an arranged marriage and concentrate on making a practical living, and Freud's desire to pursue the studies that his father thought were frivolous. Freud's analysis of the occurrence of the memory emphasized its relevance to the is-sues of love and career with which he was struggling at seventeen. One con-flict screened by the memory, he thought, was around his ambivalence about *deflowering* the girl, which apparently has the same meaning in German as in English. Another conflict was around whether to give up frivolous studies in favor of being a *bread-winner*, another cognate pun. Thus, because the mem-ory occurred to him while he was wrestling with love and career decisions, he interpreted it in those contexts.

In Freud's analysis of the memory itself, everything that fit his theory was viewed as psychologically motivated, and everything that did not fit his the-ory was viewed as an extraneous oddity added by the reality of the incident in childhood. Freud's commitment to the ineradicable traces of childhood forced him into mental acrobatics on the question of what was interpretable and what was not. If a detail in the memory did not fit the interpretation, then it was retained by chance from an actual event. If it did fit the interpretation and proved later not to have happened, that was okay because the mind shapes memory to its own ends. In fact, Freud thought that the presence of extraneous details *proved* that the events really happened, because a pure fantasy would not have irrelevancies. Freud mentioned the most common example of details proved not to have happened: like many people, he saw himself in his own memory. An ineradicable trace could not logically depict the rememberer, since we do not see ourselves when looking at events. The existence of this phenomenon proved Freud's contention that memories are influenced, and are therefore interpretable as symbolic representations of those influences. Thus, Freud's interpretation of a memory was confirmed both by fitting the data *and* by not fitting the data. Both the malleability and the non-malleability of memory are irrefutably proved because some elements fit the interpretation and some do not. It is really quite difficult to perceive what value Freud found in describing this narrative as a memory rather than as a fantasy, except that the former supported his argument that innocuous memories of childhood are screen memories for something that has been suppressed.

As is common for Freud, he forced the material at hand into the point he was making, but then he straightforwardly posited the alternatives as well. At the end of "Screen Memories" (1899), despite his argument that psychoanalysis reveals and needs to reveal what really happened, he summarized the entire argument that memory is something we do, not something we have:

> It may indeed be questioned whether we have any memories at all *from* our childhood: memories *relating to* our childhood may be all that we possess. Our childhood memories show us our earliest years not as they were but as they appeared at the later periods when the memories were aroused. In these periods of arousal, the childhood memories did not, as people are accustomed to say, *emerge*; they were *formed* at that time. And a number of motives, with no concern for historical accuracy, had a part in forming them, as well as in the selection of the memories themselves. (p. 322)

Later, Freud (1901, 1910) extended this modern idea, analogizing remembering one's childhood with a nation's historians writing its history. He noted all the other agendas operating on such writers besides rendering what happened, and saw the individual's personal history as similarly responsive to agendas other than accuracy.

Despite his forays into communication theory, it seems a fair summary of Freud's position on early memories to say he believed that they are informed by unfortunate childhood events, which they sometimes reveal and typically screen, and that these events and their repression contribute to fixations of libido that result in symptoms. Analysis of memories, like the interpretation of dreams and of unconscious motives, is undertaken to free the libido from its *cathexis* (attachment) to symptoms. This analysis takes place in the context of a *cathected* or valued relationship that does not induce repression, allowing the libido to return to the service of the ego (Freud, 1917b). The implication of an approach to interpretation that "transforms what is unconscious into what is conscious" (p. 455) is that, when applied to early memories, it emphasizes what really happened to and by the child. Freud (1914), in discussing technique, continued with his view that early memories were to be recovered rather than to be viewed primarily as fantasies or as communications. Even when he described the primary role of the analyst as having evolved into a softener of resistance, rather than a pursuer of memory, he said that this role is undertaken to facilitate the patient's role, which is to relate "the forgotten situations and connections" (p. 147). And again, when the patient repeats in the transference various problematic role relationships, Freud views these as "his way of remembering" (p. 150), as if the goal were to unlock the storage cabinet.

ADLER

Adler's (1931) view of early memories was very different from Freud's. Where Freud saw most childhood memories as the residue left over after massive repression, Adler saw them as precious gems preserved for their usefulness.

> Every memory, however, trivial he may think it, represents to him something *memorable*. It is memorable because of its bearing on life as he pictures it; it says to him, "This is what you must expect," or "This is what you must avoid," or "Such is life!" Again we must stress that the experience itself is not so important as the fact that just this experience persists in memory and is used to crystallize the meaning given to life. (p. 19)

Adler's theory of neurosis may perhaps be summarized as follows: Children meet circumstances they cannot manage and, if not taught to improve such circumstances through cooperation and courage, they develop a sense of being inferior. This sense of inferiority leads to compensatory goals of superiority. Symptoms make sense once we understand the way in which, from the patient's point of view, they confirm his or her peculiar sense of superiority. Symptoms thus cannot be resolved directly because they always serve a goal of achieving superiority, and it is this goal that must be changed. Early memories are central to understanding the individual's specific sense of inferiority and the situations that occasion it. Almost all inferiority can be attributed to physical defect, pampering, or neglect, with birth order a predictably important context. The patient's autobiography, as revealed especially through early memories, reveals, sustains, and justifies his or her quest for superiority. Neurotic compensation for inferiority looks very much like the pervasive human desire to overcome weakness, and different theorists have tried to distinguish them from each other. Nietzsche (1886) would say the difference between the two is in whether the triumph is successful or whether the weakness is neurotically glorified. Rank (1936) would say the difference is in whether the triumph is enjoyed or produces neurotic guilt feelings for being effective. Adler (1931, p. 38) says that the difference between neurotic and healthy triumph is in whether it is on "the useful side of life," which means whether there is a tendency to enrich other people.

Some of Adler's examples of early memories make it hard to understand exactly how he proposes to use them in therapy. He notes, "We are like archaeologists who find fragments . . . and from these fragments proceed to infer the life of a whole city" (p. 71). He asserts their importance to his approach to treatment stating, "I would never investigate a personality without asking for the first memory" (p. 75). And he summarizes his interpretive approach by saying that the patient's "memories represent his 'Story of My Life.'" The patient "meet[s] the future . . . with an already tested style of action" (p. 73). However, the link between memories and therapy seems only to be that the memories enrich the analyst's understanding of the patient and this understanding then must be useful. In some of his examples, he shows a clear and even startling relation between the memory and the symptom. For example, a man fell and hit his head and then could not speak above a whisper; his earliest memory was of falling and not being able to speak for several minutes. Adler interprets the lack of speech as the man's "trademark" (p. 88) method for getting attention after a fall. Adler says the man must learn that speechlessness need not follow a fall to get comfort, but he does not say how the man is expected to learn this. With another patient (pp. 91–92) he spells out the connections between memories, trademarks, and autobiography for the man and expects that this will produce change.

Certainly, Adler explicitly rejects transference and transference interpretation as a precursor to change (p. 72). "We shall not be able to help him either by spoiling him or by slighting him: we must show him the interest of one man toward a fellow man." Indeed, his approach is remarkably similar to some of the current cognitive-behavioral approaches. He infers beliefs from memories that are mistaken or outmoded guides to behavior, and translates these into statements such as "Other people always humiliate me" or "All my life I was unfortunate" (p. 74). These are then shared with the patient to show him his mistakes.

Like Freud, Adler is unsure whether early memories need be seen as having really happened, but in the main he comes down on the side of history. He does write, "It is indifferent . . . whether [it] is really the first event he can remember—or even whether it is a memory of a real event" (p. 20). And he gives an example that could as well be a dream: "The coffeepot fell off the table and scalded me." He comments, "We should not be surprised to find that the girl whose autobiography began in this way was pursued by a feeling of helplessness and overestimated the dangers and difficulties of life. We should not be surprised either, if, in her heart, she reproached other people for not taking sufficient care of her." Irrespective of their historical accuracy, Adler (p. 19) points out, "The memories of early childhood are especially useful in showing how long standing is the individual's own peculiar approach to life." However, his commitment to history is evident when he continues, "and in giving the circumstances in which he first crystallized his life-attitude," as if that crystallization happened for real and at a given time and as if these are embedded in the memory. Also: "We can judge from them whether the child was pampered or neglected," which implies real pampering and real neglect as opposed to what the child made of the parents.

In the main, though, I see memories as Adler does, as outmoded expectations or as maps to problematic situations. We differ in the extent to which we share our insights with the patient, in the variety of problems we think confront patients, and in the extent to which we view the pattern of the memory systemically. I think some patients can benefit from being told what I think about their memories, as I discuss in chapter 11, Finding a Place to Stand, but some cannot. I think people suffer from many more kinds of complexes than the inferiority complex. And I do not necessarily view a memory as the subject does, that is, from the subject's point of view; instead, I see the role of subject in the memory's system of figures as a casting decision, and as less important than the systemic interaction among the various characters in the memory. I also offer a systematic approach to interpreting memories, even though my results are often roughly similar to those of Adler (1931) and Bruhn (1990).

MAYMAN

Mayman was not the first ego psychologist to attend to early memories (e.g., see Chess, 1951 and Kris, 1956a and 1956b), but his contributions may be considered representative of these developments in psychoanalytic theory. As a psychologist interested in projective techniques, it was natural that he would investigate early memories as an assessment strategy. Consistent with ego psychology, he found in early memories durable representations of the patient's experiences of the interpersonal world, defense mechanisms, identity elements, and psychosexual themes (Mayman & Faris, 1960). He inferred from these the patient's overall mental health, underlying conflicts, and coping strategies.

Ego psychology was anticipated by Freud as he moved in treatment from prying hidden material out of the patient to chipping away at the patient's resistance to revealing that material (1917b). Ego psychology assumes that the manifest content of memories, dreams, and overt behavior is at least as important as what is repressed; the manifestations of the individual's efforts to adapt to, construe, and relate to her environment tell us what we need to know, and these same functions are what are available for observation and intervention. Furthermore, focus on these adaptations, constructions, and relationships facilitates a working alliance that does not unnecessarily foster a domineering or voyeuristic therapy relationship. As Mayman (1968) wrote, "Like any good disguise, surface appearance represents a skillful blend of the images one wishes to hide" (p. 303).

By focusing on identity, defense, and adaptation, ego psychology brought psychoanalysis out of the skull, as it were, and into the social world. This was handy for therapists, who happen to be in the social world of patients and not in their skulls. The emphasis led to a focus on defense and identity and, equally importantly, on development and social interaction. Isomorphic with this interest in the world outside the skull was a developing science that wanted data, not just speculation and case studies. This in turn led to early memory research that was *nomothetic* as opposed to *idiographic*.

In assessment theory, *nomothetic* instruments are those that seek lawfulness across population norms, while *idiographic* instruments are those that reveal a particular individual. Dreams, of course, are typically not scored or coded for content, and we ridicule dream books that offer guides to symbols. Dreams are the ultimate idiographic assessment instruments. Other assessment instruments, such as personality inventories, are useful only if they are scored, and only if the scores are compared with the scores of other people. In interpreting a Minnesota Multiphasic Personality Inventory (MMPI) or a Sixteen Personality Factor Questionnaire (16PF), one rarely if ever looks at the individual items, and the scores on the scales only have meaning in comparison to other people's scores. These are the ultimate nomothetic instruments.

Nomothetic instruments are reductionistic and lose data in the service of clarity and for the benefits of comparing an individual's scores with those of other people. Idiographic methods are harder to compare across individuals, but they do not discard data and they are ideal for intra-individual information. Actuarial prediction and statistical methods of research are nomothetic; the functional analysis of behavior is idiographic. The actuarial user does not care if a particular individual is misclassified, only that on balance there are more correct classifications than there would be without the actuarial. The behaviorist does not care why *most* people scream at their kids, only why this particular client did.

No technique is entirely nomothetic or idiographic. When a 16PF is administered, it is incumbent on the psychologist to consider whether the group it was normed on adequately represents the person taking the test. Idiographic elements are also present when the psychologist considers the circumstances under which the test was administered and any peculiar meaning the subject may attach to these circumstances. Conversely, a therapist hearing a dream compares it with all the other dreams she has heard. Indeed, one way to think about cultural competency in therapy is to inspect the *norming group* for adequate representation of the individual at hand, where norming group, in the absence of nomothetic data, means all the people the therapist has known well. If the current patient is too different from the therapist's norming group, the therapist may not be culturally competent to treat that patient (especially if the therapist does not notice or recognize the difference).

My point with respect to early memories is that a great deal of research has been done to quantify or categorize early memories nomothetically, but it is not clear that this research is fully relevant to the idiographic clinical enterprise. A colleague and I have similarly criticized Rorschachers who attend so carefully to codes and scores that they downplay the idiographic uses that distinguish the inkblot test (Karson & Kline, 2004). Nigg, Lohr, Westen, Gold, and Silk (1992) carried out what is perhaps a typical, successful, nomothetic study of early memories. Early memories were gathered from borderline and nonborderline patients, coded for the presence of malevolent figures, and shown to reveal more malevolence in the borderline sample than in the nonborderline sample. This useful study, like its brethren, accomplished several things at once, adding to the impressive experimental literature another datum to strengthen each of the following assertions. One, borderline pathology is a discrete class. Two, it is characterized by the relative presence of malevolent figures. Three, early memories are constructed. Four, early memories can be reliably rated. Five, the content of early memories conforms with general expectations.

I respect these kinds of nomothetic studies, but how much good do they really do me clinically? They definitely help support my general orientation toward psychopathology and the relationship of narrative material to the inner

life of the patient. But with a specific, individual patient, I am not going to diagnose borderline pathology by coding her memories for malevolence and
checking normative data. Krohn and Mayman (1974) wrote that the two main
uses of early memories were to uncover "internal psychic templates that determine an individual's range of experience of others" and "the overall maturity and integrity of object relations" (p. 445). The myriad of studies that code
memories and correlate the codes with other data support their use for the latter purpose but not the former. For the former, an idiographic interpretative
scheme is needed, such as the one I present in chapter 8.

Studies that code memories and then show statistical effects that link the
codes with variables of interest may seem more *scientific* than a scheme for
interpreting memories. At least one historian of science (Laudan, 1981) views
this perception as a sign of the times, rather than as a sign of what is scientific. The culture of science apparently swings back and forth between
deduction—formulating explanations and testing them by gathering data and
running statistics—and induction—gathering instances, considering their
context, and formulating explanations. Both hypothesis-testing and induction
are central to the scientific enterprise, even if in contemporary psychology
there is less glory in wondering *what* happened that in wondering why. Even
though Skinner developed radical behaviorism specifically to look inside
Watson's *black box*, his name is still associated with the disinclination of
early learning theorists to consider private events (Chiesa, 1994). The real
black-box psychologists, these days, are those who refuse to examine detailed
incidents, and instead rely on nomothetic studies to answer questions like
whether siblings should be placed together in foster care or how early memories should be interpreted. These psychologists want summaries of coded
data submitted to statistical analysis, and they refuse to look inside the data at
what is happening in context. In my view, radical behaviorism has fallen
somewhat out of favor in recent decades almost as much for its commitment
to induction (and its dearth of null hypotheses) as for its rejection of mentalistic explanations.

Thus, I am not going to review the nomothetic experimental literature,
which is easily accessed via an Internet search, but I do want to discuss one
study in particular, because it summarizes the use of early memories as an approach to Krohn and Mayman's overall maturity and integrity of object relations. Shedler, Mayman, and Manis (1993) investigated the failure of personality inventories to distinguish genuine mental health from what they called
illusory mental health, a failure related to the dependence of personality inventories on the conscious self-report of subjects. I have made a similar point,
suggesting that people who report mental health, aside from trying to look
good, may be healthy either in the developmental sense or only in the sense

of being asymptomatic, while those who report symptoms may be developmentally unhealthy or may merely be strong enough to be open to experiencing turmoil (Karson, 1980, p. 504). Shedler et al. demonstrated this effect by comparing inventory data with Mayman's overall assessment of subjects' mental health after reading their early memories. Mayman personally categorized sets of memories as essentially healthy, essentially distressed, or undecided, and his classification was a better predictor of a physiological measure of stress management (coronary reactivity) than were the personality inventories. Of particular interest to us is the second study reported, where Mayman's accomplishment was reproduced by a panel of undergraduates. The instructions given to them constitute a model for approaching a set of early memories as a general measure of overall mental health.

> The clinician [of Study 1] treated the memories as a projective test (like the Rorschach or TAT). He assumed that the memories do not simply represent factual accounts of real events. Rather, they are seen through the lenses of the subject's present psychological make-up. These "lenses" may influence the selection, content, and telling of the memories.
>
> The central issue in judging between psychological health or distress is how the person sees himself or herself in relation to the world, and whether the relations with the world are associated with good or bad feelings:
>
> Is the world seen as somehow threatening, dangerous, malevolent, or frustrating? Is it associated with injury, disaster, traumatic punishment, or frustration? Does the person represent himself as at the mercy of external forces? These kinds of representations of self in relation to the world may indicate distress.
>
> Alternatively, is the world seen as comfortable, safe, secure, benign, and gratifying? Do others, especially parents, come across as sources of gratification, comfort, or security? These kinds of representations of self in relation to the world may indicate psychological health. [They may also indicate physical health, in that rating of these representations predicts health service utilization and actual physical illness (Cousineau & Shedler, in press).]
>
> Another important aspect is narrative believability. Sometimes when a subject says he or she is happy in a memory, you will be convinced of this happiness. But sometimes when a subject says that he or she is happy, the actual details will not convey the feeling of happiness, or they may even seem to contradict the subject's explicit statement. Similarly, a person may describe a parent as warm and comforting, but the details needed to convey an impression of warmth and comfort are not there. Trust your subjective impressions rather than the subject's explicit statements. (Shedler et al., 1993, p. 1122)

With my own students, I summarize these instructions for evaluating a set of early memories for overall mental health by asking them to imagine that they are souls waiting to be born. As potential lives pass by on the conveyor belt, they have to decide if the life in front of them is desirable, or if they will pass and take their chances that the next one will be more appealing. They cannot get any information about the cultural, economic, or physical conditions of the life in question. In fact, all they can get are the early memories, devoid of anything other than their psychological relationships with other characters and with the world at large. If a set of memories would make us pick the life they came from, we diagnose overall essential mental health.

As an example of a set of memories that I think can be reliably classified as unwell, consider the following from a sixty-five-year-old woman. These were collected according to Mayman's protocol for assessments, and they illustrate the prompts he recommended:

Earliest and Next Earliest:
1. We got a big tub for washing clothes and bathing. And when you sit on it, it hurt, it was like sitting on sandpaper. I didn't like taking baths.
1a. She had a baby. I liked that. And then it disappeared. I found out later she died, I think she was about 10 months. I didn't find out until I was 16: We didn't ask in those days. No there was no violence in the family. I didn't think anything of it. I didn't even know it was my sister. It could have been anybody's baby, it was only a baby.

Earliest and Next Earliest of Mother:
2. I was babysitting my brother when they went out. I just remember listening to the radio. Everything was OK except Petey. He kept crying and wanted mom. We shut him in his room and shut the door. Sometimes we'd open the door because he cried more with the door shut.
2a. I remember Christmas. She bought me a doll.

Earliest and Next Earliest of Father:
3. He was a strong willed man. He'd tell you what to do and you did it or you'd get it. There would be no allowance. He'd say, do what I say not what I do.
3a. He used to give me money, quarters, and say, "Get yourself some ice cream."

Best or Most Pleasant Memory:
4. I don't have any nice memories. I just took life for granted. One day at a time. It's the same today. I just don't care one way or another. I mean, if someone wants to have a party I don't have to go to be happy.

Worst or Most Unpleasant Memory:
    5.   I don't have any worst memories.

Sure, these memories have a few, spare, positive features, such as receiving the doll for Christmas and the quarters for ice cream. But these are overwhelmed by the imagery of the unexplained disappearance of a baby, the irritation associated with bathing, and banishing a sad child to his room. This woman was seeking custody of her grandchildren after the state removed them from the care of their mother, her daughter. In that context, these reports-without-comment suggest obliviousness to conventional expectations of parental fitness. As an autobiographical representation of her own expectations of domesticity and childrearing, they help explain why her own children were involved with child protection services, as her children apparently acquired no more parenting skills from the subject of the evaluation than did she from her own parents.

Mayman's (1968) approach to early memories can be summarized with these quotes:

> Early memories are not autobiographical truths, nor even 'memories' in the strictest sense of this term, but largely retrospective inventions developed to express psychological truths rather than objective truths about a person's life.

> Early memories are expressions of important fantasies around which a person's character structure is organized; early memories are selected (unconsciously) by a person to conform with and confirm ingrained images of himself and others. . . . The themes which bind together the dramatis personae of a person's early memories define nuclear relationship patterns which are likely to repeat themselves isomorphically in a wide range of other life situations. (p. 304)

Among the very few writers who have suggested a way to use early memories in therapy beyond the function of general understanding, Mayman's fellow ego psychologists Fowler and Hilsenroth (1995) indicate how they can be used to anticipate transference problems. However, their approach is not informed by a systemic understanding of the therapy relationship (Bateson et al., 1956; Langs, 1978; Buirski & Haglund, 2001). Incidentally, Robert Langs (1959, 1965a, 1965b, 1967) was one of those early-memory researchers who developed a method of scoring them (Langs et al., 1960) and reported correlations with other measures. Ironically, in light of his later (1978, e.g.) emphasis on the communicative context of narrative material over and above its utility for relating historical facts, he does not seem to have considered the communicative context in which memories were elicited when he was studying them. Fowler and Hilsenroth interpret memories only from the subject's point of view rather than as a pattern that can manifest itself in a number of different configurations. More importantly, they are not careful about the contextualizing information and apparently assume that the emergence of the pattern will be solely a function of the patient's pathology.

Fowler and Hilsenroth (1995) give an example of a woman who remembered her father forcing food down her throat and then beating her for not eating it. They interpreted this memory as showing that "Sheila experiences nurturance and support from men as an invasive, cruel, and abusive impingement; when a man acts to support her, she feels like he is literally trying to shove something down her throat" (p. 91). They anticipated that a supportive male therapist (there were no women available) would be so perceived. Unfortunately, their interpretation ignores the representation of the father in the memory, who is not at all supportive and is depicted as abusive. It is not support she experiences as abusive but things being shoved down her throat. When the therapy quickly went sour, their interpretation encouraged the therapist to ask himself whether he could have prevented her intense and pathological reaction to his supportive stance rather than ask himself whether he had inadvertently, metaphorically tried to force anything down her throat.

In two other examples (Fowler & Hilsenroth, 1995), these of successful therapies, the therapist and patient discuss a problematic memory's interaction in anticipation of its replication in the treatment relationship. This discussion helps the duo weather the eventual storm. However, in both cases, the therapist is again presented as entirely innocent. For example, a man who recalled having food taken from him by his parents despite his protests was considered likely to experience the therapist as intrusive. This stance reifies the patient's identification with the role the memory casts him in. Consider the differences made possible if the therapist thinks, instead, "At some point we are bound to intrude on *each other* and a restorative move after such a misstep would have the intruder taking responsibility for bullying the other, or the person who feels violated articulating that feeling in a way that does not demolish the relationship." Fowler and Hilsenroth's approach encourages the therapist to pathologize the patient, running the risk of evoking a homeostatically defensive response or a submissively compliant response.

BRUHN

Bruhn (1990, 2005) has been prolific in developing and reporting a procedure for eliciting and interpreting early memories. He describes his approach as Cognitive-Perceptual Theory, which is an amalgam of Kelly's (1955) theory of personal constructs, cognitive-behaviorism, and Maslow's (1962) or other humanists' approach to human growth. He acknowledges his indebtedness to Adler, Mayman, and others, but where he characterizes Adler as looking for "fictive final goals" (1990, p. 42), Bruhn is primarily interested in interpreting early memories to find the subject's "major unresolved issue."

Bruhn (1990) stresses that memory is informed by perception and vice versa, and that both are informed by expectations that are presumably derived from experience. Like other nonbehaviorists, he seems ambivalent about whether early memories are pure fantasies or fantasies "firmly rooted in a substrate of reality" (p. 42). This confusion stems from his acceptance of the storage and retrieval metaphor for memory. He is perfectly clear, however, in his agreement with Mayman (1968) that the proper and useful interpretation of early memories does not depend on the events depicted in them ever having happened. What is being interpreted is the subject's narrative autobiography, not the effects of causal incidents.

Bruhn thinks that early memories depict either a lesson learned or a major unresolved issue (p. 43). As issues are resolved in therapy, he expects early memories to change, so as to represent the issue from a resolved point of view, or to move on to depict the next unresolved issue in the person's life. He cites empirical research to support this contention.

Writing primarily about assessment, as opposed to therapy, Bruhn emphasizes six principles by which early memories are organized, and one central method. The six principles that organize memories, which Bruhn uses to interpret them, are attitude, mood, time, people, place, and activity (pp. 44–47). *Attitude* means what cognitive-behavior therapists mean by *core beliefs*, the inferred rules of action and expectation that govern behavior. *Mood* refers to the current situation of the subject, although Bruhn means that the subject's feelings cause her to retrieve memories congruent with them rather than meaning that the situation that causes the feelings also occasions the production of similar memories. *Time* refers to the age of the subject in the memory, *people* to the cast of the memory, *place* to the setting, and *activity* to what the subject is doing in it.

Bruhn's *method* of interpretation is to reduce each memory to a précis that links the expectation to the situation, which is precisely the method I have employed since Langs (1978) recommended "replaying the theme" of a patient's narration when the therapist does not know what else to say but feels required to say something. Bateson's (1979) view of stories is relevant: "A story is a little knot or complex of that species of connectedness which we call relevance" (p. 12). The idea, whether Bruhn's, Langs's, or Bateson's, is to retell a memory's story so that it includes its important aspects and can be easily applied to other situations. I describe the précis and the when-then grammar at greater length in chapter 8. My use of this method differs from Bruhn's in my systemic approach to the memory's content. I emphasize the *pattern*'s relationship to the situation, not so much the *individual*'s relationship to other characters, and I punctuate the story from different points of view from the subject's.

Like Mayman, Bruhn emphasizes the need not to settle for vague or what I call *subjunctive* memories ("We used to do such and such"; "My mother was always there") (1990, pp. 130–132). Also like Mayman, he interprets the memories as a set that relate to each other, but he emphasizes the first memory as primary in a way that makes sense only if the first memory is stable, a proposition that has only mild support (Langs, 1967).

Bruhn's humanism is evident in his statement, "Cognitive-Perceptual theory is a contextual theory that emphasizes a person's innate need to grow and extend his or her range of competence. The CP model is concerned with how this process becomes derailed and what can be done to facilitate growth" (1990, p. 48). He adds, "As employed by CP theory, [early memories] help to determine where on the developmental track the individual's progress has been derailed and what can be done to correct the matter" (p. 48). Thus, in Bruhn's view, early memories detail the derailment of the individual's natural process of growth. He describes early memories as a "blueprint" (p. 61) upon which a life is built, but like Adler, he sees people as building only one kind of edifice. For Adler, it was a structure to repudiate inferiority; for Bruhn (and Maslow, 1962; Horney, 1950; and other humanists), the kind of structure a person builds with his or her identity is a natural outgrowth of the individual's humanity. A humanist views the ultimate purpose of identity development as analogous to the oak tree that an acorn is designed to build, with a fairly stable concept of health and of what constitutes staying on track. Jung (1926, 1928) also used the architecture metaphor, but he was flexible as to what kind of edifice the blueprint was *for*.

Chapter Six

Early Memories as Roadmaps

Does the Eagle know what is in the pit?
Or wilt thou go ask the Mole?

—W. Blake: *The Book of Thel*

INFERRING CHARACTER FROM INCIDENTS

Mayman (1968) and Bruhn (1990) thought that an estimate of overall mental health, or some other characterization of the person, requires an entire set of memories. Otherwise, there is too great a chance that a clinician will overly rely on a single unusual memory. It is quite common for a healthy person to have a few malignant memories that represent lacunae in an otherwise positive view of the world, just as it is quite common for healthy people to have neurotic problems or complexes, or for generally agreeable people to get angry sometimes. Conversely, a seriously disturbed person in the developmental sense of identity diffusion and dynamics of rage and abandonment can produce a few memories of comfort and joy. For categorization purposes, clinicians need the whole set.

For therapeutic purposes, in contrast, one can rely on a single memory if it offers some guidance to the presenting problem or to the therapy relationship. The therapist uses the memory not as a guide to the patient, but as the patient's guide to a type of situation. For this reason, I do not put special emphasis on the memory reported as the earliest. I am not trying to understand the patient as a fixed entity so much as I am trying to understand the *patient's* understanding of a type of situation.

I do sometimes emphasize the sequence of memories reported, not because of their temporal relationship in childhood, but because of their temporal relationship in the reporting. Often, two memories are linked, one as a comment on or extension of the other, just as two dreams are often linked, or two scenes from the same dream. For example, a patient reported as her earliest memory licking beaters with her mother as they were making cookies together. The meaning of this pleasant memory may change dramatically depending on the subsequent recollection. Consider these possibilities: The patient next recalls dropping one of the beaters and ruining her Sunday outfit, evoking her mother's scorn. Or the patient next recalls riding in her father's truck and being allowed to steer. Or the patient next recalls steering her father's truck and crashing it. Treating each of these hypothetical subsequent memories as the second scene of the first memory would be more productive than considering the first memory in isolation. Put differently, I am still interpreting one memory at a time as the patient's map of a kind of situation, but sometimes it is a matter of judgment how to punctuate the beginning and end of "one memory."

Most schemes for interpreting early memories are too abstract for effective use in therapy. They typically require the clinician to review a set of early memories and make statements about the type of person who provided them, whether that typology centers on her object relations, her power dynamics, her infantile wishes, or her unfinished business. Then, specific events encountered in therapy are understood in light of the type of person the patient is considered to be. When memories *are* interpreted without the unnecessary intermediate step of categorizing the person, they are often, unfortunately, taken almost literally: "Her father treated her in some manner that she now expects from other men or from other authority figures." My approach attempts to avoid the level-of-abstraction problem; it emphasizes the pattern in the memory rather than the literal exchanges in it.

A person's conduct in any incident must be interpreted in the context of the situation that elicited it, and the interpretation should indicate how the subject is likely to behave under similar circumstances. Thus, in behavioral parlance, an interpretation of a specific incident should indicate which aspects of the situation served to define the situation (what are the discriminative stimuli), which response tendencies were operating (the learning history of the subject in the presence of these discriminative stimuli), and which reinforcers were effective (potentiated) under the circumstances as a result of deprivation (as with hunger) or prior conditioning (as with money, although once conditioned, a reinforcer like money can also be enhanced through deprivation).

There are often logical problems with inferring character from remembered incidents. To abstract from a functional analysis of an incident to the broader statement, "This is the type of person who . . . ," is allowable only under certain conditions. What such a statement really says is that the operative context of the incident is common enough, and the state of potentiation is ordinary enough, and the recent learning history is unremarkable enough, that we are able to infer that the context of the incident is likely to be substantially repeated. And if the context is likely to be repeated, the person is likely to engage in similar conduct in the future.

If we say that a particular man who has committed a robbery is a dangerous person (abstracting from an incident of robbery to a personality trait), we are in effect saying three things about him. One, we are saying that the situational aspect of the robbery was not particularly unusual and is likely to recur. A man who acquires a pistol and robs a liquor store may live in a world of pistols and liquor stores. In contrast, a man who sees a woman counting a wad of money on the subway platform as his train is pulling out and reaches out to grab it is experiencing a once in a lifetime event. We may label the first robber as *dangerous* and the second robber as *opportunistic* or *impulsive*, but what we really mean is that the relevant defining (or discriminative) stimuli are common for the first and unlikely to recur for the second.

Two, if we say a robber is dangerous, we are suggesting that his potentiations are not noteworthy. Two men who rob liquor stores may be distinguished by their subjective need for the money. One has no more need for money than most people; the other is a heroin addict in whom the need for a fix has created a deprivation state in which money is temporarily an unusually potent reinforcer. The former is characterized as dangerous because his need for money is not unusual. With the heroin addict, the drug dependency may be enhancing the reinforcing effect of money, and if the drug dependency can be changed (either through sobriety or legal, inexpensive alternatives), then other people's money will not be such a powerful attraction. Because the potentiated reinforcing effects of money are unusual for the addict, we may be less likely to classify him as characterologically dangerous.

Three, if we say a robber is dangerous, we are suggesting that he is not in the thrall of a recent learning history. Such a history, often labeled as situational stressors, might include an escalating argument with the store clerk or a dare from fellow adolescents. On this score, robbery is not such a good example, as most people will not be moved to robbery under any set of recent experiences. But if we see a man attacking a soda machine, a recent history of losing his money to it is likely to explain the conduct better than some characterological description, because extinction (no soda emerges) of reliably reinforced behavior (soda machines almost always work) explains his frustration without input from his personality.

The problem with going from incident to character cannot be addressed without knowing how commonplace are the occasioning context and the recent history of the individual. It is acceptable to infer character from incident when the inference has been validated by empirical research (Shedler et al., 1993, for example, or Bruhn, 1985), as long as the clinician remains aware that the current case may be a statistical exception. It is *always* acceptable to go from incident to similar incident, to use behavioral patterns in one set of circumstances to shed light on expectations in similar circumstances. Clinicians may still differ, of course, in their assessments of which situations are alike and which are not.

THE THEORY OF LOGICAL TYPES

Going from incident to character trait violates the Theory of Logical Types (Whitehead & Russell, 1910; Bateson, 1972, pp. 201–206). This theory states, in a nutshell, that much mischief ensues when a thing is confused with its class, with its name, or with an abstraction. Maps, which are abstractions of a higher order than territories, must not be confused with the territories they represent (the word *book* is not a book). In addition, classes of things can be aggregated together for an even higher logical type (*noun* is a class of words like *book*, and words are classes of things). The Fallacy of Logical Types occurs when clarity is lost about the distinction between a class and a member (*noun* is a word but it is also a kind of word; *concept* is a concept). Some people fallaciously treat the flag as if it *were* the republic for which it stands. This fallacy plays a large role in personality assessment, since psychologists are prone to treating an indicator of a condition as the condition itself, and *conditions* are classes of *indicators* (some writers have compared depression to fever, suggesting that depression is an indicator and not a condition). As a colleague once clarified for me on a forensic unit with respect to a detainee, "He's still psychotic as ever, but now he has learned how to pass the MMPI." She meant that the patient's low scores were indicators and not the condition of interest, and that we should be interested in whether the condition still obtained, not in whether one particular indicator did. Subjects required to pass a polygraph to increase their freedom are caught in the fallacy, as are all subjects whose psychologists ignore error rates and Bayes' Theorem. Juliet showed her mastery of the Theory of Logical Types when she said, "Tis but thy name that is my enemy," distinguishing the boy, Romeo, from the class, Montague, and the map, *Romeo Montague*, from the territory, a passionate, well-spoken young man.

   Going from incident to character is permissible only if the defining characteristics of the incident are commonplace, as noted above, or if the step from incident to character has been validated by research. Validating the categorization of people into types is hard enough to accomplish with inventory and actuarial data, which are well suited to this kind of treatment because of scoring reliability. Instead of using early memories for a difficult purpose (categorizing people) for which they are not well-suited, early memories should be used to illustrate the patterns at work under particular kinds of circumstances.

The step from incident to character is very much like the step from individual to culture. If one views a person as a collection of response repertoires (Skinner, 1953), or figures (Jung, 1926), or internalized representations of others (Mahler, Pine, & Bergman, 1975), or some other systemically intertwined arrangement of potential responses, then the total personality may be viewed as analogous to a country (Karson, 2001). Dawkins (1976) makes a similar point in considering the person to be a *vehicle* for genes. Each person, like each country, contains all or nearly all the various elements of humanity, but in different people as in different countries these elements are arranged differently. In one person, the diva may be in charge of the archives and information is hard to retrieve; in another, it is the clerkish librarian, and information is easily retrieved. In one person, a diplomat may be assigned to manage interpersonal relations, while in another, the most belligerent warrior figure may have this task.

Countries differ from each other not so much in whom we find there but in how the various kinds of people are arranged and in what the local customs are for behavior in different kinds of circumstances. Individuals differ from each other not so much in what feelings, impulses, needs, and desires we find in them but in how these psychological facets are arranged. Systemically, a response repertoire is part of a system within the individual. Behavioristically, the relevant environment for an operant includes other response tendencies and repertoires within the person, just as the relevant environment for a gene includes the other genes. A gene with the potential for improving the animal's search for food will not survive if its interaction with other genes is deadly, and a behavior with the potential for successful management of a situation will not become more probable if its internal effects are disorganizing and disruptive.

Once the analogy between person and country is delineated, then it becomes clear why it is hard to infer character from an early memory. Generally, one cannot make intelligent statements about, say, Spanish culture, by observing a single Spaniard, and one cannot make intelligent statements about an individual based on a single incident. However, under certain circumstances that are commonplace or where the inferential leap has been validated by research, one can do just that. For example, one might observe many Spaniards (ethnographic study of many citizens is analogous to multiple observations of an individual behaving under many circumstances), or

one might sample a large number of Spaniards for some standardized protocol validated comparatively with practices in other countries (surveying citizens of a country is analogous to personality testing). Generally, though, an
individual is a class of responses and an incident needs special treatment to
provide information about the class of which it is a member. Tolstoy (1869)
makes a similar point at the end of *War and Peace*, where he explains the fallacy of trying to understand the behavior of a nation by writing about gener-
als and statesmen.

MAPS AND TERRITORIES

A map is a set of rules for conducting oneself, where the consequences of
those rules are depicted or spelled out. If I find that driving south on Speer
Boulevard leads me under Sixth Street via a tunnel, but not to a point where
I can turn left on Sixth, I can memorialize this information for someone else
or for my own later use by drawing it or by writing down the rule. I can also
dramatize this information as a filmmaker, rather than as a graphic artist
might, by visualizing the tunnel going under Sixth and by re-hearing my internal comment of disappointment as I drove beneath the street I intended to
turn on. When I say a memory is a map, I do not necessarily mean a literal
map like a drawing; it may be a map of the sort that dramatizing it would be.

Viewing early memories as maps for navigating certain kinds of situations
has the advantage of being in line with why we have memories in the first
place. In the classic, oversimplified situation, a person encounters blueberries
behind a certain ridge, and it is an advantage to return to that location the next
time she is hungry, to reduce the energy output necessary to acquire the nu-
trition available. The capacities to be reinforced (pleasure in food makes the
lure stronger), to be controlled by deferred consequences (so she does not get
distracted on the way), and to generalize across different stimuli (in case she
approaches the location from a different angle) are all features of her big brain
and are all advantages when it comes to finding the blueberries again. "Finding the blueberries again" is often described as "knowing where the blueberries are," and is often further described by the unfortunate storage metaphors
discussed in chapter 3. She is said to contain the knowledge of where the
blueberries are. The only evidence of her "knowing" where the blueberries
are, though, is her finding them again, or her directing others to find them
again. Finding the blueberries again is facilitated by a visual narrative, like replaying a silent movie of the trip behind the ridge. Helping others find them,
or helping oneself find them later, is also facilitated by speech, by recording
speech as writing, and by drawing literal maps. The original visual behaviors

of seeing what is happening on the way behind the ridge is reinforced by the end result of finding the blueberries. Visualization of trips that do not culminate in interesting destinations quickly extinguish; such trips are said to be forgotten, that is, they are not remembered because visualization of them is not strengthened by their outcomes. The original visual behaviors emitted on the hunt for food, and strengthened by reinforcement, are then emitted later under the influence of hunger (the person fantasizes about blueberries and how to get them). Thus, the origin of memory as a survival strategy is in the making of maps or their equivalents.

Early memories do not come with labels, at least not with explicit ones, and they need inspection to determine what kinds of situations they are maps of. Roadmaps generally tell the user which landscape they are a map of. Otherwise, the user would have to locate her present position on the map and also her desired destination, and taking note of differences between the map and her observations, deduce whether the map was a good guide to her current environment. She does much the same, but in her imagination, when she looks at a map that purports to be of a small section of a familiar city and pronounces it incorrect. The map's suggestion of turning south to get to higher-numbered streets does not comport with her imagined (remembered) travel in Manhattan.

A good map is one which, if the user follows it, gets her to where she wants to be. This is most obvious when a friend draws a map of how to get to his house. If she has trouble finding his house (and assuming that this was indeed her goal), it is either because she was not skilled at reading a map or because he drew a bad one. Who is to blame is largely a matter of social preference. If most people could have followed his map successfully, we are likely to impugn her skills; if most people would have gotten confused by the map, we are likely to blame him. If they are allied in their goal, it does not matter as much who is to blame as it matters who is more capable of improving: which partner can become more adept at drawing or map reading, respectively. With early memories, when the mapmaker and the map user are the same person, blame is useless. What matters is the conversation between the two parts of the person about how to improve the map or how to limit its use to appropriate circumstances.

An important part of the mapmaker's job is selecting which information to include and which to exclude. All maps reduce information, else they would have to be the same size as the landscape they describe, which would make them useless. The choice of information depends largely on cultural norms. Most of us expect major intersections to be marked on graphic maps, or distances between instructions to be specified in verbal maps, or that something will be included to help us anticipate the next turn we have to make. In New

England, people will tell you about buildings you will pass, which means you can only follow the map if you are already familiar enough with the neighborhood to recognize the landmarks. In the Midwest, you are likely to hear a much more sensible litany of major intersections and road signs, which depend for their utility only on the ability to read. The conventions used in a map like an early memory, where the maker and user are the same person, can become quite idiosyncratic.

An oral map is a set of directions or a verbal description; it is as subject to the rules of mapping as are graphic and dramatized maps. The friend who says he lives on the southeast corner of Ogden and Tennessee is a mapmaker. Oral maps are often maps of behaviors that produce a desired result ("turn left at Fifth"), but sometimes oral maps are maps of visual maps. The person visualizes a drawn map he may have seen previously, and uses words to describe what he is privately seeing. This may produce a visual map in the listener's imagination, which the listener may then describe to a third person who wants to get to the mapmaker's house. Each new map involves a selection of information, an omission of information, and a reliance on shared understandings or assumptions with the next user.

The more shared understandings the mapmaker and the user have, the less information they need on the map. When use of the compass became common, European maps switched from an east-at-the-top orientation (wherefore the designation of the East as the *orient*) to a north-at-the-top orientation. It then became necessary to draw an up arrow with a large N at the top of it in a prominent position on the map. Nowadays, such an orienting logo is unnecessary, and an unmarked map in mainstream America is presumed to have north at the top when the writing is upright. When my partner tells me that the flavored almonds she wants from the grocery store are located "above the romaine," she is capitalizing on our shared understanding of which store I am going to and of where the romaine is in that store.

In drawing maps for oneself, which would include the creation and rehearsal of early memories, there are bound to be some peculiar conventions. This point is obvious when we write a note to ourselves. There are so many expected shared understandings between the writer and the anticipated reader (also the writer) that a great deal can be left out. When we find an old note to ourselves that we can no longer understand, it is because the reader is not as similar to the writer as we had expected. The less intimate the relationship between mapmaker and user, the more information, keys, and legends the map must contain. When the mapmaker and user are as intimate as possible, that is, when they are the same person, the less information and the fewer keys and legends the map will contain.

Early memories constitute the sort of map where a lot of information is omitted because of a shared understanding between the maker and the user. They are sometimes hard to understand because of this. Even if the individual had written a specific rule of conduct, rather than dramatize it in an imagined narrative, the rule would be hard to understand without more contextual information. Imagine a man writing in his diary as a little boy, "Note to self: breaking stuff is fun." He may have known that this bit of wisdom was good for navigating his life only under certain circumstances, but he would not have needed to note those circumstances in his diary, because the writer (the boy) and the intended reader (a slightly older boy) would both have known that he is not the type of person, say, to break expensive stuff, or to break stuff when no audience is watching. Thus, an important element of interpreting such a diary entry would be to understand what sort of situation it applies to. By the same token, an important element in understanding the rules of conduct dramatized in an early memory is to understand what sort of situations they apply to. This is what I mean by asking in chapter 8 what the memory is a map of.

The context of remembering can provide an answer to this question of the map's relevance. The stimulus situation that evoked the memory is likely to have something in common with the stimulus situation that created the behavior originally. Indeed, it is well known among memory researchers that the stimulus under which a memory is "stored" must be like some current stimulus or prompt if the memory is to be "retrieved," even if what researchers *should* say, eschewing the storage metaphor, is that the conditions under which the response was learned must usually be like current conditions for the response to be emitted again. I lived in Durham, New Hampshire, for ten months when I was four years old and did not return until thirty years later, whereupon I drove directly to our old house, making four or five correct turns without any errors. Presumably, some of the visual stimuli I saw at age thirty-four were similar enough to visual stimuli I saw at age four that the stimuli at thirty-four evoked some of the same behaviors that the stimuli at age four created. These behaviors included some visual expectations (a map) and a series of operants that might be referred to as getting home. I also lived for less than a year in San Antonio, Texas, but the current situation—seeing parts of Durham as we approached the town—made it likely that the evoked map was a map of Durham and not a map of San Antonio. Similarly, if I start following a map dramatized in an early memory, my current location can provide clues as to what it is a map of. Of course, a set of rules is a map of a psychological situation rather than a physical situation, but the logic connecting the current situation with the past one holds up.

Besides examining the current context for clues to what the memory is a map of, we can also examine the memory itself for such clues. We do this with literal maps, as well, of course, when we examine a map for information not for getting from one place to another but for information regarding what situation it is a map of. Many published maps have labels at the top like *Vermont* or *Colorado* to help us with this, but some maps do not. For example, I had a book of maps of Boston, with each page representing a different section of the city. One could look at the map of the entire city in the front of the book to locate the page representing any portion of the city. Or, as I did one day, trying to quickly find a page to devise an alternate route over the river, I just fanned through the pages until I saw a strip of straight green that I assumed was Commonwealth Avenue near downtown, since I knew that Commonwealth in that area is a parkway. The green strip was a clue that on that page was a map of downtown. Street names were a less obvious clue to someone frantically scanning the pages of the book. Early memories often contain analogous clues as to the terrain being mapped.

Early memories depict the erroneous assumptions, associated with early childhood, that are misguiding the patient's current conduct. A map published by major cartographers is unlikely to be incorrect with respect to serving as a guide to navigation, although anyone driving in a major city must be prepared for changes in the city since the map was drawn. Early memories are not nearly as accurate as published roadmaps, even when they are first visualized in vivo. And circumstances that define the consequences of various behaviors change even more rapidly and dramatically than do the routes in major cities. Thus, it is quite expected and even inevitable that early memories become outmoded as maps of psychological landscapes. This tendency is their weakness for guiding behavior in the present (just as the remote past is always a weak guide) and their strength for our use as therapists. I recognize that, for many circumscribed psychotherapy problems, one need not understand the faulty map the patient is using as long as one can point the way in the present. However, if psychoanalysis has taught us anything about psychotherapy, it may be that patients are often attached to their outmoded maps and refuse to give them up, even when they keep leading to dead ends. In these cases, a peek at the map can help the therapist, and thus the patient, understand where the outmoded map is leading her astray.

Chapter Seven

A Systemic View of the Psyche

There is a season and a time to every purpose under heaven.

—Ecclesiastes

EXAMPLE: JELL-O OR SYMPATHY

Let's look at an example of using systems theory to understand the interactions in a memory. A twenty-five-year-old white woman named Jean identified her primary complaint for therapy as difficulty asserting herself. She frequently found herself, like many women (Gilligan, 1982), ignoring her own needs and trying to fulfill the needs of others. Her earliest memory was, "I was in the hospital, in a crib-like bed. I had an operation but I was feeling okay. My parents were there. My brother was there. He is a year older than me. I remember the nurse coming in and asking if he wanted some Jell-O. I feel like he declined, but I said I would like some. But the nurse said I couldn't have any and took my brother to get some anyway."

To approach the incident (as opposed to its recollection or its report) systemically means that we treat the characters in the memory as if they were real people and we treat them as if they are all involved with each other in such a way that they mattered to each other. If the characters were not important enough to each other to affect each other's reactions, then there would be no system. If something like the incident did actually occur, it seems unlikely that the real nurse's behavior would have been crafted to facilitate a systemic purpose for the family. But if the nurse's actual conduct were not geared to a systemic purpose, either it would have been de-emphasized or eradicated over time, or it would have changed in Jean's imagining until it *did*

97

fit the system between the figures. Thus, the nurse in the memory should be treated as if she were an integral part of the system, even though the nurse in the actual hospital probably was not.

A straightforward approach to this memory seems to shed some light on the woman's problem. Jean acquiesced to her brother's getting Jell-O even though she wanted some and he did not. One might suggest that she was trained from an early age not to make waves when her needs were not getting met. This might lead to some therapeutic speculation as to her version of womanhood as gleaned from her family, or to her association of not getting her needs met with her being an ill person. A therapist might use the memory to encourage her to rethink her identity as an ill person and to connect getting her needs met with being a well person. A therapist might challenge her cultural definition of how to be a woman without referring to her personal psychology at all.

Looking at the events on a family systems level, rather than from the perspective of Jean or one of the other individuals, we see a system trying to meet the needs of its children, but where each child thinks the other child is getting preferred treatment. The obvious narrative indicates that the girl was jealous of the boy's getting Jell-O, but it also seems likely that the boy was jealous of the girl's getting sympathy. In fact, it seems likely that the nurse was trying to give the patient some time alone with the parents. The boy does not want Jell-O; he wants what the girl's getting. The girl does not want sympathy; she wants what the boy's getting.

The function of their mutual envy, speculatively, may be to distract everyone's attention from the insufficiency of resources. Most children would rather believe that goods are being withheld or unjustly distributed than believe that the goods do not exist, because the latter precludes any possibility of getting the goods. The children's mutual envy keeps alive the hope of getting the goods and protects the parents from feeling as if they are simply not providing enough. Not providing enough is certainly understandable in light of the daughter's having had an operation on top of the challenges of trying to meet two young children's needs under the best of circumstances. However, what is understandable to us is not always understandable to children. Some parents provide enough for their children, both physically and emotionally, but are not very good at saying, in effect, "That's all, it will have to do." Instead of facing their understandable limitations, some parents prefer to believe that the only limitation on what they provide is their children's dissatisfaction with it, saying, in effect, "I've given you everything a child could want, but you are obstinately dissatisfied with it." The children's mutual envy may thus protect the parents from facing their limitations.

It is important to emphasize as clearly as possible that the purpose of this speculation is not to hypothesize what *happened*, it is to hypothesize what *to do* in the future. A systemic hypothesis is designed to stimulate an intervention (Selvini-Palazzoli et al., 1980). If the intervention does not work, a new hypothesis is developed; if it does work, then the problem is solved. Whether the hypothesis is true is not really relevant. Here, the hypothetical function of the mutual envy is articulated to help the therapist see what to do about the presenting problem, a question that will be taken up with respect to Jean and other patients in chapter 12.

A systemic view of the psyche should pave the way to a systemic view of the interaction within an early memory. Each figure in the memory plays a role in the pattern; each represents an aspect of the individual's functioning; each one's role can be inhabited by the self from time to time. The pattern itself will be seen to have intrinsic self-regulating and self-perpetuating features, else it would not be a sustained pattern.

PEOPLE ARE SYSTEMS

What I am saying is that systems theory is applicable not only to the relationship between patient and therapist, but also to the interrelationships of the characters within a memory. That statement guides my approach to interpreting early memories, but it also implies an integrative approach to psychology that, if not understood, will make my interpretive approach sound strange. I treat the characters or figures in memories as if they were people, and I treat people as if they were societies of characters or figures. In the rest of this chapter, I present an integrative approach to psychology to set the stage for interpreting memories.

One of the main things about human beings is that our big brains make it possible for us to do many things at once. Indeed, even pigeons have big enough brains to do several things at once. A pigeon can be taught to lift its leg whenever a light goes on and to bob its head whenever a buzzer goes off. Leg-lifting and head-bobbing can become almost completely independent of each other, as if the psychologist-light-leg system just happened to pass through the same pigeon body as the psychologist-buzzer-head system. For example, if the reward for leg-lifting is discontinued, leg-lifting will extinguish on a smooth curve pretty much regardless of the changing contingencies associated with head-bobbing.

Our bigger brains allow us to do many more things at the same time than pigeons. Many of these things we do are relatively independent of each other, just as many things that pigeons do at the same time are relatively independent of each other. A crucial thing we are always doing is imagining things, and this constant background behavior often runs independently of anything else we are doing. Within the imagination, various response repertoires also operate fairly independently, analogous to leg-lifting and head-bobbing. The father I imagine acts fairly independently of the mother I imagine, as do all the other characters one might find in my imagination from time to time. This independence justifies my treatment of these figures as if they were people with their own proclivities, histories, and systemic roles.

Imagination may be important to us for a number of reasons, but perhaps the most crucial is that it allows us to try out behaviors tentatively, and privately, without having to risk the aversive consequences of a mistake. Trying things out in fantasy is like doing a crossword puzzle in pencil instead of in ink; mistakes are easily remedied. If we want to ask the boss for a raise or a stranger for a date, we can imagine different ways of going about it and select the one that works best in our imagination. To the extent that the boss or the stranger in our imagination is like the one in reality, their reactions in our imagination will be a good guide to how to act publicly. To the extent that we discover that the figure in our imagination is not like the one in reality, we refine the way they behave in our imagination, so that next time imagination will be a better guide than it was before.

Idiosyncratic features of our childhood environments will have lasting effects on the implicit rules that govern behavior in our imaginations. Take, for example, a child with prolonged exposure to situations where deference is required to exert any influence over others and where any show of pride or even a sense of well-being is demolished. Such a child will try out interpersonal behaviors in an imaginal world in which other people respond very badly to anything but deference. He will emit public deferent behaviors even when someone with a more accurate imagination could see that assertive behaviors would work better. Essentially, this is what is meant by psychopathology, to the extent that psychopathology means disadvantageous behavior that comes from an idiosyncratic learning history. (I realize that this emphasis on accuracy omits the aspects of psychopathology related to conflict and to pain.) This is also what is meant by transference, to the extent that transference means the expectation that old rules of behaving will apply in therapy.

The implication is that it serves the individual to have an imagination that accurately reflects reality, and that imagination's failures in this regard are meaningfully related to the person's learning history. Since remembering is a form of imagining, or imaging, it follows that memories that are old, that were created in childhood, despite being renovated as the years go by, may retain some of the old rules of relating that the person initially learned to apply to reality.

All people are basically the same, in the same sense that all cultures and all countries are basically the same. Every country has people of every stripe;

countries differ in how these people are organized, what roles they are given, and how they interact with each other. The main difference between two countries may be that in one, the psychopaths are in charge and in another, the psychopaths are in prison; or in one, the soldiers run the judiciary while in another, the soldiers run the army and answer to the judiciary. What accounts for a national character is not the people, but how they are organized. Similarly, every person has tendencies of every stripe; people differ in how these tendencies are organized, what situations they occur in, and how the various tendencies interact with each other. The difference between a normal man and a rapist is not the presence of morality, sexual desire, or the desire for power, it is in the arrangement of these features with the psyche. In a rapist, the figures of Lust and Cruelty appear as partners, and both dispel the presence of a moral figure. In most people, genuine Cruelty dispels Lust.

The analogy between a person and a country becomes even more salient once we recognize the tendency of the human imagination to personify behavioral tendencies. When I am focused on my teaching technique, I may actively attend to imagined consequences that different classroom behaviors may engender. Typically, though, I passively daydream while I am ostensibly paying attention to something else—driving to work, attending faculty meeting, watching a movie. In my daydreams, I do not imagine myself trying to engage recalcitrant students; instead, I see Ed Bordin's welcoming smile. I do not imagine making my lectures more extemporaneous and personally relevant; I see Howie Wolowitz standing in front of our psychopathology class limiting himself to examples that happened that morning over breakfast with his children. I do not imagine playing games in class; I see Keith Johnstone getting workshop participants up and moving. In my imagination, my behaviors organized around engaging students are personified by Ed Bordin, and so on with the others. Thus, to say that in most people, cruelty dispels lust is to say that in most people, the figure that for a particular individual personifies genuine cruelty will not appear in early memories, dreams, or fantasies, in a collaborative, harmonious, or joint action with the figure that for that individual personifies lust.

Every person has a good teacher, or several kinds of good teachers, somewhere in their repertory; in other words, everyone has had exposure to at least a few instances of good teaching. The question is rarely whether someone is capable of being a good teacher, but when, under what circumstances. If *typical* teaching circumstances evoke a set of responses associated with *bad* teaching, because, say, the social situation elicits shyness or the power differential elicits arrogance, then we say the individual is a bad teacher. Metaphorically, we talk about there being a good teacher *inside* the individual, and we wonder what needs to happen to bring out that particular figure. In the context of imaginal material, the figure of the good teacher might be represented by the likeness of Edward James Olmos from the film *Stand and Deliver*, or Sidney Poitier in *To Sir, With Love*. In an early memory, the same figure might be represented by a smiling or welcoming kindergarten teacher, or by the helpful uncle who showed the person how to tie his shoes.

The clinical question, then, is not whether certain figures or response repertoires are expressed by the person, but under what circumstances and in the company of which other figures they appear. This feature of the systemic view of the psyche can be summarize as "when—not whether." When is the individual angry or nurturant (when do the personifications of Wrath and Nurturance appear)? After ascertaining that someone is psychotic or pathologically shy or narcissistic, the important clinical question is *when*. *When* (under what circumstances) is she psychotic or shy or narcissistic? Prolonged careful observation can help us answer that question, and so can early memories. The question is important because its answer implies a treatment plan, either in avoiding or changing the circumstances associated with the problem or in arranging for circumstances associated with a solution.

These figures that populate the psyche, which I am saying are fundamentally similar in all of us, may be introjects of parental images, or they may be hierarchically organized response repertoires, or they may even be ahistorical archetypes. It does not matter for most purposes. What does matter is that noting their arrangement in psychic patterns, also known as complexes, can help us understand the person's expectations of reality. While we are all the same in terms of the building blocks of our psychologies, we are all different in how those blocks are arranged. The idea that we differ from each other more in the ways our parts are organized than in the parts we possess may be illustrated by looking again at the analogy to a country. A presidential election can make America a very different country from the one it was the day before the election, but both countries are composed of almost exactly the same individuals.

Some clarification of the relationship between figures in the psyche and psychological concepts may be in order. Any group of figures that appear together on a regular basis can be called a constellation or a *complex* (Jung, 1926). I prefer to use the terms interchangeably, but some people use *complex* only if there is a neurotic component to the grouping, in other words, when the figures are locked together in a web of interaction that works to the individual's disadvantage. In many people, certain figures typically accompany certain others, and some of these groupings are common enough to get their own names, for example, *inferiority complex*, *Oedipus complex*, or, from transactional analysis, *rescuer triad*. Locating and tracking certain figures is central to certain theories. The figure of the infant is the central focus of many object relations orientations (Mahler et al., 1975), for example, while the figure of the idealized self would always attract the attention of students of Karen Horney's (1950) work.

One figure that any approach would be interested in would be that of Ego. Somewhat different from the Freudian *ego*, the figure of Ego, which of course means *I* in Latin, is merely whichever character in the drama is cast as the self. In other words, all the figures in a memory can be seen as aspects of the person, but it is a matter of interest which one of the roles is currently being identified with. This can vary from time to time, as when a person who usually identifies with the submissive role in a dominance complex occasionally has dreams of dominating others. A clinically interesting phenomenon occurs when the number of roles in a complex is very limited, so that to appear at all, Ego has to choose the lesser of various unappealing roles. *Identification with the aggressor* fits this problem: when the roles are reduced to perpetrator and victim, many people find it less aversive to be cast as a perpetrator (Bettelheim, 1943).

Jung (1926) says that complexes are the architects of dreams. He means that the dreamwork is laid down onto, integrated with, or informed by preexisting narrative structures, plot lines, and lists of characters. Other theoretical languages might say that the blueprints of dreams represent not complexes but personal constructs (Kelly, 1955), wishes (Freud, 1900), transference patterns (Langs, 1978), or previously punished behaviors (Skinner, 1953). My view is that complexes are also the architects of early memories.

A mystical question of Jung's is whether figures are *ahistorical*. Some Jungians think that the individual's psyche comes populated with preexisting figures, called archetypes, and that while these are pictured differently from person to person according to the specific cultural context, the underlying figures are the same in everyone. Other Jungians think that figures in the psyche are *historical*, meaning that they are internalizations and representations of childhood relationships and experiences. If different people across cultures tend to have the same figures, it may be because of common environmental factors or common species practices, not because of preexisting archetypes.

The interesting part of this question of historicity is how things go when figures are treated ahistorically—that is, as if each one is an autonomous being—versus how things go when they are treated as less than autonomous, as functions of biology and personal history. In my experience, figures tend to react the way people do when they are treated as if they are not autonomous: they try to prove that they are. Thus, even the most die-hard radical behaviorist will not treat people as piles of molecules. If she does, she will not get back from them a response that makes her happy. The same goes for figures as for people. Figures in the psyche are probably internalized images of others and of experiences with others, but it is better to treat them as independent citizens of the psyche.

Case Example: The Tornado

What does it mean to treat a figure as if it were autonomous? An adolescent boy, Jack, reported a memory of a little girl lifting her dress for him when he was four years old, allowing him to see her genitals. He was afraid he would get in trouble and looked away. A tornado was visible on the horizon and his mother called to him to get indoors. This usually prudish teen had recently gotten into trouble for gently poking the behind of a girl in his high school. A helpful question to ask this boy might be, "What does the tornado want?"

To encourage Jack to think about the tornado's point of view may lead to a solution, just as it might in conflict resolution between two humans. Likewise, the next time this complex manifests itself in his daily life—for example, when he feels inhibited about expressing sexual interest in a girl to her face—he may not have to be afraid to look at the danger of expressing such interest. He may not have to avoid that danger by stealing a touch and running off. Preparing to restrain himself only makes his fear and impulsivity worse, according to the memory, since in the memory the tornado does not bear down on him until he averts his glance. Jack needs to learn *how* to express sexual interest, not how *not* to. In a sexual situation, if he has been thinking about what the tornado wants, he might ask himself who would be angry if he failed to ask out a girl he liked. If the answer is no one at all, it might dispel the tension. If the answer is a specific person (which might include himself, of course), he might try to ask her out in a way that accounts for that anger, rather than panic as it approaches.

Jack is tempted to say, "I panicked because I feel guilty about sex." He thereby reduces his fear to an extension of his own impulsivity, treating the figure of the tornado as if it were unimportant in its own right. This treatment may give him an illusion of control over his prudishness, but it will not bring the tornado into a dialogue that can lead to change. That would be fine, of course, if the tornado figure really were external, not a part of him. For example, there is no reason to wonder what a real tornado wants, to greet it, to engage it in dialogue, or to try to change it. But here, the tornado is a part of him that deserves as much respect as the part of him that he identifies with. The figure is more like a wife than a stranger, more like an impulse than a weather phenomenon, in the sense that it is related to him and wants not only what is good for him but also what is good for itself. Instead of trying to explain away the figure of the tornado in the memory, the boy needs to know what it wants, why his sexual restraint makes it angry, and why he considers sexual interest to be a transgression. He needs to resolve the complex in a way that does not cost him all the energy and power embodied in the tornado, as his prudishness has done.

It seems peculiar at first to treat figures in a memory as if they were real people who have settled on the depicted mode of interaction, and I suppose it does require some imagination and a sense of play. The scientific rationale for this treatment is based on behavior theory and the organization of response repertoires and on the application of systems theory to the imagination, but spelling this out is as unnecessary as it would be to spell out the biochemistry of a cough before recommending a lozenge. I want to note the parallel between treating the figures of a memory as real people and treating individuals in an organization as real people. There is no reason to do so when one is working with the entire organization as an organic entity. For example, imagine a new regulation covering absenteeism, which proclaims that the next most junior employee must cover for anyone who is sick, late, or on vacation. Considering the effect of this regulation on the entire organization, one can predict that problems between employees are bound to erupt under such a system. This prediction will just become muddled if one tries to consider the personal psychology of each individual worker. However, when one is resolving conflicts between two specific employees (or figures), one of whom is angry at the other for needlessly saddling her with additional work, then it is more productive to consider each individual's personal psychology, if only to keep the employees from resenting you. They will not appreciate having their feelings dismissed as a mere by-product of a confusing policy. Similarly, there are situations where it makes good sense to consider an individual's psychology as a whole, analogous to considering an organization as an integrated entity, but there are other situations, including all psychotherapy cases, where it pays to consider the individual interactions among the figures in the psyche.

Chapter Eight

Step-by-Step Interpretation

My physicians by their love are grown
Cosmographers, and I their map. . . .

—J. Donne, *Hymn to God, My God, in My Sickness*

In this chapter, I offer interpretive steps that address first the communicative aspects of reporting early memories and then the systemic interactions within the memories. I illustrate these steps with one of Goethe's early memories, which I have selected because of its historical interest in Freud's writing.

GOETHE'S EARLY MEMORY

Goethe presented an early memory near the beginning of his autobiography, which Freud (1917a) interpreted in an important paper. The memory involved neighbor brothers named von Ochsenstein, of whom Goethe wrote, "My people used to tell of all kinds of pranks in which these men . . . used to encourage me" (p. 147). The one Goethe chose to relate took place just after a crockery fair had come to town, which meant that the kitchen had been resupplied. Toy versions of the same crockery had been purchased for the children of the family to play with.

> One fine afternoon, when all was quiet in the house, I was playing with my dishes and pots in the hall [a place which had already been described, opening on to the street] and, since this seemed to lead to nothing, I threw a plate on to the street, and was overjoyed to see it go to bits so merrily. The von Ochsensteins, who saw how delighted I was and how joyfully I clapped my little hands, called out, "Do it again!" I did not hesitate to sling out a pot on to the

paving-stones, and then, as they kept crying "Another!" one after another all my little dishes, cooking-pots and pans. My neighbours continued to show their approval and I was highly delighted to be amusing them. But my stock was all used up, and still they cried "Another!" So I ran off straight into the kitchen and fetched the earthenware plates, which made an even finer show as they smashed to bits. And thus I ran backwards and forwards, bringing one plate after another, as I could reach them in turn from the dresser; and, as they were not content with that, I hurled every piece of crockery I could get hold of to the same destruction. Only later did someone come and interfere and put a stop to it all. The damage was done, and to make up for so much broken earthenware there was at least an amusing story, which the rascals who had been its instigators enjoyed to the end of their lives. (pp. 147–148)

Freud interpreted this memory as a screen for Goethe's destructive feelings for his little brother, whose presence in the family the young poet resented. I think this may fairly be called an example of Freud fitting the memory into a preexisting hypothesis that early memories must either reveal or screen (Freud, 1899) primal urges. Freud was convinced of the correctness of his interpretation, and published it, after a patient of his recalled destroying crockery in a fit of sibling jealousy; if destroying crockery meant an urge to destroy the new baby with his patient, then it must mean the same with Goethe. Rom (1965) interpreted the memory from an Adlerian perspective, noting Goethe's delight in the acoustic and visual aspects of the memory, and also noting his delight in pleasing an audience through "extraordinary actions." Rom said the memory presages the development of a great poet.

COMMUNICATIVE CONTEXTS

As noted in chapter 4, our interpretations of the incidents depicted in early memories are secondhand. What we are really interpreting are *reports* of early memories. These reports are themselves instances of behavior, and to interpret the report of an early memory, or any narration, or any *behavior*, we need to know the context in which it occurred. Thus, to interpret Goethe's, or anyone's, early memory is, as in Churchill's description of the Soviet Union, "a riddle wrapped in a mystery inside an enigma." The "riddle" is the incident depicted; the "mystery" is the man's recollection of the incident, its occurrence to him on a specific occasion; and the "enigma" is the man's report of his recollection of the incident. (In Goethe's memory, it is not even clear, regarding the "mystery," that he *recalled* the event in question. When he writes, "my people used to tell of all kinds of pranks," it suggests that he is repeating a family story. However, for the sake of this discussion, I will treat this as a recollection.)

A similar triad has already been proposed with respect to the interpretation of scale scores on personality inventories (Karson, Karson, & O'Dell, 1997). That triad was described as *measurement*, *characterization*, and *declaration*. *Measurement* referred to the variance attributable to trait strength in the individual (whether transitory or enduring). Shy people tend to endorse shy items. *Characterization* referred to variance attributable to self-concept. People who believe they are shy, regardless of how shy they are, tend to endorse shy items. *Declaration* referred to variance attributable to what the subject wants the psychologist to think. People applying for sales jobs tend not to endorse shy items. Motivational distortions can be of all three types. For example, there can be a measurable characterological tendency not to reveal one's shyness; an insistence that one behaves socially boldly because it fits one's self-characterizations; or an attempt to feign, enhance, or malinger social boldness because of situational factors or to influence the psychologist in some way. With respect to early memories, the measurement factor is analogous to what happened as a child; the characterization factor is analogous to the individual's sense of herself and her world that facilitates her maintenance and production of the memory; and the declaration factor is analogous to the performance aspects of the report, to the relationship between the behavior of reporting and the environment that occasioned it.

All too often, psychologists seem to want to exclude the performance or communicative aspect of answering questions and get on with the interpretation of personality characteristics. Many therapists treat reports of events—memories—as if they are either entirely suspect or as if they are trustworthy representations of reality. The latter style is especially noticeable in case presentations, where therapists discuss family history as if it were a matter of fact. "He's the third of four boys" is probably true, but cannot really be isolated from the fact that the patient claims to be the third of four boys. Like hearsay exceptions that allow testimony in court when the witness would have little reason to lie, we accept such statements as true (Karson, 2005). My problem with this is not that I doubt that the vast majority of such factual statements are accurate (although I do know of one long-term therapy organized around grieving a mother's death that was considerably disrupted when the mother called the therapist). My problem is that acceptance of such statements as factual creates a mindset in which therapists either doubt or accept statements as factual, rather than learning to interpret them as communications that happened for a reason. Their meaning must be understood in the context of the motivation for saying them, rather than examining the motivational context and then allowing the context to dominate the content or the content to dominate the context.

Parenthetically, much the same thing happens when psychologists interpret scores from personality tests. Typically, they look at the fake-good and fake-bad indicators and either they decide that the personality scale scores are valid and then ignore the motivational context, or they decide the fake-good or fake-bad scores are too high and ignore the personality scale scores. What is more interesting is understanding the relationship between validity scales and personality scales. What the patient looks like when he tries to look good can be as informative about his personality as what he looks like when he does not particularly try to look good. Admittedly, we will often come to similar conclusions in interpreting, say, an elevation on a scale that measures paranoia, whether we say that it indicates paranoia or we say that the subject is performing the role of test subject like a paranoid. But the latter formulation leaves us better positioned to take the situational variables into account. This has implications for cross-cultural testing, where many mistakes depend on the psychologist overlooking the context of the assessment and its meaning to the subject (Stuart, 2004). The analogy to therapy would be that we may come to similar conclusions if we say he is performing the role of therapy patient in a paranoid manner rather than saying that he *is* paranoid, but the former is preferable because it keeps us alert to situational variables.

INTERPRETIVE STEPS: WHY NOW AND IN THIS MANNER

As noted in chapter 5, early memory researchers usually abstract memories from their communicative contexts, then code them in some way, then correlate them with some measure of interest. One of many problems with such research is that it tries to get at what I am calling the riddle by bypassing the mystery and the enigma. A more sensible strategy would be to work backwards. If the memory can be interpreted or accounted for by attending to the communicative context in which it is reported, then there is little incremental validity to be obtained from investigating why it occurred to the individual or why it happened (*if* it happened) in the first place. The earlier the memory, the less likely the events in it occurred as depicted, and the less interested we should be in unanswerable questions about what happened at the time. Even memories of events that occurred the same day as the therapy session, though, should be interpreted first as verbal behavior that occurred in the therapy office, then as remembering behavior that occurred in the therapy office, and only last as an incident. Thus, we should begin an interpretation by asking why the memory was reported in this manner at this time.

Also, working backwards from the report ensures that we will work with relatively reliable material. In other words, we can never be sure what, if anything, happened to the child; we *can* be certain that the subject has the narrative within his repertoire at the time it was reported but we *cannot* be certain that it forms a part of his self-definition; we can be quite certain, though, that the memory was reported to us under observable conditions, because we were present when the report occurred. Similar considerations induce family therapists to work with reports of misconduct rather than with misconduct itself. Discussion of who yelled at whom just leads to arguments about what happened that night. Discussion of how other family members found out about the quarrel deals with communicative avenues and styles that exist in the therapy room. It may be argued that ignoring the quarrel or childhood experience in favor of how it was communicated is like looking for one's keys where the light is better rather than looking where they were dropped. However, that is a false analogy. The family therapist considers the problem not to be that the couple had a quarrel—everyone has quarrels—but rather to be how the spouses communicate about their quarrels. So focusing the discussion on what is observable is very much aligned with the therapist's concept of where the keys are. And the psychologist should be less interested in what did or did not happen a long time ago than in which current situations make an old pattern of behavior seem relevant and operative. Psychologists, in my view at least, should be interested not so much in *whether* a subject is depressed, histrionic, or paranoid, but *when* (under what circumstances) he or she is depressed, histrionic, or paranoid. A narcissist, for example, is someone who is narcissistic often and under a wide variety of circumstances, but everyone is narcissistic sometimes (except me: I'm special that way). Treating reports of early memories as communicative incidents with contexts of their own highlights this question of *when* the pattern in question is called up.

Again, the first level of interpretation of any memory report should investigate the function of the reporting behavior in its occasioning environment. In Goethe's case, imagining him sitting at his desk writing his autobiography, we must ask what point he was trying to communicate to, or impression he was trying to leave with, his imagined audience. I do not know nearly enough about Goethe to speculate as to who was in his imagined audience nor to speculate about the circumstances under which he was writing. I can suggest that he seems to be saying that a good story is worthy compensation for broken crockery; that someone tried to saddle him with cookware but he was too boyish to endure it; and that his boyhood was very happy. It seems surprising that Freud, who clearly believed that Goethe was a great, perhaps the greatest, writer in world history, did not consider that he was *writing* when he wrote this memory. In that context, the memory, at the start of

Goethe's autobiography, would seem to be a statement: "While you are read-ing the story of my life, I want you to think of me as an iconoclast who makes stories that people remember to the end of their lives." After all, Goethe (1808, lines 534–537) wrote in Faust: "You will never conquer [the world] unless you feel it, unless a surging from your soul, a primal joyful en-ergy compels the hearts of all your listeners." Perhaps he was making the same point in his autobiography.

In the clinic, we must ask what metaphorical commentary on the clinical relationship is expressed by the report of the memory (Bateson, 1972, p. 209; Langs, 1978). Had Goethe reported this memory in a therapy session, its com-municative meaning would depend on the circumstances of the relationship. For example, imagine the report occurring just after Goethe had expressed an-noyance at his therapist for misinterpreting something. In that context, the re-port would seem to be saying that Goethe appreciated the robust acceptance of his aggressive annoyance, but that he still resented being ignored (left to play on his own with imitations).

Had Goethe reported this memory in a psychological assessment, it would be impossible to interpret it without knowing the referral question. If he were applying for a job as an air traffic controller (impulsive, expressive icono-clasts need not apply), the psychologist might wonder why he chose this par-ticular story to tell, and whether that choice indicates poor judgment about the interview or ambivalence about the job. If he were being screened to be a foster parent, the psychologist might appreciate the representation of tol-erance for misbehavior in children. Nomothetic and categorical research on assessment instruments is welcome, but it invites psychologists to consider test responses independently of the referral question, which is usually the most prominent aspect of the communicational context in which these re-sponses are emitted. What we should be doing is conducting a functional analysis of the test responses in relation to the occasioning environment, the latter including the test stimulus, the setting, and, especially, the referral question.

INTERPRETIVE STEPS: SYSTEMIC

To the extent that a report of an early memory is not a commentary on its oc-casioning environment and not a performance for the psychologist, it may contain patterns of conduct relevant to the individual's problems. Whether the reported incident happened or was constructed or some combination of the two, something must account for the memory's durability. In my view, it is more important that the remembering behavior is still in the person's repertoire than that the underlying incident happened, so much that I have little concern over whether it really happened or not. What interests me is that it is reported in response to an autobiographical query in the context of a referral question or treatment relationship. Thus, the individual is implicitly identifying the story in the early memory as fundamental in his or her autobiography (Adler, 1931).

Early memories are roadmaps to psychological terrains that are often outmoded, but to which the person will revert for guidance in trying times; in other words, in situations where more current roadmaps are not effective, the individual will resort to old ones. To the extent that they are preserved by the individual from childhood experiences, they are preserved because they were useful. After all, the survival value of memory itself is in preparing for new situations, and viewing early memories as patterns for expecting and negotiating new terrain accords with most theorists. Adler (1931) noted the purpose of a memory is to "prepare [the person] to meet the future with an already tested style of action" (p. 73). Mayman (1968) discussed enduring relational paradigms and character structure. Bruhn (1985) emphasized that people recall what has utility and relevance in the present.

My approach differs from these others in that I do not abstract from reported incident to type or character or trait or life plan, but I maintain an emphasis on the incident itself as a roadmap to future incidents. This is consistent with a behavioristic functional analysis, where response tendencies are assessed in relation to the occasioning environment, the learning history, and potentiations. My interpretive scheme asks, first, which kinds of psychological terrains is this memory a roadmap *of*? Second, which figures populate that particular terrain? Third, what is the systemic interaction among the figures? How is their systemic interaction self-regulated and self-perpetuated? Fourth, what predictive statements about that terrain can be made in the form of "when-then" (described below in Step 4)? Fifth, what specific elements of the memory are necessary to understanding it nonreductionistically? Sixth, in what way, if any, is symptomatology put in context by understanding the wisdom (compromise formation, regulatory function, or reinforcing effects under the circumstances) of the symptomatic behavior? Seventh, taking the memory on its own terms, what interventions if any are suggested and possible? Finally, if therapy is anticipated, how might the memory help the therapist and the subject understand what is happening when the therapy relationship gets complicated?

The remainder of this chapter will illustrate how to answer these questions, using Goethe's memory as a partial example. It is only a partial example because there is no referral question or treatment setting to guide our answers. The following chapter provides three more examples.

INTERPRETIVE STEPS EXEMPLIFIED

An interpretation will be more or less useful depending on the selection of the landscape to which it is seen as a guide, according to the characterization of its figures, and according to the plausibility of the interventions suggested. If two clinicians argue over whether a particular memory is a guide to a landscape of sibling rivalry or a guide to a landscape of boredom, they are at least disagreeing about the relevant issues to understanding and applying the memory. Similarly, two behaviorists may disagree as to which stimulus is controlling a particular operant, but at least they are arguing over the relevant problem. Ditto when two systemic therapists argue about how best to punctuate a marital interaction. Therefore, the steps below need not be undertaken with a goal of producing a correct interpretation as long as they are used to develop plausible, useful interventions.

1) What Psychological Landscape Is the Memory a Map Of?

The physical location of the events in the memory often relates to the type of situation it is a guide to. Thus, a memory that takes place in the kitchen might be a guide to situations where nurturance is expected or where chores are done and a memory that takes place on the front porch may narrate rules of conduct for the boundary between public and private. I cannot emphasize enough, though, that I am not advocating a *this means that* approach to interpretation. The purpose of understanding the landscape that the memory is a map of is not to get it right, but to help the patient connect the guidelines implied by the memory to the situation that needs guidance. If the map of a particular memory does not help navigate a particular situation, try another map. The patient is more likely to try out the guidebook implied by a memory if the connection to the troubling situation is pointed out by the therapist, just as the patient is more likely to use any theoretical template for understanding her problems if its connection to her particular case is articulated.

While I think there are many right answers to the question of what landscape a memory depicts, there are many wrong answers too. Thus, even though I reject a "this means that" codebook for symbols, I think that early memories remain in the individual's repertoire of responses because they are useful in making sense of particular kinds of different situations. Learned in response to certain kinds of stimuli, they are generalized to appear in response to similar stimuli. Since memories are largely visual and auditory, what is seen and what is heard in recall should bear some resemblance to what was seen and heard when the memory was created. This makes memory somewhat different from stepping on the brake, in that the stepping behavior can provide a clue as to what was being done when the behavior was learned, but not a clue as to the situation (except the inference that it was in a car). Visual behavior, when repeated later, does contain such clues, because the content of visual behavior *includes* information about its environment.

Early memories are maps of psychological landscapes. The situation that produced the memory, and the subsequent situations that refined it, are defined by the stimuli that occasioned it and the other occasions to which those stimuli generalize. We summarize these sets of stimuli with phrases such as *in intimate relationships, during sibling rivalry,* and *when confronted with ambiguity. Psychological landscapes* include the kinds of contexts that typically interest us as clinicians. An early memory of being dropped off for the first day of kindergarten might be a guide to the subject's expectations and to the patterns operating in a variety of psychological landscapes. These might include, among others, the landscape of independence, of transition to a new stage of life, or of entering academia. The referral question will help us select our description of the landscape. For example, a referral question about why the subject is still living at home at age twenty-five might lead to an interpretation of an early memory of being dropped off for kindergarten as a guide to what happens when a new stage of life is contemplated. A referral question about a learning disorder might contextualize the same memory as a guide to entering academia.

Absent a referral question or a presenting problem, it would be hard to specify a plausible psychological landscape for Goethe's memory. Nonetheless, *playing alone in one's house* suggests a landscape of imagining or writing, since a writer when writing is usually alone in his imaginal world seeking that which might be enlightening or amusing. Defining writing as the psychological landscape is linked to the pseudo-referral question of why Goethe was such a great writer, which, humility aside, was probably his justification for writing an autobiography in the first place. The interface with the public that is achieved by throwing things out the window suggests a psychological landscape of letting others read what he has written, letting others observe the content of his play. The memory, then, may be a guide to his expectations of interpersonal and psychological outcomes when he is writing or sharing what he has written.

2) Who Are the Dramatis Personae?

Much can be inferred about the expectations of the individual and the operative pattern merely by knowing how the drama was cast, just as much can often be inferred about the nature of a film by knowing who is in it (at least, when they are the sort of actors who always play the same type of roles).

Which images, figures, forces, or response repertoires appear in the land-scape? Is a memory of being taken to kindergarten populated with a benevo-lent, welcoming teacher? An indifferent, preoccupied teacher? An upset mother? An enthusiastic child? A diffident child? Just knowing who is in the memory can help us understand it. A patient whose memory of her first day of kindergarten includes a smiling and reassuring teacher is going to have a much different experience of transitions regardless of whether the content in-volves learning to fingerpaint or dealing with a bully.

Listing the characters in the memory also ensures that none of the relevant figures will be excluded from a systemic analysis. All too often, therapists find themselves trying to help a patient with a problematic relationship with-out considering the other characters in the drama. I saw a British woman in therapy who came for help about her relationship with her parents; for sev-eral weeks, I was lost in confusion about her connection with them. She would relate stories about them from her childhood and from recent vacation visits that sounded more like interchanges with strangers than with her own parents. At one point, I thought maybe I had lost track of her narrative, and that she really *was* talking about strangers. Finally, I just asked her, "These are your parents you're talking about now, right?" Yes, she replied. Maybe, I thought, *parent* had some unexpected meaning in England that I did not know. "The people who raised you?" I clarified. "Oh no," she said. "I was raised by my nanny." Her stories of childhood made sense only if one in-cluded the unspoken presence of the nanny, and her current stories only made sense by noting the nanny's absence.

More common than my example, of course, is the effort to help clarify a relationship without taking into account even the expected figures. Patients (and therapists) will discuss a problematic relationship with their fathers as if that relationship can be abstracted or separated from their relationships with their mothers. In an effort to discover the relevant characters, in my assess-ment work I not only ask how many children adults have, I also ask how many the women gave birth to or the men have biologically fathered. I have met too many people who let the former phrasing exclude those children who had already grown to adulthood or those who had been removed by the state. I ask who else is in the family, but I also ask who else spends the night in the same residence on a regular basis, and whether that list has changed in the last year. I have met too many assessment subjects who grew up with stepparents and parental roommates they did not consider to be *in the family*.

Sometimes, the characters in the memory are not personified, but are rep-resented by animals, objects, or natural forces. Thus, to treat a memory with a tornado in it systemically requires us to treat the tornado as we would in a dream, as representative of a systemically connected psychological construct such as anger. Recent memories that include a tornado are likely to do so simply because a tornado is an unusual occurrence. Older memories that include a tornado are more likely to incorporate it into a systemic relationship, because if it were not systemically connected to the other figures in the memory, its recall might have extinguished for lack of usefulness. Still, many early memories of unusual events must be interpreted primarily as a reflection on how things go when there is a tornado or how things go when there is an injury. These are maps to emergencies, surprises, losses, disabilities, and so on. When an inanimate force or an animal does participate in a memory as a member of a meaningful system, its amenability to intervention is often limited. Below, I will discuss how to use a memory as a guide to intervention, but for now, I just want to note that certain figures are easier than others to engage in dialogue and to advise as to alternative courses of action.

When we consider the systemic interrelationship among the figures in a memory, we will want to ensure that we understand the contribution of each of them to what is going on, just as we would in a family system. In Goethe's memory, the figures are the playful child and the enthusiastic, mischievous audience. The parents are notable in their absence. So far, one might say that Goethe's memory suggests that when he is being creative, the figures that occupy the creative space are the playful child and the mischievous audience. Parental influences seem only distantly relevant.

3) How Is the Systemic Interaction Among the Figures Self-Regulated and Self-Perpetuated?

Patterns are patterns because they persist and recur. There must be something about them that sustains their integrity, or they would dissipate. Indeed, the heart of systemic thinking is to consider how recurrent patterns of behavior self-regulate and self-perpetuate. *Self-regulation* means that patterns have elements that keep them from escalating to the point where the underlying interaction is destroyed. *Self-perpetuation* means that patterns do not morph into something different. Systemic thinkers are used to applying these concepts to families and their members. For example, the standoffish wife and critical husband are seen as self-perpetuating because his criticisms make her withdraw and her withdrawal makes him more critical. Eventually, they have a quarrel, and each apologizes in preference to divorce, with the apologies being a form of self-regulation that keeps them from escalating to the point where the marriage ends. They make love and start all over again.

Systemic thinkers are less practiced in applying cybernetic ideas like self-regulation and self-perpetuation to the internal figures of individuals than to the individual members of families. The logic of applying these ideas to individuals is that a person is as much a system as is a group of people. The individual's response repertoire is organized in some way, and this organization is as amenable to systemic thinking as is an organization made up of people. We already think of individuals systemically when we talk about the endocrine system or the nervous system, assuming as we do that the component parts of each are in harmony with each other. A person regulates many variables, such as temperature, water, and salt, cybernetically, in other words, as a thermostat does. Excess heat, for example, sends messages that produce perspiration that cools the person. The exact nature of those messages, where they are transmitted and received, and how they produce perspiration are not as interesting to us as the higher-level observation that we sweat when we are hot and shiver when we are cold. Analogously, the exact method by which response repertoires are organized in the brain is less interesting than the higher-level depiction of the process in the metaphorical terms of an early memory.

In Goethe's memory, it is plausible to suggest that, under certain circumstances metaphorically represented as *home when all is quiet*, his iconoclasm evokes cheering, and his cheering evokes iconoclasm. This formulation treats the relationship between his internal states as one treats the states in a marriage. If we were to transpose his internal pattern to a marriage, we might say that one spouse's iconoclasm evokes the other's cheering and vice versa; in the interpretation of an internal system, we treat both the iconoclasm and the cheering as his.

One consequence of applying systems theory to family interactions is that systems thinkers have learned to characterize a marriage rather than, or in addition to, characterizing the people who comprise it. For example, they might describe the marriage with the pattern of a husband's criticism and a wife's aloofness as a hunt and hide relationship, or as a criticism-avoidance marriage. Then, the individuals are seen as playing roles in this type of marriage. This way of thinking, rather than thinking of the individual personalities involved, facilitates the goal of changing the interaction between the people rather than changing the people themselves. The marriage is an invention of two people, and any attempt to punctuate the transactions as starting with him are no more valid than attempts to punctuate them as starting with her. Applying this kind of systemic or circular thinking to the individual requires us to describe the pattern in an early memory rather than just the component parts.

To exemplify this kind of internal system, one might imagine Goethe encouraging himself to write, with such encouragement producing iconoclastic impulses. He might say to himself that the morning is free from other responsibilities and it is a good time to get some writing done. This impulse is connected to the absence of parental figures, which for the adult Goethe, who had many more worldly responsibilities than the average writer, might mean that he is able to escape those responsibilities for a while. This absence of parental or conventional responsibilities in turn could produce a twist to his writing that makes him want to break things metaphorically, in other words, to be iconoclastic, since this is the period in his week when he is not answerable to convention. Conversely, one might punctuate the pattern by imagining him first feeling rebellious and wanting a break from his many worldly responsibilities. The pattern in his memory suggests that it is these breaks with quotidian duty that he associates with creativity, with being alone in a quiet house. At these times, he produces behavior that is met with encouragement.

Thus, the memory suggests that self-encouragement is associated with rebelliousness and rebelliousness is associated with self-encouragement. The system is regulated by the damage done: he only throws out the new crockery, none of the crystal. Balking at the crystal plays a cybernetic function, just as balking at divorce will keep a marriage together. Goethe's internal system—his interlinking of encouragement and his naughtiness—is self-perpetuated by his talent. If his iconoclasm did not produce applause, the system would disintegrate, just as the marital example would disintegrate if the husband's criticism did not produce aloofness in the wife, or vice versa.

Using memories as maps can guide intervention, as will be discussed below. For now, I want to emphasize that if a driver is lost and asks us for directions, we have to start from scratch when we see twenty roadmaps in the back seat and have no idea which one got her here. But if one map is unfolded on the driver's lap, we can comment with something analogous to, "Ah, that map you're using is outdated. These roads are all one way now." Or, "that map you're using is upside down," or "that map is of Manhattan and you're in Brooklyn." A systemic understanding of the memory helps us understand how it applies to the current situation and also helps us understand what's wrong with it as a guide.

4) When What, Then What?

In my view, many systemic formulations can usefully be framed as *when-then* statements. This grammar helps locate observations in their context. "When she is on her own, she depressively experiences herself as having to answer to a harsh authority" is more contextualized than "She is suffering from major depression." Contextualizing the statement with the when-then grammar also opens the door to points of intervention. The diagnosis, made at a higher level of abstraction, calls for abstract ideas about what to do for her: individual therapy, family therapy, medication. As noted in chapter 2, it is like diagnosing a lurching car as having problems operating and recommending car repair. The when-then grammar invites one to consider changing the situation or changing the mode of interaction among the relevant figures.

The when-then grammar also reminds us that the behavior of concern to us is not exhibited by the person all the time, on all occasions. A paranoid man is not always paranoid; a depressed woman is not always depressed. By demanding to know when he is paranoid or she depressed, we assert that paranoia and depression are things these people do, not things they are. Since it is easier to change what people do than what they are, this is a good thing to remember. If the man is paranoid whenever he takes an exam, then it is certainly worth considering whether on balance a better treatment than resolving his troubled self-experience may be to avoid exams. Ditto if the woman is depressed only when she talks to her brother.

Applying the when-then grammar to the relationship between the figures in Goethe's early memory, it might be said that when he feels iconoclastic, he senses encouragement. When he feels encouraged, he gets iconoclastic. Concerning the relationship between the complex and the situation that evokes it, that is, between system and landscape, one might say that when Goethe is alone in his own house, the pattern of iconoclasm and encouragement emerges. Leave him alone in the bathtub and expect to come back to a watery floor. In other words, when he is alone and has an opportunity to be creative, he is likely to escalate in self-encouragement and iconoclasm until some damage, but not serious damage, is done.

Now, one way to respond to narrative material, whether memories, dreams, or incidents, is to state a précis or theme of the story (Langs, 1978; Bruhn, 1985), as we were taught to do in the eighth grade. Using the when-then grammar can highlight the applicability of the *then* pattern to situations covered by the *when* clause. The idea of a précis is to summarize the gist of the story in such a way that the essential elements of the narrative are retained, but also in such a way that the story can be used as a guide to other situations. For example, a précis of Goethe's memory might be that when he was playing by himself at home, he noticed the quiet, and then began throwing his crockery out the window, which led some neighbors to applaud his naughtiness so vigorously that he proceeded to eject all the crockery he could lay his hands on.

Stating a précis has several advantages. It forces the clinician to put a story in terms that can be applied to other events or that can be used to see a pattern. It organizes the story into terms that are easier to recall than a longer narrative might be. It invites the therapist, when he or she has nothing to say after hearing a story, to replay the précis, which invites elaboration or recognition from the patient. Finally, it forces the clinician to decide which elements of the story are important and which trivial, the better to remember and recall the important elements.

5) Which Elements of the Memory Are Necessary to Understanding It Nonreductionistically?

A memory needs to be summarized for later use (shorter behavior sequences are easier to learn than longer ones), for application as a guide, and for detecting patterns. There are levels of mapmaking to consider. First, seeing and hearing an actual event is a map, as the visualization and auditory behavior will already reduce and organize the information available. This perceptual behavior is then replaced by the behavior of seeing and hearing it in the imagination, and this higher order map of imagining becomes territory to the even-higher-order map of verbally describing what was seen and heard in the imagination. Now, the former map (the memory report) again becomes the territory, and a still higher order map (the précis) is created. Whether the original event was an actual experience or a suggestion that led to visualizing behaviors in the imagination, by the time a therapist gets around to using this material in therapy, there are maps of maps of maps. Each level of mapping constitutes as loss of information, introduction of expectations (whether accurate or erroneous) by the new mapmaker, and introduction of new emphases, depending on what the new map will be used for. This analysis makes it clear, I hope, why my approach to early memories in psychotherapy is one of neutrality as to whether they really happened and one of emphasis on how the memory guides the patient's expectations of reality and when the patient uses that particular guide for navigation.

It is not possible to specify, independent of context, which elements of a memory are important and which trivial. Good maps vary in their content according to how they will be used. A map for determining where on a property to build a house will have contour lines that would be unnecessary and confusing on a road map, whose use is to get from one place to another in a car. Referral questions and therapeutic goals will help determine which details are important and which are dispensable.

The therapist's effective use of the patient's narrations, whether they be early memories, dreams, reports of symptoms, or identifications of stressors, will be enhanced by two levels of technical skill. One, the therapist should create a communicative environment with the patient in which the patient's report of narratives is affected maximally by the desire to get help and minimally by fear of how the therapist will react to the details. Such an environment may generally be described as nonjudgmental and welcoming. Many analysts quite logically consider consistency and confidentiality also to facilitate the development of such a communicative context. Even under the best of circumstances, of course, the patient's narrations will be affected by personality, predilections, and circumstance. Nonetheless, it is a truism of therapeutic technique that, aside from the distorting influences intrinsic in any report of anything, the contribution made by the speaker's fear of the listener's reaction should be minimized.

Two, the therapist should strive to make his or her own map or précis or synopsis of the narrated material as much as possible inclusive of the important information. How the therapist determines which information is important cannot be described simply, as it depends on the theoretical understanding of what causes presenting problems, how therapy helps, and how to use the patient's verbalizations. Still, the important thing for now is to emphasize that the therapist's précis should include the important things, and one source of finding out what is important is to ask the patient.

The task is to restate the patient's narrative in a way that does not leave out important information. Leaving out important information can happen either by omitting it entirely or by abstracting it beyond recognition. As noted, the therapist's theoretical orientation (call them personal expectations if you prefer) will dictate to a large degree what is considered important. If the therapist views all problems as trauma-based, for example, he may emphasize in his own version of the memory anything that sounds traumatic, and de-emphasize anything that sounds metaphorical. If the therapist is cognitive-behavioral, he will emphasize implicit beliefs. Frequently, there will be specific details in the patient's narration, and the therapist will not know if these are incidental details or meaningful ones. The patient may, for example, introduce a memory by saying, "When we lived in Iowa. . . ." There is no way for the therapist to know what living in Iowa means without obtaining the patient's associations. If the patient tells a memory about an encounter with a vicious dog on his way to church, it is hard to see how the therapist can justify leaving out the detail about it being a church. Thus, the therapist's job of treating an early memory nonreductionistically is not easy, but in general I think therapists will do better on this score if we remain aware of the problem.

Which information to preserve also depends on the therapeutic context. For example, if the referral question were a troubled marriage, the fact that Goethe's crockery was cookware might signal an aggressive assertion of a hypermasculine posture. Whatever the interpretation in that context, the précis should probably mention this stereotypically feminine feature of the crockery. If the referral question or operative context involved the birth of his new sibling (as Freud hypothesized), then the précis should mention that the neighbors were brothers. Absent a specific referral or therapeutic context to guide us, we can only listen to the memory and let that which strikes us as unexpected loom larger in our précis than that which seems fully determined by the context. For Rom (1965), the useful detail may have been the merry response to the visual image of the shattering. For a Lacanian, it might be the name of the neighbors; were they like oxen yoked together in slavery only to be freed by Goethe's iconoclasm? For someone like me who has spent twenty years working in the child welfare system, it might be the absent parents.

To interpret the memory nonreductionistically—to ensure our précis leaves out as little as possible that is important—we may ask ourselves whether the memory would be substantially different if we changed an element. "Why this and not that?" we can ask ourselves. What if the crockery were toy soldiers instead of cookware? If we think, in effect, "Now that's a substantially different memory," then we may also say the detail is important. In dream interpretation, such details are almost always meaningful (though still not necessarily worth preserving in the précis), because the dreamer is at liberty to improvise any details. Since memories are cobbled together with a combination of apperceived expectations, actual events, and sensible features, the person's freedom to choose meaningful details is constrained. Goethe's production of a useful guide to iconoclasm, naughtiness, and celebration may have been stuck with the crockery he happened to have available as a child, just as newly evolved characteristics in a species are often makeshift or jury-rigged around what happens to be available anatomically.

6) What Is the Wisdom of the Symptom?

It was originally a Jungian concept that a symptom constituted the guerrilla warfare of the psyche against the oppressive forces of imposed order. Instead of asking what we as doctors know that the symptom-bearer does not know, Jungians asked what the symptom-bearer might know that we do not. A child who elects mutism may *know*—not of course in the sense of verbalizing, but in the sense of reliably and successfully responding to—that her parents' marriage works better when they are exasperated with her than when they are not, or that people do not listen when she speaks. The suicidal patient may know that something has to die.

The conception of the individual as a collection of figures or response repertoires allows this wisdom to be imputed to the symptom, rather than to the person who expresses it. The gene that produces sickle-cell anemia protects against malaria. At one point, the anemia was wise, making what were on balance good cost-benefit decisions. This is not to say that many symptoms are not unwise; many symptoms in fact are downright foolish. They are foolish, typically, when the maps that guide them are outmoded, as when anemia persists but malaria is no longer a threat. The girl who grows up, leaves her family, and relapses into mutism is not wise (assuming the symptom has indeed outlived its usefulness). However, the symptom itself may enable other parts of the woman to remain functional, as when she finds that it is now her own marriage that appears to function well when she does not say what is on her mind. In this respect, it still makes sense to inquire in what respect the symptom is wise.

Symptoms are also wise in other ways. In the psychoanalytic sense of compromise formation, symptoms balance impulses and restraints. They are wise in the systemic sense of metaphorical communication and cybernetic regulation, meaning that symptoms communicate needs in ways that are deniable and they also can keep systems operating smoothly. Behaviorally, symptoms are often wise in the sense that their expression garners more (often unacknowledged) rewards than does their suppression. Rewards, in this context, can mean the very same kinds of results and partial expressions of impulses described by psychoanalysts and systems theorists.

It is often difficult to guess the wise purpose of a symptom (Selvini-Palazzoli et al., 1980). One thing that makes it hard is that we rarely get a chance to observe the symptom in action, which is one reason many family therapists like to see the wheels go round right in the session. Prescribing the symptom in the session is not only a clever way of exciting the system to rebel by finding alternatives and demonstrating that the symptom is controllable, prescribing the symptom also allows the therapist to see it in its interpersonal context. When a metaphorical representation of a symptom can be discerned in an early memory, the memory also imparts its psychological context and relevant systemic counterparts. This makes for clearer hypothesizing in Selvini et al.'s sense of speculating as to the systemic function of a symptom.

Recall that a systemic hypothesis is judged not on its accuracy but on its plausibility and its suggestion of interventions. With that in mind, we may speculate that the quietness of the house and the sense that his initial play "led to nothing" may have set the stage for Goethe's behavior, which brought merriment and liveliness into the scene. Quietness and pointlessness sound like depression, or at least like existential angst, and Goethe's aggression may have served the purpose of livening up his experience of his house. This view is somewhat reinforced by Hirn's (1900) statement that later in the autobiography, "the old poet frankly and unreservedly describes how, when lacerated by the conflict between hypochondriac, suicidal thoughts and an ineradicable love of life and cheerfulness, he resorted to an old homely remedy of writing down his sufferings" (p. 73). The implication might be that playful aggression in the quiet of one's home is akin, to Goethe, to making poetry, and that one function of the symptom (which varies in its appearance from tossing crockery out the window to writing poetry) is that it produces cheerfulness that dispels depression. For the sake of using Goethe as an example, one might imagine that he is brought to a clinic as a boy for being oppositional. In that context, this memory suggests that the wisdom of his oppositionality may be that it brings liveliness to the scene. In any event, it seems worth considering that the memory of breaking crockery and the memory of writing himself out of a suicidal state were constructed, in Jung's (1926) metaphor, by the same architect (i.e., by the same underlying pattern or complex).

7) What Plausible Interventions, If Any, Are Suggested by the Memory?

One thing that the psychoanalytic concept of transference has in common with systemic theorists' notion of equilibrium is that a pattern must be changed from within. The psychoanalyst allows the transference to develop, in this view, so she can enter the problematic pattern. Trying to change a pattern without entering it is likely to arouse a reaction that maintains the status quo (Watzlawick et al., 1974; Karson, 2001). Any moves toward change must be made by existing figures within the pattern. Otherwise, an intervention would be like rolling a die as a move in a chess game: irrelevant and ignored, and likely to lead to reification of the current pattern of rules ("no dice").

This simple, basic proposition—that patterns must be changed from within—accounts for the fate of good advice. Advice works when there is a figure within the pattern who is wise and respected. In the guise of that figure, the adviser may speak and expect to be heard. Patterns that contain such a figure are rarely of concern to clinicians, because the presence of a wise figure usually means that the pattern is amenable to input from the environment. Advice also works, of course, when there is no fixed pattern, when the person is not invested in a particular solution.

Thus, it is a violation of the implicit rules of the pattern in Goethe's memory to suggest, say, that the child should be more careful or that the neighbors should be more responsible. The figures presented in the memory are of a carefree child and rascally neighbors. Such *deus ex* machinations might work in the abstract, but they do not address the problem as presented. They are analogous to a family therapist saying, "If the boy were obedient, he could please his parents." Of course, one long-term possibility is to introduce a new figure into the complex, so that this new figure can make moves. Indeed, one way to look at psychoanalytic therapy is that it tries to introduce the figure of the therapist into problematic patterns.

Taking Goethe's memory on its own terms, a difficulty with suggesting an intervention is that no figure in the memory is unhappy with what is going on. The relevant figures have no motivation to try something different. For the sake of the discussion, then, I will suggest consideration of other figures, as a family therapist might do if a mother and adult son were both happy with their interdependence and the therapist wondered about the father. Technically, it would not be the father who was being neglected in such a scenario, but the filial needs of the son and the romantic needs of the mother. By mentioning the father, the family therapist would be trying to give a voice to these dormant figures.

In Goethe's memory, one dormant figure is the boy's allegiance to his parents, or, I should say, the boy who is allied with his parents. That boy may be unhappy with the incident. (As presented, Goethe seems to expect that his parents, too, will appreciate a good story over cheap earthenware, but I am again assuming for the sake of this discussion that there is a problem needing intervention.) Any intervention within the memory on its own terms will depend on giving that boy a voice. When an adolescent comes home after curfew, scolding does not work, behaviorally, because punishment is only effective in the presence of the punisher. Scolding only increases the adolescent's tendency not to think about his parents when he is out late. Systemically, scolding does not work because it satisfies and quiets the part of the adolescent that is allied with the parents. Out on the town, the allied adolescent thinks, as it were, that the parents can look after themselves. The parents are more likely to be effective if they gently inquire what the adolescent might imagine it is like for them when they do not know his whereabouts. This intervention fosters the voice of the teenager who cares about them.

The dormant part of Goethe concerned about his parents might be asked, "How long did it take Mommy to go to the crafts fair and select all that earthenware?" This part of the child might then select something to toss out the window that is less destructive but equally iconoclastic. For example, he might play loud contemporary music, or sing naughty lyrics. I imagine in the actual story, however, that this part of Goethe was already activated, wherefore the crockery and not the crystal got tossed.

8) How Might the Memory Anticipate a Therapy Relationship?

Early memories involve young children and therefore often involve parenting relationships. These, in turn, are often relevant to individual therapy, since the role of patient has much in common with the role of child. When individual therapy is recommended, early memories can often guide the therapist through potential potholes and landmines. They can also serve as alliance builders if the therapist and patient can refer back to early memories when things get rough for a joint understanding of what they are going through.

Thus, Goethe's therapist might want to anticipate a misalliance in which the patient acts entertaining and the therapist feels entertained, but the background quietness and sense of directionlessness is never explored. This of course would only make sense if the crockery destruction and its parallels in his life were problematic. As a successful solution to the meaninglessness and vanity of life, there would be no point in trying to address the underlying existential dilemma or to pathologize the solution. An in-therapy test of the function of entertainment might be the therapist's own sense that something is being avoided in the room. The therapist might then comment, "I notice that we were both silent for several seconds, and then you said something funny to dispel the moment," speaking from the position of the neighbors but changing their message from encouragement to one of welcoming intimacy.

Chapter Nine

Interpretive Examples

To see a World in a Grain of Sand
And a Heaven in a Wild Flower

—W. Blake, *Auguries of Innocence*

Having introduced the steps I use to make sense of an early memory, in this chapter I will apply these steps to three examples. I call the initial appraisal of the communicative function of the memory report Step 0, in order to maintain the numbering of the content steps from the previous chapter, and to differentiate it from the others as to the kind of interpretive step it is.

Interpretive Steps
0) Why now and in this manner?
1) What psychological landscape is the memory a map of?
2) Who are the dramatis personae?
3) How is the systemic interaction among the figures self-regulated and self-perpetuated?
4) When what, then what?
5) Why this and not that?
6) What is the wisdom of the symptom?
7) What plausible interventions, if any, are suggested by the memory?
8) How might the memory anticipate a therapy relationship?

CASE EXAMPLE: BEE IN THE HOUSE

Joe was a twenty-six-year-old white man who came to our clinic, seeking help for the way he had always felt stigmatized by a lifelong diagnosis of attention deficit disorder with hyperactivity (ADHD). His sales job required almost no reading and he was quite successful at it, having squeaked through college with a business degree. In spite of his financial success, Joe was haunted by the feeling that he would be doing more socially useful work if he were better educated. He might have been better educated (according to his own definition of the term), except that he refused to take stimulant medications. Although he acknowledged that they helped him focus, he resisted their implications for his identity. He attributed a superficial love life to his repeated decision to end relationships before discussing his hyperactivity. However, he had numerous close men friends who were aware of his diagnosis.

When asked his earliest memory, Joe responded: "I stepped on a bee. I thought it was a thumbtack on the floor, but it buzzed. My babysitter was there and I ran and hid from her. All I wanted was my mother. I remember running across the house to my brother's room." His next earliest memory was a pleasant recollection of playing alone in his room, creating a fantasy world for his stuffed animals. He reported an early memory of his mother at Christmas, arranging the morning festivities. He remembered his father carrying him piggyback over a creek. Joe also recalled disappointing his mother when she had to come to school because his hyperactivity got out of control.

We will apply the interpretive steps to the first, problematic memory, but it is important to remember that the other memories, not to mention Joe's clinical presentation and reported history, indicated his overall mental health. If all or almost all of a person's memories are scenes from the same essential drama, it is not a good sign of flexibility in responding. If, on the other hand, the problematic memories stand out against a background of warm, rich, specific, textured imagery, they are far less likely to indicate serious psychopathology (Mayman, 1968; Shedler et al., 1993). Nietzsche (1879) said, "It is possible to shape the picture of a person out of three anecdotes." I would suggest that if you can do it in one anecdote, you may be dealing with a personality disorder. I mean that if the person has only one mode of experience, one map for navigation, then their approach to life is likely so inflexible as to constitute a personality disorder. Another way of saying the same thing is that a personality disorder means that the person is always in a complex, always caught in a drama that supersedes reality, always negotiating the world's demands with a limited set of figures and a predictable set of interactions. As Jung (1926, p. 96) said, "Everyone knows nowadays that people 'have complexes.' What is not so well known . . . is that complexes can *have us.*"

Step 0) Why Now and In This Manner?

Is the memory occasioned primarily by the therapist-patient interaction, or is it Joe's association to his early childhood in the context of the presenting problem? Joe told his memories in response to direct questions rather than as free associations. This makes their occurrence less likely to be a reflection on the psychological transaction in the room. Spontaneous verbal productions could be responding to nearly anything in the immediate environment, but answers to direct questions are likely to be responses to the stimulus of the question itself. Joe's memories in this context were probably a reflection of what he was trying to communicate to the therapist about his autobiography and what he typically thinks about when he thinks of his early childhood. Nonetheless, the presence of the babysitter in the memory as an inadequate comforter raises questions about whether the hired help (i.e., the therapist) will be able to comfort him. There may be an implicit critique of the therapist in reporting a memory where someone hired to care for him cannot do the job, a critique that may suggest that the therapist is being too businesslike and too impersonal.

The memory may have been selected under the influence of concerns about how personal, versus how professional, the therapy relationship would be. The clinic was modeled after my private practice and involved clerical staff as little as humanly possible in the transactions: there were no initial intakes; therapists managed the finances and the billing and the filing personally; patients did not check in with a receptionist upon arrival. Still, there were some aspects of the clinic that were unavoidably impersonal, such as the public waiting room and the fact that checks, though handed to the therapist, were made out to the clinic. Thus, the memory could be used as a map for navigating this personal versus professional issue, which was, at least reportedly, the central reason for therapy in the first place. Joe was worried that, in life, he was more a patient than a man, more an object of professional than personal interest, and that hyperactivity was more central to his identity than *Joe* was.

Step 1) What Psychological Landscape Is the Memory a Map Of?

Joe's memory takes place in the family home, suggesting that it has to do with his personal life. This framing of the memory's application may be especially useful in light of the referral questions regarding his difficulty getting close with women and how stigmatizing was his diagnosis. These questions raise concerns about letting people into his home life and about different self-definitions between his social and personal environments. Focus on the home as the landscape of the memory also highlights the issue of whether the source of injury was domestic (a thumbtack that he first expected belongs in the home) or imported (the bee that actually injured him does not belong in the home). The psychological landscape may have to do with the aftermath of injury, or with what happens when the outside world comes inside, or with what happens when comfort is sought. In light of the referral question about hyperactivity, I would emphasize the extent to which the memory referred to his "running across the house," a behavior that looks like hyperactivity but in this case is not.

Step 2) Who Are the Dramatis Personae?

The figures in the memory are the injured boy, the babysitter, the brother, the bee, and the mother who is not there. Often in a memory, as in a dream, a figure represents itself or its relational counterpart. A mother may represent herself or the part of the individual that typically relates to the mother. A dream about one's spouse may refer to the spouse or to the part of the dreamer that is married. The brother in the memory may refer to the affiliative aspects of Joe. Delineation of the figures will become relevant when we attempt to include them in a systemic formulation.

Step 3) How Is the Systemic Interaction Among the Figures Self-Regulated and Self-Perpetuated?

One way to answer this question is simply to make sure that the narrative description of the complex is coherent regardless of where it is punctuated, that is, regardless of which starting point is selected. Factors that govern the regulation and perpetuation of the system should then become more obvious. In this memory, to begin with the mother's absence, her absence brings in a babysitter. Importing the outside world leads to injury, which in turn leads to seeking maternal comfort. Finding mother absent, there is a lot of activity and sibling comfort is sought instead. Presumed, eventual fraternal comfort makes mother's absence less troubling, and therefore easier for her to be absent in the future, which was our starting point. Punctuated differently, the seeking of comfort from other boys in the midst of excess activity (running through the house) makes mother's presence unnecessary, which brings in the outside world in the form of babysitters and bees, which produces injury and, with mother absent, brotherly comfort, which again was our starting point. To start in yet a third place, the outside world is brought indoors, leading to injury. This leads to excessive activity and seeking brotherly comfort, making mother's presence unnecessary. Mother's absence leads to importation of the outside world. The system seems to be regulated by the presence of some comfort within the house; without it, it is easy to imagine Joe dashing outside or demanding that his mother stay home when he might need her. The system is perpetuated by his sense that the babysitter cannot comfort him, since turning to her for help would change the pattern's dependence on maternal absence and fraternal comfort.

Step 4) When What, Then What?

The systemic interchanges should be summarized in template statements, that is, statements that may apply to other situations. When the outside world is brought in unexpectedly, Joe gets injured, links his mother's absence with his impulsivity, and seeks comfort from peers. When Joe seeks comfort from peers, he loses his sense of connection with his mother. When Joe feels he is in the care of hired help, he unexpectedly encounters the outside world and feels un-consoled with respect to the pain this causes. When Joe is unexpectedly injured, he finds himself in the care of hired help. The suggestion that emerges is that if his reaction to injury did not look so much like hyperactivity (running through the house), his mother would have been there to comfort him.

Step 5) Why This and Not That?

Does it matter that it is a bee he steps on, and not some other object that does not belong in the house? It is hard to see how it could matter, although if Joe were to mention that his father was a beekeeper or a worker drone or some other interesting association, then it might. In this memory, I see no particu-lar reason to preserve the specificity of the bee, although *stepping on a bee* is an easy way to cue the entire sequence for later applications.

Step 6) What Is the Wisdom of the Symptom?

If there is a symptom in this memory, perhaps it is Joe's not letting the babysitter comfort him and instead running through the house to his brother. What function might this serve in the system? It may preserve the role of the mother-who-is-not-there. If the child in the memory allows himself to be comforted by babysitters (or teachers, doctors, or reading specialists), then the absent mother will no longer be a figure in the story; instead, it would just be a story about the time he got stung by a bee and was comforted by the babysitter. The symptom wisely keeps him attached to his mother, and keeps her in the home even if only as a vacuum.

Interpersonally, this pattern could easily apply to a real family (as opposed to the constellation of characters that populate the memory). Children reject the ministrations of strangers not only because they are not precisely sooth-ing, but also because acceptance eliminates the spot being reserved for mother. Such rejection is compounded if the mother has communicated to the child any disappointment when the child allows himself to be cared for by others. Then, the rejection of soothing by others is a way of protecting the mother from herself feeling rejected.

For an intrapsychic understanding, it can be a good exercise to imagine how the complex might play out without involving other people. This exercise ensures that our understanding treats the figures in the memory as aspects of Joe. One way to eliminate other people and to concentrate on Joe's inner world is to deal with a sequence of events in which he is alone, such as driving home from work, dozing on the sofa, or taking a shower. Imagine Joe driving home, thinking about what he wants for dinner. He imagines cooking something for himself, maybe quesadillas. He realizes it would be lot simpler to stop by Del Taco on the way home and buy dinner, but he envisions a hair in his food, so he decides just to go home, where he realizes he will wind up eating chips and salsa while watching a basketball game on television. This story I am making up takes place over the course of a few seconds while he is driving his car, and only involves figures in his imagination. When his imagination took him to Del Taco, which I am proposing as the psychological equivalent of a babysitter compared to homemade quesadillas, his imagination then introduced a bee in the form of an unexpected import, the hair in the food. This led him to his brother's room, metaphorically, which I am depicting as chips and basketball. I tend to engage in this exercise of playing out the complex intrapsychically only to be sure I understand how it might have become a part of him, to practice thinking about people as a system of figures.

The wisdom of the symptom might also be considered in Weiss's (1993) control-mastery terms. Very briefly, Weiss sees therapy as a series of tests or opportunities, where the patient gives the therapist a chance to do something right that needs doing. One finds such tests in other venues as well, including teaching and childrearing, in other words, wherever the trustworthiness of the person in greater power needs testing. In this context, it strikes me that running through the house instead of being comforted by the babysitter is giving the rest of the system a chance to fix something, a chance to demonstrate their understanding of the difference between activity and hyperactivity.

This memory makes me think of how often in the life of a hyperactive child the parents must mistakenly attribute the child's impulsivity to his disorder rather than to circumstances or to normal development. I imagine the scene of the memory happening for real, and I see a babysitter who shrugs at the sudden exclamation and sudden dashing through the house as yet another instance of Joe's hyperactive unpredictability. In fact, I imagine Joe's whole problem, his whole reason for wanting to be in therapy and his self-consciousness about his condition, as a function of his parents not carefully enough distinguishing between his hyperactivity and his activity. He may associate his father, for example, with treating all his impulsivity as a case of "boys will be boys," and his mother with treating all his impulsivity as the result of his cortical sluggishness. (I agree with those like Barkley [1998] who view ADHD as an impulse disorder caused by cortical sluggishness—the cortex governs self-restraint—which should be treated with stimulants for the sluggishness and therapy and education for the family members.) Joe may feel he cannot take medication without labeling not only his ADHD as disordered, but also his spontaneity, his brassiness, and his extraversion. Joe may have needed a father who was more willing to pathologize his impulsive barefooted attitude toward life and a mother who was more willing not to pathologize his normal inattentiveness and roughhousing. (Meichenbaum & Turk [1987] teach parents that even normal children follow orders only about half the time.)

Step 7) What Plausible Interventions, If Any, Are Suggested by the Memory?

For an intervention to be plausible, it must be something that someone in the memory could actually do or say in context. It is no good to say that the father could have been there and warned Joe about the bee, for example, because the father is not one of the characters in this story. Neither is it any good to say that Joe should let the babysitter comfort him, because the whole problem with the situation is that Joe will not do this. Such suggestions amount to telling the patient to get over it.

A couple of interventions occur to me, though I am sure there are many others that are plausible. The babysitter could follow Joe to his brother's room. This would probably lead to angry words from Joe, but this is a storm the babysitter might be able to weather if she reminds herself that Joe has just been hurt and wants to impress upon her the fact that she is not his mother. The babysitter might even cautiously make it clear that she is not trying to replace his mother. "What would Mommy do?" is a pretty good way of showing a child one's willingness to help without usurping the role. (For foster kids, you might have to ask, "What would *a* mommy do?" but it is the same idea.) These then are steps the babysitter might take to approximate comfort in a way that does not replace the mother. In my quesadilla fantasy, the part of Joe that is willing to spend a little money to save time and effort might preserve some but not all of the benefits of a home-cooked meal over chips and salsa by stopping at the store on the way home and buying frozen food to heat up at home, or by getting takeout from a mom-and-pop type restaurant where the food preparers are not disaffected teenagers who may not be too careful about getting hair in the food.

Another intervention suggested by the memory is that the mother could, when she returns home, conscientiously and patiently find out about all the bumps and bruises that happened while she was away, and inquire as to their origin. In *my* imagination, Joe's mother has extinguished on this brand of parenting, because the list is always so long and the cause always seems to go back to his not looking where he was going. For the sake of suggesting a plausible or doable intervention, I hold off for now on suggesting that the mother help Joe distinguish boyish from hyperactive behavior or teach him to protect himself and the objects around him from constant bumps. Instead, I think just getting the litany of hurts will be initially restorative, and I would ask of the mother in the memory only that she not use the list as an excuse to provide object lessons in how Joe should behave. At most, I hope that she could eventually classify each story as normal or as hyperactive, and respond with sympathy to the former and with sympathy to the latter. I am pretty sure that the two forms of sympathy would develop some distinctions if she were discriminating accurately. In my quesadilla story, this would be a solicitous voice inside Joe that asks, "Okay, then, what else sounds good?" instead of just running to the chips.

Step 8) How Might the Memory Anticipate a Therapy Relationship?

Since there are figures in the memory charged with Joe's care, the translation into therapy is fairly easy to make. The therapist should behave, as always, neutrally, anonymously, confidentially, warmly, and consistently enough to allow Joe's complex to emerge in the therapy, and then the therapist should attempt an intervention analogous to those suggested for the babysitter or the mother. The therapist can offer two different kinds of sympathy for hyperactivity accidents and for life's vagaries. The therapist can offer comfort while carefully distinguishing it from real love, so that Joe does not have to reject it. Alternatively, the therapist can invite Joe's actual parents to family therapy sessions to teach them how to do these things, although at twenty-six, he may balk at family work.

What the therapist should *not do* is to explain the complex to Joe, as if the suggested intervention for the events in the memory were to call in a professor of psychology to lecture the babysitter, Joe, the mother, and the brother on family systems theory. On the other hand, the *babysitter* might explain a few things to Joe, doing so in the guise of the therapist. The therapist could perhaps say, in the babysitter role, "I notice that whenever you are hurt unexpectedly, you run away from me," which could lead to a discussion of the reasons for running away from the therapist. Conversely, the therapist may find *himself* unexpectedly hurt and actively retreating from *Joe*. I imagine a particularly tender moment in which the therapist blurs the distinction between therapeutic comfort and paternal love, which Joe might rebuke by stinging the therapist with a comment about the fee. Caught in the complex, the therapist could easily be driven into a flurry of active intervention, rather than processing the sting interpersonally. This flurry would be the equivalent of running through the house, which the therapist could usefully manage by relinquishing this avoidant defense and returning to Joe.

Joe's therapist might benefit from thinking through beforehand how to manage an accusation that he or she is just in it for the money. Reflecting on the babysitter's situation, not just one's personal situation, could help the therapist manage this accusation in a way that is most beneficial to Joe. I prefer something along the lines of, "Well of course I'm in it for the money, but why would you think it was *just* for the money?" Or, "You wondered about my motives right after you unexpectedly encountered evidence of a previous patient having sat in your chair." Then, assuming the evidence is something the therapist should have kept out of the office, the therapist can adopt the role of the unprotective mother and apologize for letting it in and note that this naturally led Joe to question the therapist's motives. Later, the therapist can draw the analogy between the evidence of a previous patient and the bee in the memory.

The therapist may also want to think through how to handle the recommendation for stimulants. It may be impossible, once the issue comes up, not to become either the oblivious father or the pathologizing mother. My preference is to metacommunicate about the dilemma rather than to try to resolve it, but there is no reason, in theory, why the therapist should not differentiate adult hyperactivity from adult spontaneity and recommend stimulants, prepared to discuss Joe's anticipated accusations of pathologizing him. The real problem is not when a complex enters a therapy, but when a complex subsumes the therapy. Thus, I can easily imagine Joe's therapist exercising therapeutic privilege, in the face of an interpersonal bump in the road, by pathologizing Joe, either as hyperactive or as insecure. For example, Joe discovers the previous patient's Kleenex shreds on his chair, then misses the following session. The therapist does not wonder what he did wrong, but instead chalks up the missed session to Joe's impulsivity. This would replicate the complex rather than help Joe resolve it.

CASE EXAMPLE: DRAINING EGGS

Kirk was the father of two children, an eight-year-old boy and a six-year-old girl. Both had been placed in foster care by the Department of Social Services (DSS) following a report of neglect by their mother, from whom Kirk had been divorced for two years. Since the divorce, he had not seen his children often, but upon learning that they had been removed from their mother's home, he was seeking custody of them. He agreed to attend batterer's treatment to address a history of mild physical altercations with his ex-wife. He was already involved with Alcoholics Anonymous (AA) for periodic drunkenness, and had not had a drink since the divorce. Finally, he was seeking individual psychotherapy to address his lifelong adjustment problems. These might be summarized as the stark contrast between, on the one hand, his middle-class upbringing with above-average intelligence and, on the other hand, his mediocre work history, which included a series of odd jobs and use of the welfare system. He dropped out of college after one year. Now thirty-two, he had enrolled in a small liberal arts college, using his inheritance from his grandfather to pay tuition and living and expenses. His grades were highly variable, which he attributed to feeling like an odd duck among the undergraduates.

Kirk's earliest memory began with a description of the family home, an historic landmark built by a famous American. When asked for a specific incident, he switched to kindergarten, and remembered that he had been given the task of draining raw eggs to prepare then for an Easter display. He thought he had a better method for draining them than the one his teacher had described, but the first two eggs he tried it on both cracked. When he went to the teacher for more eggs, he was upset to learn that he had broken the only two she had. The teacher said it was not a big deal, but Kirk was aware that the students waiting to paint the eggs were sorely disappointed.

Step 0) Why Now and In This Manner?

Kirk was, in short, being accused of inattentiveness to his children. By putting his children in foster care instead of giving them to him, the state was holding him responsible for the substandard care his ex-wife had provided. In effect, the state was telling him that he should have known about the poor quality of care they were receiving, that he should have visited more often, and that he should have done something about it. In that context, the first part of the memory can be viewed as a protest that he comes from the type of family that does not belong in the child welfare system. The second part of the memory communicates that when children do not get their needs met, it is not his fault. As a metaphor for the neglect his children suffered, the memory is a claim that there was no way for him to know about the limited resources (depicted as only having two eggs) provided by his wife (depicted as the kindergarten teacher), and that he was therefore not responsible for the disappointment of these children. As the oldest of three children himself, there were presumably hundreds of stories he might have told where something unfortunate happened to a younger sibling that was not his fault. Even though choosing this particular incident may have largely served his agenda to deny his culpability, the memory may have other features that tell us something more about Kirk's psychology when he is in a position of responsibility. Thus, an interpretation of the memory itself seems warranted, to understand his personal expectations beyond what he may be communicating about his innocence.

Step 1) What Psychological Landscape Is the Memory a Map Of?

This memory in two scenes moves from an historic home to school. The emphasis on the home's exterior and on its prominence suggests that the memory has something to do with familial pride or, at least, with the family's public façade. The school scene might indicate something about Kirk's own academic life, but it also has to do with responsibility toward children. It is also a terrain of competence, because of his having to handle the eggs adroitly, and this emphasis appeals to me because it may be relevant to his work history.

Step 2) Who Are the Dramatis Personae?

The characters in the memory are the creative child (who wants to try his own method of draining eggs), the teacher who has fewer resources than one might imagine, and the expectant, then disappointed students.

Step 3) How Is the Systemic Interaction Among the Figures Self-Regulated and Self-Perpetuated?

The pattern is perpetuated by the teacher's dearth of resources, by the creative child's not knowing about the lack of resources, and by the other students' hopefulness. If any of these were different, the pattern would dissipate, as can be illustrated by retelling the story in a circular narrative.

The systemic interaction of the three figures can be punctuated by starting with any of them. The teacher's lack of resources makes her self-conscious or defensive about telling the creative child the importance of using her method of draining the eggs. His ensuing freedom to experiment wastes the eggs, and the expectant children are disappointed. Their potential for disappointment makes the teacher self-conscious about having so few eggs. Starting with the child cast as Ego, his desire to experiment keeps him from inquiring about the potential costs. His bad feelings about disappointing the other students make the teacher want to make light of the failure. Her minimizing the failure keeps him from suspecting in the future that there are scant resources. From the students' starting point, their disappointment in not having eggs to color makes the teacher want to meet their needs in the future. She protects them from future disappointment by concealing the dearth of resources, like a parent who would rather reassure a child that it will not rain on his birthday than have to deal with his worrying that it might. Her concealment leads to experimentation and the waste of resources.

Oddly perhaps, the system is not only perpetuated but also regulated by the dearth of resources. Having only two eggs means the creative child cannot overdo his wastefulness. The fact that he is also essentially an experimenting rather than a rebellious child also ensures that he will stop breaking things once he runs out of legitimate things to break.

Step 4) When What, Then What?

When family pride is at stake, a complex emerges in which failure is chalked up to creativity rather than to a lack of resources; this explains away the failure and maintains the family pride. This statement applies to Kirk's excuses for his ex-wife's lifestyle, which he saw as free and natural rather than as neglectful. It also applies to his problems in college, which he attributed to his disinclination to do "busy work" or to "kiss ass" to get good grades.

When the limited quantity of resources is ignored, or when authority figures are defensive about what they are able to provide, wastefulness and disappointment follow. This statement of the memory's theme has direct relevance to the problems that grew out of the parents' refusal to take stock of how the children were doing. Both parents, mother daily and father whenever he saw them, ignored signs from the children that they were being neglected.

When children are given responsibility beyond their years (as Kirk was for draining the eggs), parents are let off the hook and children's needs are not met. A good example of this theme in operation involved the children's rotting teeth, which were a consequence of their mother's attitude that children have to make up their own minds on issues of self-care. Kirk's attitude was that the children could have called him if they needed to see him.

Step 5) Why This and Not That?

Does it matter that the memory takes place at school? That it is related to Easter? That it has to do with eggs? In my view, it makes sense to preserve the school detail because of Kirk's own educational concerns. The relationship between eggs and birth and childrearing, like the relationship between resurrection and Kirk's getting a second life after starting with AA, are both appealing on the level of poetry, but neither association seems to me to be dictated by the memory. These associations seem to come from me.

Step 6) What Is the Wisdom of the Symptom?

The creative child accepts the blame for the limited resources in the system, and the disappointed children facilitate this acceptance by blaming him and not the authority figure. This helps all the children preserve an idealized image of the parent figure. In general, children would rather think of their parents as withholding than as not-having, perhaps because a withholding parent can always change his mind, while a not-having parent cannot meet child's needs under any circumstances.

Step 7) What Plausible Interventions, If Any, Are Suggested by the Memory?

At first, it appears the onus would be on the teacher to do something different. It may seem strange that she is concealing the number of eggs, given that this does not strike us as an embarrassing sort of secret, but to empathize with her, we must recall that it is this concealment that leads to the creative child absorbing the blame for what is imperfect about the family. In this memory, the child, who has already been saddled with certain parental functions, may be as likely to change his behavior as the parent figure is. The child blames himself partly because, had he known that there were only two eggs, he would not have tried his experimental method of draining them. Thus, likely interventions on the memory's own terms would be for the teacher to learn to acknowledge her limitations or for the child to inquire as to the depth of available resources. By extension, the child figure can also inquire as to the depth of familial pride: "How well must I do in school not to embarrass you?" is the kind of question that can occasion reasonableness in parents to combat the parents' unspoken requirement of *summa cum laude* at Harvard.

In life, the adult's acknowledgment of scant resources or the child's inquiry about their depth might take several different forms. Near the end of a visit with his children, for example, Kirk initiated a game of checkers with his son while holding his daughter on his lap. The hour-long visit ended before they had completed their game, which made all three of them feel frustrated, father and son because the game was incomplete and daughter because she expected to do something with her father once the game was finished. The initiating child within Kirk had not been told by the parental figure within Kirk that there was not enough time left in the visit to play checkers, which led to the disappointment of all concerned. This probably happened because Kirk hated to acknowledge to his children that the visits were time-limited, as this feature symbolized the visits' embarrassing circumstances. Kirk would rather blame the part of him that suggested fun but impractical games than blame the part of him that had allowed his contact with his children to fall under the scrutiny of the state.

To prepare for such circumstances, Kirk could be taught to articulate his limitations to his children, allowing him to discover that they are less devastated by his limitations than they are relieved to know the actual parameters of the visit. Conversely, Kirk could be taught to ask, "Is this realistic?" and let the children answer him. Even if their answers were incorrect, they would be less disappointed knowing they had provided input for the creative child's decision-making, just as the students in his memory would likely have been less disappointed if he had consulted with them prior to using his experimental method of egg-draining. Similarly, regarding custody, Kirk was presenting as a man prepared to take his children home with him. In light of the family pride at stake, the complex dictated that he should ignore any limitations on his readiness to have them live with him. The children could be encouraged, in family sessions, to inquire as to how he was prepared to handle any concerns they might have regarding the proposed living arrangements. Kirk might be asked to develop a realistic schedule, which should include his work, school, and self-care obligations, to present a picture of how much parenting he was actually prepared to do.

Step 8) How Might the Memory Anticipate a Therapy Relationship?

Kirk might cover up the therapist's inevitable limitations by trying to do all the work himself in some manner that will lead him to accept responsibility for failure. Such limitations might be unavoidable, like the length of sessions the therapist is able to provide or the availability of the therapist between sessions, but more likely, they will be of the sort that would make the therapist lose pride for acknowledging them, like a limitation on sympathy or understanding. Since the therapist, being human, would prefer to ignore such limitations, and since Kirk might prefer to be blamed for them, the therapist should be alert to the need to take responsibility for and to articulate his or her limitations. Signs of creatively defining the patient role by Kirk might alert the therapist to this aspect of the treatment. For example, if Kirk suddenly decides to read poems he wrote in the session, or unexpectedly brings in his children's drawings to discuss, the therapist might wonder if there are not enough eggs in the room.

Conversely, Kirk might induce creativity in the therapist to disguise his own limitations. If the therapist departs from standard protocol or technique, and especially if the therapist starts justifying these as creative efforts to help, it may be a way to distract the duo from Kirk's lack of resources. This would be most likely to occur if an unholy alliance developed between them, as for example often happens when therapists are working with parents who are fighting for custody: The therapist can become an advocate for the patient, working to obtain custody rather than to resolve parenting impairments, and this can lead the therapist to ignore the patient's parenting limitations. Advocacy can also seem to justify going overboard with respect to boundaries and technique.

CASE EXAMPLE: FOOLING THE BABY

Ms. L, the mother of an infant, was accused of complicity in her daughter's serious abuse after her husband confessed to shaking the baby and breaking several bones over the course of several weeks. The authorities believed the abuse could not have been perpetrated outside of her awareness, given the small size of their living quarters and the husband's statement that she was nearby in an adjoining room for much of it. He would get frustrated when the little girl would fuss or would not nap or would wake up at night. The case did not, by any means, turn on a single memory, but I have selected it because it seemed particularly illustrative at the time.

Ms. L's reported earliest memory was quite brief: "I remember my father feeding me with a spoon. I was in my high chair. He would trick me, saying, 'One for me, one for you.' I can see his face lighting up when he pretended to eat the baby food." I inquire, following Mayman (1968), for earliest, next earliest, earliest and next earliest of mother, earliest and next earliest of father, happiest, and unhappiest. Here, I present only the earliest for the purpose of helping to illustrate my approach to interpretation.

Step 0) Why Now and In This Manner?

Ms. L was undergoing a psychological evaluation to help determine her fitness as a parent. Her choice of a memory that constituted a positive parenting exchange may largely have served her effort to make a good impression. It may be noteworthy that her idea of good parenting seems to align with most people's, suggesting that her judgment is intact on this issue. Still, as a psychologically healthy person, there were presumably hundreds of stories she could have told in response to my query, and the one she did tell may have elements that were occasioned by her associations to childhood and by her associations to the referral question. These bear further exploration.

Step 1) What Psychological Landscape Is the Memory a Map Of?

Ms. L's memory unfolds in a landscape of being fed by her father in her high chair. This might imply a landscape of parent-child nurturance or just domestic need gratification in general. The events in the memory may serve as a guide to what she expects to happen when domestic needs are supposed to be met.

Step 2) Who Are the Dramatis Personae?

When she is in a space where domestic need-gratification is anticipated, the figures that appear are a contented child and a playful, nurturing father.

Step 3) How Is the Systemic Interaction Among the Figures Self-Regulated and Self-Perpetuated?

In Ms. L's memory, it seems that her gratification depends on being tricked and she may expect that any trickery has a gratification component. This connection is found in many happy children; as soon as they get a sense that we are tricking them, they smile with anticipation that the experience will be gratifying. For them, as in Ms. L's memory, trickery is a prelude to fun and reward.

As it happened, Ms. L was very slender but not excessively skinny, and she acknowledged that she constantly watched her weight. I asked her if she had ever gotten too skinny for her own good, and this otherwise intelligent woman told me that her understanding was that you cannot really gain weight if you only eat at meals. She explained that her desire to keep her weight down was fully satisfied by forgoing all snacks, so she never went overboard. Her self-deception about the nature of calories had allowed her to eat well since adolescence. In other words, her belief that one cannot gain weight eating only three times a day was analogous to her belief that her father was eating the baby food, and both self-deceptions produced eating on her part, despite her concern about gaining weight as an adult and despite whatever made her hesitant to eat in the memory (presumably, her budding autonomy needs). The systemic connection between healthy eating and self-deception was regulated by her hunger, to which she was fortunately responsive enough not to escalate into anorexia, and by her intelligence, since she could go only so far in her self-deception before her skepticism would arise. She seemed to know that the three allowed meals could not include a surfeit of fat and carbohydrates if weight gain was to be avoided.

Step 4) When What, Then What?

When Ms. L needs nurturance, her internal parent deceives her for her own good. And when she is being deceived, she anticipates nurturing play. When she is in a domestic scene where nurturance is expected and available, this pattern is occasioned, and deception and nurturance are expected.

Step 5) Why This and Not That?

Ms. L's memory report is so brief that the précis hardly needs to leave anything out. Still, is it happenstance that it is her father and not her mother in the memory, or is it important? In other words, should we be thinking about a kind of parenting or a kind of fathering that is paired with being fed? Does it matter that the game was deceptive (the father not eating but pretending to)? Does the memory change substantially if we substitute a father playing airplane with the spoon and getting the baby to eat by making it a game? I thought the deception was intrinsic to the memory, but I thought so because the referral question, simply put, was whether or not she had been deceived by her husband.

Step 6) What Is the Wisdom of the Symptom?

Ms. L's presenting problem was her gullibility, in that she never questioned whether her husband was mistreating their daughter. Her early memory suggests that the systemic function of her gullibility may have been to garner her the nurturance she needs. What the memory did not prepare her for was the possibility that deception might be used for nefarious ends.

Step 7) What Plausible Interventions, If Any, Are Suggested by the Memory?

In Ms. L's memory, a dormant figure is the child's hunger. We might retell the story with three characters: the deceptive, nurturing parent, the gullible child, and the hungry child. The hungry child might not be happy because she is being tricked, even if lovingly, into eating before she has expressed herself. The gullible child is being taught to attend to the parent rather than to her own hunger. "Am I hungry?" she should be asking herself, not "Is it time to eat?" or "Does Daddy want me to eat now?" "Are *you* hungry?" one might ask Ms. L.

Interestingly, her husband was a clean-cut, likeable young man with a good job and membership in her church. They were ostensibly a good match, and he courted her according to their joint rules of propriety. I wonder if things would have been different if she had asked herself—or if anyone had asked her—whether she was in love with him, and how she felt when she was with him. In her defense, at the trial of her parental fitness, I testified that, having evaluated the husband after the violence but before his confession, I could not tell from the interview or the background check that he was seriously disturbed (although it was clear from the testing). If I, a clinical psychologist, could not tell how disturbed he was by interview alone, I testified, how can we hold her, a layperson, responsible for not knowing? I thought his benign presentation, her distance from how she felt, and her gullibility adequately explained her not knowing what was going on in the next room.

Incidentally, *his* earliest memory was of being proud to be able to recognize and name the cartoon character on his shirt. He added, "The same day I got sick and threw up at the table." The combination of external benign functionality (naming the cartoon character) and internal sickness (throwing up) fit his presentation, and also may have guided him when his daughter was fussy or uncooperative: he acted superficially competent but was uncontrollably ill. His benign presentation was a testament to his training in putting a cute shirt over his disruptiveness. In becoming angry at her fussiness, he acted as if he thought his daughter should keep her unhappiness to herself, as if she should put a cute façade over her own discontent.

Step 8) How Might the Memory Anticipate a Therapy Relationship?

Ms. L's therapist may need to metacommunicate with her about the fact that therapy requires nurturing when it is time to nurture rather than when it is most wanted. Otherwise, the therapist is likely to find her happy and feeling well-fed, but under terms that replicate rather than change her expectation that deceptions are to go unquestioned. In other words, she must learn to attend to her internal cues as signals that occasion the satisfaction of her needs on demand. Therapy, however, is best provided on a schedule. Treating Ms. L might become a paradox: ask for nurturing when you need it as long as you ask on Thursdays between ten and ten fifty. Unless this paradox is discussed, the therapy could easily become yet another instance of her letting the authority figure decide when she should be satisfied.

Chapter Ten

Enhancing the Working Alliance

I suppose I ought to just hang up my stethoscope, because if you can walk in here and tell me what's wrong with you, I'm out of a job.

—J. Goodwin, Doctor Valliance in *The House Not Touched by Death*

I was angry with my friend:
I told my wrath, my wrath did end.

—W. Blake, *A Poison Tree*

I am always at a bit of a loss when asked my theoretical orientation. With colleagues, I prefer, "It depends," because I think different theoretical orientations are useful in different circumstances and for different purposes. At bottom, I suppose we all should be evolutionary–quantum physics–systemic–behaviorists. But just as a carpenter is not well served by thinking in the language of quantum mechanics while sawing wood, or prospective lovers well served by Darwinian concepts on their first date, therapists may be better served by thinking intersubjectively, cognitive-behaviorally, or even in Rogerian terms, regardless of the likelihood that a behavioristic explanation is the most fundamental. Indeed, a behavioristic explanation of the existence and persistence of these other theories would be that they must be doing someone some good, or their use would peter out. (Of course, the same can be said of astrology, so the good they are doing need not by any means be related to navigating reality.) Still, when a teenager stops doing homework, I tend to think systemically. When an adult, middle-class woman secretly cuts herself, I tend to think psychoanalytically. And when a man cannot stand up in front of a group of people and discuss his work, Horney's perfectionism comes to mind.

147

If a patient or potential patient were to ask me my theoretical orientation, I would like to answer, "Same as yours." Of course, I would never actually say so, because the patient would likely assume I was unctuously soliciting business. What I would mean, though, by such a statement, would be that the patient's orientation to the problem must be taken into account and even adopted by me if I am to intervene effectively. An excellent roadmap of Denver will not help a patient who believes he is in Boston.

Perhaps you have experienced a similar phenomenon in reading this book. Perhaps you have found one of my theoretical orientations sensible and clear and one or two others obscure and useless. If you believe, as many psychodynamic therapists do, that behaviorism is simplistic and dry, maybe chapter 3 seemed like a waste of time to you. If you believe, as many behaviorists do, that psychoanalytic theory is akin to astrology and superstition, then it is hard to imagine why you are reading this book at all (unless it was assigned in a required class). The only reason I became a behaviorist, as it happens, was because twenty-five years ago I was trying to induce a behaviorist supervisee not to answer the question "How are you?" when a patient started the session with it. I asked him what I could do to get him to try not answering, and he said he would need me to read *Science and Human Behavior* and provide a behavioral rationale. The result was that I became a behaviorist and he tried not answering the question. He and I wrote a paper linking psychoanalytic technique and behavior theory, but behavioral journals rejected the paper as too psychoanalytic and psychoanalytic journals rejected it as too behavioristic.

If mental health professionals do not want to hear ideas cast in a different epistemology, what chance is there that patients do? There are basically two ways we manage this problem in psychotherapy. First, we teach the patient a new epistemology, on the grounds that his is not working. We show him, as it were, what city he is lost in and what maps he can use for navigation. We engage him in an alliance around viewing not only his symptoms as the problem but his way of solving problems as the problem. This approach has a few drawbacks. One, it runs the risk of replicating what one writer said of Freud's psychoanalysis, namely, that one could travel to Vienna and the great man would show you how you fit into his theory. Though interesting, such demonstrations rarely lead to change. Two, engaging the patient in a dialogue about his epistemology (call it what you will) requires certain strengths on his part, whether these be described as a capacity to metacommunicate, a conflict-free ego sphere, or the presence of wise figures within his complexes that can be accessed during the sessions. The drawback is that if the patient is capable of discussing his problem this rationally, it is probably not the kind of problem that would bring him to therapy. Before seeking therapy, he would probably already have run into someone who could have this conversation with him.

In other words, there are few truly ego-dystonic symptoms brought to therapists, and those that are truly ego-dystonic are usually easily dispatched with by use of behavioral and cognitive-behavioral techniques or by giving good advice. Because these rare problems are alien to the person's view of his world, and because good advice on the subject is not, he follows the advice or the treatment regimen and the problem soon resolves itself. As noted, these kinds of problems usually run into good advice long before they get to a therapist.

The second basic way to manage the patient's reluctance to hear ideas not cast in his own epistemology is to learn the patient's epistemology and to speak his language. This can be accomplished by trial and error via interview and dialogue, as one learns how to see things from the patient's point of view. Rare, though, is the patient who can join with us in this enterprise. I saw one unusually psychologically sophisticated woman in therapy who linked excitement and fragility, such that when part of her was excited, another part felt fragile. I pointed this out in reference to a story she told me about her mother, and she said, "You must be right, because at this moment you seem excited by the point you're making, and I'm feeling very fragile." Most patients are not that adept at applying maps to their lives, their problems, their families, and their therapies.

Thus, these next four chapters are about using early memories as a guide to learning the patient's epistemology, as a guide to the patient's expectations of the interpersonal world, and as a mutually accessible map to that world that the patient can accept as relevant.

COMMON FACTORS VERSUS TECHNIQUE

In this chapter, I am not going to review the theoretical contributions or research on *common factors*, those aspects of therapy that apply across all types of treatment and which may account for the general effectiveness of psychotherapeutic treatment independent of any particular school. For such a review, there are many sources in the clinical literature (see, for example, Grencavage & Norcross, 1990, or Jørgensen, 2004). Instead, I intend to assume the acceptance of the key features of this literature and to discuss the use of early memories in therapy with that assumption in mind. I also intend to discuss tensions that arise between the importance of technique, which depends on specialized knowledge and clinical skills, and the importance of the common factors, which depend largely on good faith and relationship skills.

I think a fair summary of the common factors literature might run as follows. Talking about problems tends to resolve them for reasons that transcend any particular school of therapy. These reasons include the patient's faith in the process and the patient's general mental health; the therapist's warmth and ability to inspire faith in that process; a process that provides the patient with a graceful way of relinquishing problems, partly by providing an explanation for having the problem, a rationale for relinquishing it, and a technology that allows change to happen; a collaborative relationship that embraces the other common factors; a chance for emotional expression that is welcomed; and a chance to try out new solutions.

The common factors literature has emphasized from the start (Rosenzweig, 1936) that the truth of the therapist's comments and point of view is not nearly as important as its consistency. The therapist provides the patient with a coherent rationale that explains his problem, that accounts for its longevity, and that involves certain rituals that make sense of its resolution. What the patient cannot afford to do, psychologically, is wake up one day and say, "This is silly," and stop smoking, start eating, stop cutting, commit to a relationship, and enjoy work. The patient in effect has built up too much investment in his problem, and a simple resolution ("don't tear paper") would make the patient feel stupid for not changing earlier. Instead, the therapist must explain to the patient that he has been unable to change because of his *core beliefs, organizing principles, unconscious conflicts, learning history*, or whatever, present some rigmarole for resolving same, and presto-change-o, the patient improves. All the patient typically needs, in this view, is a *graceful way out* (Haley, 1973), an *alibi* (Frank, 1971), or a plausible explanation (Selvini-Palazzoli et al., 1980).

Those of us who care about theory and technique find this point of view somewhat dismaying. It makes us wonder how we are different from astrologers, bartenders, and cab drivers, all of whom are quite capable of employing the common factors, some with more psychobabble, some with less, and providing relief. If all we have going for us is the patient's faith in psychotherapy and our faith in ourselves, it is pretty disheartening and makes a mockery of the years of training we undergo. In fact, it makes me worry that we are pretty much in the same boat as the patients: having invested years of time and trouble in our behavioral preferences, we cannot easily shed them.

The problem of whether technique provides added value to the therapy relationship beyond the common factors reminds me of some theater friends who were criticizing a performance of *Hamlet*. The characters' personalities had not been completely thought through, some of the speaking was singsong, and the swordfight was unexciting. I commented that, for some of the audience, it was probably nonetheless the greatest experience they will ever have in a theater. My friends recognized that their criticisms only really applied to a sophisticated audience and that for people seeing *Hamlet* for the first time, it was still a great play and great theater. I drew the analogy to the interpretation of an early memory. I think such an interpretation is incomplete if it does not answer all the questions raised in chapter 8, and if the interpretation is not applied to the presenting problem and to the therapy relationship. Nonetheless, people all over the world are telling their therapists about things that they think happened to them as children, and the telling helps.

Common factors may account for a lot, even most, of what is helpful about talking about life's problems, but perhaps technique still provides added value. Common factors proponents do not all agree, of course, on what percentage of therapeutic effects are attributable to these relational issues. This is partly because general therapeutic effects are hard to quantify, and because the common factors are hard to isolate. Like almost everything else in psychology, proponents of one view can point to supportive research, but so can their opponents. Still, accepting as we are for the sake of discussion that the common factors are an important aspect of therapeutic efficacy, it would seem to make sense to adopt a therapeutic methodology that emphasizes them. However, this emphasis cannot be explicit. If a patient comes in with a complaint that his romances always dissipate after three or four months, he is not going to commit to therapy if I tell him, "I can help you if you have faith in me and faith in therapy regardless of what you think your problem is." Well, he might, but I would not want him to. I do not want to be an astrologer or a bartender or a cab driver.

THE WORKING ALLIANCE

Bordin's (1979) concept of the working alliance has been especially useful to me in bridging the generalities of the common factors research with the specifics that I think are necessary for good technique. Bordin reduces all the common factors to a working alliance that he says has three elements. These elements are mutual goals, relevant tasks, and emotional bonds. In Bordin's view, this working alliance applies to all forms of psychotherapy, which he defines as a relationship between a person seeking change and a change agent, where the matter to be changed is psychological. His definition of therapy, altered slightly for different types of change, is easily extended to other change relationships, including parenting and education, where he also thinks the working alliance is crucial.

In elaborating the three elements of the working alliance, I think the elegance of the approach deserves some mention. With only three things to monitor, the therapist's job becomes fairly manageable. If something goes wrong in therapy (or in the classroom or with one's children), there are only three places to look: the goals of the relationship are not mutually accepted, the things the change agent is asking the other person to do are not seen as linked to achieving the goals, or something has disrupted the emotional bonds between the two people.

Bordin's concept of the working alliance bridges the gap between general and specific, between common factors and technique, because its employment requires the therapist to articulate goals, to ensure that the process of psychotherapy is explicated or at least understood as specifically related to achieving the goals, and to monitor and explore disruptions in the emotional relationship between therapist and patient. In a sense, the patient's necessary faith in therapy is operationalized as a belief that the therapist's assignments—whether the cognitive-behaviorist's homework or the psychoanalyst's free association—will produce the desired results. Operationalizing the patient's necessary faith in treatment in this way forces the therapist to articulate the rationale for the therapy in a manner that makes sense to both the patient and the therapist. It also forces the therapist to adopt a stance toward treatment that is more or less equivalent to the psychoanalytic idea of analyzing resistance. It does this because once the therapy has gotten underway, the working alliance concept requires the therapist to monitor breaches in the alliance and to repair them, rather than proactively to solve the patient's problems. Thus, in my view, Bordin's approach is one that capitalizes on the common factors while leaving plenty of room for technique.

INQUIRING ABOUT EARLY MEMORIES IN THERAPY

Early memories are relevant to all three elements of Bordin's working alliance, as I will try to illustrate below with a case example. As a preface to this example, I note that early memories can help a therapist and patient define the goal of therapy in a way that makes sense not only in the terms of the patient's description of his current life circumstances, but also in the context of the patient's sense of the trajectory of his life's voyage. The relevance of assigned tasks can be enhanced by pointing out the analogy between what we are asking patients to do and what they might have done in the scenario of an early memory. Finally, as representations of object-relational paradigms (Mayman, 1968), early memories can help us understand the emotional relationship we enter with a patient.

The working alliance concept guides my inquiry into a patient's early memories. I try not to ask about them, or about anything else for that matter, until the task of answering the question seems relevant to the goals we have established. The immediate goal of virtually every therapy is to see if we think there is a problem suitable for psychotherapeutic treatment. A little lip service toward naming this initial goal goes a long way, in my experience, toward justifying the kinds of things we ask patients: what actually happens, how long have you had the problem, who knows about it, who does not, and what would or do your parents say about it. All these questions seem relevant to the patient when we remind her that we trying are to decide if her problem is suitable for therapy. Having located a problem amenable to treatment, our next goal, typically, is to sort out what kind of treatment. If the problem is primarily relational, why not invite the other party into the treatment? If the problem is situational—that is, out of character—some sort of problem-focused treatment is probably in order. If the problem is based on a pattern that is fairly pervasive, the patient might learn compensatory skills. Dialectical behavior therapy (Linehan, 1993), for example, can be seen as a technique for masking chaos with cognitive skills in patients for whom changing seriously disturbed patterns is unlikely. If the problem is pervasive and fundamentally relational—one commonality between object relations theory, self-psychology, and systems theory is that all pervasive problems are seen as fundamentally interpersonal—then relationship-based (i.e., psychoanalytic) therapy may be recommended.

If a problem-focused or family therapy patient can agree that childhood experiences influence our adult perceptions and expectations, early memories can be sought when that agreement is articulated. Otherwise, a little footwork is needed to get there optimally. In family therapy, most people agree that their first family influenced them at least with respect to their current families. In problem-focused therapy, a discussion about how early experiences create the context for current expectations will do. I recognize that most patients come with a sort of built-in working alliance, a willingness to go along with our agendas under the assumption that we know what we are doing. This means they will tell us their early memories just because we asked, and no rationale is needed. Still, I would rather share my rationale and start the treatment out on mutual understanding rather than on faith. I think the ensuing posture—partners rather than compliant subordinates—is a good one for patients to become familiar with. Also, when I inevitably expose my feet of clay, it need not wreck a therapy based on collaboration, as it will a therapy based on faith.

In relationship-based therapy, there is usually some connection drawn between the presenting problems and the patient's identity or sense of self. The patient is told, in effect, that the problem finding suitable work or gratifying romance is not a problem of opportunity, skill sets, or strategy, but a problem with who they are as people. This formulation might be followed by the proposition that who we are is the sum total of all the relationships we have been in, noting that the therapy, though specialized in many ways, is ultimately, basically another influential relationship. The more influential the therapy is, the greater the impact it will have on the patient's self-definition. To increase its influence, one recommends that the patient make himself or herself as nondefensively present as possible. Operationally this means, if it is a psychoanalytic therapy, saying whatever comes to mind, holding nothing back. The therapist may provide a list at this point of the types of things that might come to mind: incidents from the week, incidents from the more remote past, dreams, reactions to the therapist, fantasies, and memories of early childhood. Then, the therapist might simply inquire about earliest memories, as if the duo is taking this free association vehicle on a test drive.

In psychological evaluations, I follow Mayman's (1968) procedure and elicit earliest, next earliest, two of mother, two of father, happiest, and unhappiest, and sometimes include specific probes for memories of being snug, afraid, angry, and excited. I sometimes follow another of Mayman's suggestions and ask, "What stories about your early childhood do your family members like to tell?" In therapy, though, I find the formality of this list somewhat off-putting, as if I am suddenly turning the patient into a diagnostic example or a clinical *case* after working so hard initially to communicate his or her, and our, uniqueness. Thus, I tend to be much less formal in seeking early memories in the context of therapy.

I realize that the timing of my inquiry may affect the patient's recollections. However, I am not conducting research on which memory is actually earliest. On the contrary, the more the memory is affected by the referral question or by an anticipation of how the therapy relationship might go, the better I like it. The timing thus enhances the likelihood that the memory will provide a useful road map to the presenting problem or to treatment impasses.

CASE EXAMPLE: THE SNARLING DOG

Jason was a thirty-three-year-old white man who had been in therapy with a female colleague of mine for a year. His previous therapist and I worked at the same clinic, and he was transferred to me when she left town for personal reasons. Jason's chief complaint when we started was the same as it was when he began the first therapy, namely, he was constantly angry and looking for fistfights. His belligerence had landed him in jail on three occasions for simple assault. He agreed with his probation officer that therapy might help him control or defuse his anger, but the therapy was not technically a condition of probation and there was no contact anticipated between me and his probation officer.

Jason was single and worked on a construction crew. He spent a great deal of time in bars after work, but rarely drank more than one beer. He went to bars mainly to get in fights, and he was rewarded in his search about once a week. He was about five-foot six-inches tall with an extremely muscular, hardened body. His great pleasure in life was getting picked on by a bigger man and then defeating the aggressor in a fistfight. He had no interest whatever in pursuing an organized form of fighting such as boxing or karate. The fighting itself was secondary to getting picked on by someone who thought he could best Jason and then turning the tables on him. Even walking down the street, Jason never stepped aside for others, preferring to let them bump into him, hoping they would pick a fight.

Jason was paranoid, but not delusional or psychotic, managing a profound sense of insignificance by acting so aggressively that others had to take notice of him. He might have been described as either mildly paranoid or severely narcissistic. He lived in a world where his masculinity was constantly questioned and then proven by fisticuffs. Because he was well built, nice-looking, and quiet, he had several one-night stands with women, but he never initiated anything, for fear of being turned down. He was afraid he would get too angry if a woman turned him down, and it was against his morals to strike a woman under any circumstances. His periodic sexual encounters always ended after one night, as he would reject any further contact.

His previous therapy had been, by both parties' accounts, a long, exhausting maneuver as the therapist attempted to construe Jason as a patient and Jason attempted to construe the therapist as a woman. He was never frightening, and he never violated a boundary other than the conventions of speech, but he spoke to her only as a woman, never as a therapist. Whenever she pointed this out to him, which was at least a few times each session, he politely agreed with her. With me, he allowed me to adopt a therapeutic role once he realized I did not think less of him for being the patient. In fact, I had commented early on how much braver the patient is than the therapist, since the patient has to expose himself and the therapist does not. I also made a lot of headway when I mentioned in passing that he was "someone to be reckoned with." Nonetheless, sitting with him was like sitting on a keg of dynamite, and I found it difficult to pull rank on him. Thus, I occasionally fudged the ending of sessions on time until he had come to a natural stopping point. Also, for the only time in my career, I completely ignored the paperwork requirements of the clinic, keeping no progress notes at all, presumably in a misguided effort to repudiate my role.

Jason's earliest memory was of walking to church by himself for the first time. As he crossed the town common of the New England village where he grew up, he was confronted by a big, snarling dog. There the memory ends.

This is not a healthy memory. On its own terms, the boy is endangered and there is no relief in sight. We know that the child came out of it okay, but by not preserving the resolution as part of the story, the memory describes help-lessness and trembling as what the boy can expect of his world. As a metaphor, the aggression in the memory is primitive (you cannot negotiate with a dog) and the only hint of parental protection is the abstract image of the church, which in the memory is unreachable. One way to think of serious psychopathology is, in Kernberg's (1975) formulation, a disruption of the in-tegrative functions by the presence of unmanageable rage. This memory de-picts this concept, where the unmanageable rage in the form of the snarling dog disrupts the familial functions around going to church. In Masterson's (1981) formula for borderline pathology, the child is encouraged toward in-dependence and then punished for trying it. This, too, is depicted in the mem-ory, where the young boy is encouraged to walk to church independently and what he gets for his trouble is an encounter with a snarling dog.

What is far less clear to me than the disturbance in this memory is what good it does me, Jason, or the therapy to categorize it as a disturbed memory. I suppose it is helpful to know that Jason's problems are characterological, which suggests that the peculiar reinforcement he obtains from reenacting his underdog drama will not be easily replaced, and that his role in this drama is not incidentally and certainly not accidentally supported by his family sys-tem, but instead is central to its functioning. The recognition that his problems are characterological suggests the need for an essential change, meaning open-ended therapy targeting his self-definition, or some clever way of avoid-ing the problems despite his personal inflexibility. But I knew all this before he told me the memory. I think his presenting complaint, and certainly his presentation of self, made it clear that he had a personality disorder.

Using the memory to demonstrate Jason's disturbance would merely have confirmed his expectation of one-upmanship in the therapy relation-ship. It would have said, in effect, that as the doctor I have a privileged pur-chase on what is true and on who is right when disputes arise, that I am okay and he is not. In the terms of the memory, using it as an indicator of his pathology would have made me the dog and him the little boy. While, if given this choice, I like anyone else would prefer to be the dog, I think the whole point of therapy is to develop alternative scenarios to those outlined by the memory.

On this subject of who is healthy and who is not, a cute metaphor emerged early on with Jason. In discussing him at our clinical meetings, I mentioned that his family doctor was prescribing a mild sedative to help him sleep at night. The medical director of the clinic insisted that I obtain a release to dis-cuss Jason with his doctor, which I resisted largely under the influence of

Langs's (1978) then-recent ideas about the centrality of managing the *frame* of the therapy: Langs argued that any deviation in the fee, location, time boundaries, or confidentiality would dominate the patient's experience of the therapy and make the treatment space seem unsafe. A lively discussion followed around the drawbacks of violating the frame of the therapy, especially with someone who is paranoid, someone who already suspects that the therapist is not on his side. I lost this argument, and I obtained the release from Jason. He missed the subsequent session, and when he returned he began by saying that a neighbor had been "slandering him around town," adding that he was thinking of suing the neighbor for "deframing [*sic*] of character." Our psychiatrist was suitably impressed by this metaphorical representation of the release as a form of slander, and he agreed that I need not call the family doctor after all.

Instead of using the memory to (further) categorize Jason as disturbed, I used it to enhance our working alliance. The memory became a focal point for our mutual definition of the goals of therapy and for the reason I thought a close personal relationship with me was a good idea. It also became our metaphor for what could and often did go wrong in our emotional connection.

My private interpretation of the memory would be designed to produce a version of it that did it justice in terms of including what was important and specific, but that also pointed the way toward its applicability to the presenting problem and the therapy relationship. The literal landscape of the memory was the town common, and it struck me that part of the psychological landscape was being alone in a public place. There is also the psychological context of walking to church the first time, which may be rendered either as premature independence or as an abstract devotion to the family. I call this an *abstract* devotion because it is not a memory of an event that would spark gratitude or reverence toward the family ideals, as might, say, a memory of the joy of worship or the good works of the church; instead it is a memory that should, in the abstract, produce such devotion. Within this terrain, apart from the abstract and unavailable parental idealization, there is only the snarling dog and the frightened boy. Systemically, there appears to be a *runaway* in the complementarity between the dog and the boy. There are no apparent systemic brakes or governors to keep the system regulated; instead, the viciousness of the dog increases as the boy's submissiveness increases. The absence from the memory of any intervention or explanation of how the boy escaped enhances this view, since the intervention would constitute a regulation of the anger-submission interplay. The dynamic of anger-submission is thus exaggerated and the two characters play nearly polar opposites. The only resolution in sight is the dog's exhaustion, which one can only hope will precede the boy's injury. A therapeutically useful translation of this scenario into words might be, when he is required, without friendly support, to ally with the family's idols, he expects to be faced down by animalistic anger. Conversely, the situation might be described as, when he is faced down by animalistic anger, he expects to have to find his way to familial idols without friendly support.

I said something like, "That memory suggests to me that you have felt for most of your life that when you are paying respects to your family, you know, by going to church, it seems like a lonely duty that you must accomplish without your parents' help. Being alone, you expect to have to choose between being bullied and fighting back." If saying this made me the dog and Jason the little boy, if it drove him out of therapy, that was fine with me. I think I have been a lot more cheerful in this line of work than some of my colleagues by setting up conditions of therapy that are intense, intimate, and interpretive. This has driven away a lot of patients in the first session or two, which admittedly has adversely affected the size of my practice. On the other hand, my caseload has never had many patients in it who were not getting help. I would not expect or want Jason to continue in a therapy with me where I was actively pathologizing him, where I was using our power differential to justify my own privilege. I would not want him to continue in a therapy organized around how much better a parent I am than his mother and father, but if his idealization of them was so intense that he could not even discuss them in the cool atmosphere of my office, then I would just as soon end it quickly.

As it happened, Jason did seem capable of distinguishing between his parents and his idealization of them. My restatement of his memory stressed his going to church at the time and likened that to paying respects to his parents. Jason volunteered, in response, that the times he had been the aggressor in fights, and every fight for which he had been arrested, involved insults about his mother. When the other fellow slurred his mother, Jason threw a punch. Thus, by acknowledging this as a sensitive issue, he was allowing for the possibility of discussing it as problematic. This made him different from the patients, so common among criminals, who say in effect, "What else could I do? He insulted my mother." This difference may already have been evident in his pursuit of treatment even though it was not a formal requirement of his probation. On the other hand, I was soon to learn the difference between who he was when he was *talking about* this complex and who he was when he was in it.

I used the memory to diagram the bar fights that were illegal. "When you were in a bar, and a man insulted your mother, you were in the situation in the memory . . . alone . . . friendless . . . paying your respects to your mother . . . no one in sight but you and a big snarling dog. I don't know what you did when you were a little boy confronted with that dog, but the way you tell it makes me think that cowering, huddling on the ground, would not have helped. If I could talk into a transmitter directly to that little boy in the memory, I don't know, it's conceivable I would recommend that he try punching the dog in the nose. You know, get its attention, get its respect. Unfortunately, while that might be a reasonable solution to the problem presented in the memory, it doesn't work so well in a bar, because throwing the first punch, at least when the opponent is a man and not a dog, is illegal." Jason helped with this diagram by pointing out how little and angry he felt in the memory, and how little and angry he usually feels, especially in bars.

Together, we used the memory to articulate goals for the therapy. Even though it was understandable that the situation would lead to violence, whether from the dog or the boy, violence could produce only a short-term solution; the potential for violence would recur unless the scenario was somehow changed. No changes could be prescribed for the dog; its depiction as a dog conveyed the sense that the violence in this situation was not to be reasoned with. A snarling dog is more amenable to dialogue than a tornado, and even more amenable than a wolf, but not nearly as amenable to dialogue as even the angriest human. (Rorschachers will note the parallel to perceptions of human movement, which is widely interpreted as a sign of health, other things being equal, and specifically as a capacity for empathy or at least an instance of identification, compared to animal movement, which has been traditionally interpreted as impulsivity, other things again being equal, compared to inanimate movement, which is widely interpreted as a sign of psychic forces experienced as acting on the individual rather than as stemming from the subject [Exner, 2003]. In Freudian terms, the *it* is animalistic or a force of nature and the *I* is that with which one identifies.)

Any usable advice would have to be directed at the little boy, not at the dog. What could *he* do differently? I think the terms of the memory suggest that once he crosses the town common, the die is cast, and the confrontation with the dog, with its subsequent violent solutions, is inevitable. This observation conforms with the impression that once Jason entered a bar, it was too late to talk to him. Change would have to affect his going into bars or the way he went into them, not how he behaved once inside. Working together on what the little boy might do differently, we came up with the idea of spoiling the image he thought his proud parents had of him and confessing to them that he was afraid of going to church alone. A frank discussion of whether the little boy would take this good advice led to our joint recognition that he would not. His parents' pride in him, or rather his perception of their pride in him, was just too important to tarnish by acknowledging that he needed a companion. Instead, we settled on asking the boy to find someone else to go with him, someone whose identity would not automatically signal that he was frightened. That someone could be a pet dog of his own, a friend, or an adult headed for the same church. "Maybe it could be me," I suggested.

As we discussed the possibility of me personally playing a role in the drama described in his early memory, it was the first time, I think, that Jason really saw a link between coming to therapy and solving the problem of getting into bar fights. He wanted to know what it would look like, in a bar, if I were there with him. "Well, one way of understanding what happens in the bar is that you're in there alone with the snarling dog. The part of you, the voice inside you, that knows better than to provoke fights is silent in the bar. If you in a bar or you on the street were the same as you are here, you might think of more options than fighting. So what I really mean by suggesting that I might be on the scene with you is that the way you are in this room would be on the scene with you."

After thus defining our therapy goal in the terms of the early memory, the next step was to use the memory to make the therapeutic tasks seem like they would lead to the goal. Otherwise, Jason's investment in doing his part of the work would dissipate. I suggested that the only way for me to venture out onto the town common with him was for us to bring the town common into my office. And that meant bringing the little boy and the snarling dog into my office as well. The way to accomplish that, I said, was to arrange our appointments in such a way that his inner life, which is where the town common of his memory and the little boy reside, would be expressed in the therapy. I briefly explained that the most mature, thoughtful part of him was largely oriented to keeping his inner life from displaying itself. While that was a perfectly acceptable and even desirable use of his cognitive skills when he is out in the real world, where the immediate goal is usually to keep his inner life to himself, this thinking part of himself would become an obstacle to our therapeutic goal of revealing that inner life. Then I recommended that while he was with me he should say whatever came to mind, bypassing the thinking part of him, and trying to produce his inner life in my office.

In this manner, I was linking Jason's task of free association to our mutual goal of including me in his complex of facing escalating aggression. Not only did this increase his investment in free association, it also set the stage for interpreting lapses in free association as a resistance to revealing his inner life. I also mentioned the other two classic tasks of psychoanalytic therapy, namely, coming to the sessions on time and paying his fee. Part of my job, I told Jason, would be as much as possible to make this a place where he would feel comfortable saying whatever came to mind. That might mean a lot less encouragement than he might be used to when he said something useful or pleasant, because I would not want him to get the idea that my silence was an absence of praise. I wanted him to get the idea that when I was listening I was welcoming whatever came next. I told him that I thought that every person fears rejection when he reveals himself to someone else, and one way I had of helping him not worry about rejection would be to keep our interactions, as much as humanly possible, limited to the fifty minutes we designated as our therapy session. I know that sounds at first more like a slight rejection than like total acceptance, I said, but just as I did not want my silence to be a sign of disapproval, I did not want my ending the sessions or not inviting him out to lunch to be signs of rejection. The best way to accomplish this, I told him, was to let the clock and the calendar, not how much we wanted to see each other, dictate our time together. Another way I intended to minimize his natural fear of rejection was to assure him at the outset that I intended to make sessions available to him for as long as he wanted to continue therapy. Nobody can predict the future of course, but I thought he should know that as of then, I had no plans to leave the area or otherwise to end the therapy; that would be up to him unless, of course, something extraordinary and unpredictable happened.

My intention was to enhance our working alliance by, as much as possible, making the things I was saying and doing, and the things I would be asking him to say and do, seem to be in the service of our therapeutic goal. This is not just selling attendance and free association; it is a reminder of why we ask patients to do these things. In psychoanalytic terms, we are asking the patient to participate in an intersubjective system, to reveal his inner world. In behavioral terms, we are asking the patient to engage in derivative behaviors that need extinction, because their response tendencies are still so strong. In the terms of communication theory, we are asking the patient to do the things he has trouble discussing (metacommunicating about) so we can teach him to discuss them.

There are, of course, several things that need to get done in the first session or two that have little to do with achieving the mutual goals, except in the general sense. I do not pretend that they do. I note that I am a psychologist licensed by the state, and that as part of the licensure process designed by the state to monitor the practice of therapy, I am required to inform him of several things. Then, I explain the limits of confidentiality, mandated reporting, and so on.

Thus, I used Jason's memory to help establish the first two prongs of Bordin's (1979) working alliance, namely, mutual goals and task relevance. The third prong in the working alliance is the emotional relationship that develops between the therapist and the patient. Again, Bordin's idea is not so much how to build the therapy as it is where to look when things go wrong. If the patient misses a session, for example, the problem according to the theory must be that the patient and therapist are not working on mutual goals, that the task of coming to the therapy does not seem relevant to achieving mutual goals, or that there is something amiss in the emotional bonds. When Jason missed that session with me early on, after I asked him for a release to speak to his doctor, it was an example of my having asked him to do something that did not seem relevant to achieving our stated goals. This made Jason question whether I had an agenda of my own, and whether attending therapy was in the service of my goals or his.

An early memory can help the therapist prepare for what might go wrong in the therapy relationship and take preventative steps. With Jason, as with any paranoid and many narcissists, the hierarchical aspect of the therapy relationship was bound to raise concerns about dominance and interfere with our emotional bonds. If I may take the liberty of reducing Kohut (1971) to a single sentence, he is saying that proper management of the dominance and exhibitionism elements of the therapy relationship, by a therapist who maintains emotional bonds as fundamental, can bear fruit as the patient learns that there are other gratifying aspects to relationships than the constricted ones afforded the narcissist. And if I may take the further liberty of reducing intersubjective systems theory to a single sentence, its proponents (Buirski & Haglund, 2001) are telling us how to go about accomplishing this. What I am suggesting is that an early memory can provide a map of the relevant psychology.

Under circumstances that could be analogized to Jason asking me to accompany him across the town common, it is hard to see how he and I could get into any real trouble. He might fear that I would run at the first sign of the dog, that I did not really want to get to his parents' church, or that I was only coming with him for the money. These kinds of fears, where the therapist is essentially innocent of the implied accusation, and where the therapist is construed by the patient as being in a fundamentally sound, if slightly flawed, therapeutic role, are easily managed. One way of thinking about why they are easily managed is to note that, in managing them, I get to keep playing the good guy in the drama.

Analogous to a fear that I would run from the dog, after he got angry for the first time in a session, Jason expressed concern that I would kick him out of therapy. I did not say anything so mawkish as to directly reassure him. Instead, I interpreted the connection between his fear and the breach that had made him angry: usually, I would unplug my phone during a session, but this time I forgot, and it rang. I still did not answer it, of course, but Jason was angry about the intrusion I had allowed. When he said I might kick him out of therapy, I said something like, "My forgetting to protect the therapy from intrusion by leaving the phone plugged in has you wondering about all sorts of ways I may not fulfill my obligations to you." The manifest message was,

"You are right and I am wrong," but the metamessage was, "I can tolerate being wrong and I can tolerate your anger." Once such techniques are learned, they are as noted above rather easy to employ, as I got to play the accepting, benign, reassuring therapist. In the new version of the drama, with Jason and me crossing the town common together, as long as I got cast as me, I would be able to handle whatever came up.

Real trouble would occur if and when I found myself in the role of the dog. In that case, our real relationship could be expected to melt away, just as Jason's relationship with his parents melted away to an abstraction in the memory itself. No part of him would be present for reasoned discourse or emotional connection any more than such functions were available to him in a bar fight.

To avoid becoming the dog, I introduced a signal in the therapy that would warn us of approaching danger. If Jason did something to make me angry, which happened with predictable frequency, I would find an occasion to remark, "We're headed for the common." This served as a joint warning that we were on a path to a place where the only options were to bully or be bullied. Then, we could discuss what was going on, how we got there, and how we could avoid going any further. "We're headed for the common" was the verbal equivalent of a time-out signal, the communication that the current set of interactions should be halted so we could step back and look at them.

One way to characterize what it means to have a personality disorder, in terms of communication theory, is that such persons are much more frequently in a complex than are most people, where a complex, again, is a rigid set of expectations and role relationships unsuitable for negotiating the demands of the current situation. A person with a personality disorder, like a normal person in a severe complex, is unable to metacommunicate about the complex. There is no such thing as a time-out. In game theory terminology, every communication purportedly *about* the game is taken as yet another move *in* the game. With Jason, my ongoing worry was that one day he would see "we're headed for the common" as a putdown or remonstrance, rather than as a friendly reminder. I think that day was much longer in coming than it might have been because the signal was derived from his own early memory rather than imposed upon him as a therapy technique. The delay gave me time to cement our mutual relationship so as to improve its chances of withstanding his eventual suspicions about me.

Unfortunately, he blindsided me in a way I was not prepared for. In control-mastery terms (Weiss, 1993), he gave me a test that I failed. After an unusually warm and relaxed period of therapy, I began to feel as if it were a therapy on course, meaning, I suppose, that I assumed that stuff would emerge but that we could handle it. I relaxed my vigil around not humiliating him. At that time, Jason had not been in a fight of any kind for a few months, but he was still frequenting bars, playing with the idea of fighting. He would review events with me, creating the sense that I was becoming a part, a restraining and mature part, of his night life. Jason told me about a woman who had flirted with him the previous week. She was mildly intoxicated, out with a couple of friends, enjoying the flirtation with him, but probably expecting it not to go anywhere. She went to use the ladies' room, and soon he approached its door. As she was leaving the restroom, he pulled her back in and forced himself on her in a way that sounded just short of a legally defined rape but certainly took advantage of her and treated her like a piece of meat. As soon as he finished, he left the restroom and the bar. He smirked as he told me about it.

I do not really remember what I said, but it was definitely attuned to her and not to him. I think I just said, "Jesus," but I may have reproached him directly. A few seconds later the therapy was over. He said, "I knew you'd take her side," and left.

I cannot recall ever being nearly as angry in a therapy session as I was when Jason told me that story. Ironically, I had repeatedly prepared myself for the time when Jason would be unable to distinguish metaphor from reality, and here I was the one unable to do so. I mean, in retrospect, that I do not know what, if anything, happened in the bar that night. For all I know, it was all a fantasy, or a story invented to have an effect on me, or a mutually enjoyable sexual encounter spun by Jason to make the woman seem victimized. I was consumed by my own narcissistic investment in the therapy. What got me so angry was not that Jason reported violating this woman; worse happens every day. What got me so angry was that a patient *of mine* had treated a woman so shamefully. This was not a story about a woman using Jason as a plaything and his turning the tables on her. This was a story about *me*, about my investment in my patients, about my pride. My anger should have signaled to me that I had become the snarling dog from his memory, but like the dog, I did nothing but snarl. Conversely, I was abstractly attached to my idealized image of therapy as a church where people are trained to treat others well. I was the little boy faced with oppressive dominance in the form of Jason's depiction of himself, and the only solution I could find was to punch the snarling dog in the nose.

If I could have sat with my feelings, metabolized them in the psychoanalytic vernacular, I might eventually have thought of something to do with them other than escalate the aggression between us. Perhaps I would have suggested that he was trying to *show* me something in addition to telling me something, by telling the story in a certain way, with a certain emphasis. Perhaps I would have said, "It doesn't sound like very satisfying sex." Perhaps I would have reflected on a connection between our recent warmth and his telling me this story to dispel it. What I did do was to write Jason a note saying that I would appreciate an opportunity to explore what happened, but aside from the final check he sent to the clinic, I never heard from him again.

The early memory served as a useful roadmap to the presenting problem and to the working alliance, but a roadmap loses its utility when one stops consulting it.

Chapter Eleven

Finding a Place to Stand

Give me where to stand, and I will move the earth.

— Archimedes

To summarize elements of previous chapters, early memories depict systemically coherent patterns that illustrate the person's expectations of certain types of situations. In a situation, or *psychological landscape*, that is relevant to the memory, the person interprets what is happening and what is likely to happen under the influence of the same variables that produced, maintained, and revised the memory and acts accordingly. When such action is problematic, a therapist can use the memory as a guide or as a roadmap to the person's idiosyncratic construction of the relevant situation. The therapist can suggest, prescribe, demonstrate, or welcome options or alternative behaviors that will potentially lead to preferable outcomes. These alternatives must be made available to one of the characters in the memory, or else the suggestions will be irrelevant to the problem at hand.

CASE EXAMPLE: MISSING THE PICNIC

A pattern would not even exist unless there were forces operating to maintain it: otherwise, it would be a mere occurrence. Some patterns are open to intervention; some are not. As an example of a pattern that is open to intervention, a couple finds itself in the pattern of one partner always initiating sex and the other accepting or refusing depending on his or her mood. They talk it over and agree that their pleasure is diminished by this particular dance, since it makes the receiver wary of expressing affection when sex is not wanted and it makes the initiator feel angry for having to play the role of supplicant. In fact, the initiator makes only halfhearted, nonseductive overtures, the better to be protected from feeling rejected. They agree that they will take turns initiating sex, and that the former receiver will initiate sex within five days when it is his or her turn.

The patterns that bring people into psychotherapy are, almost by definition, not easily open to intervention. Otherwise, they would typically be solved (or dissolved) before requiring professional help. Thus, Leo and Mary, who had the sexual problem just described, came for help because after deciding on the new schedule, Leo continued to initiate sex every day or two and still felt angry when his wife reminded him of the new agreement. Leo's earliest memory of his father was a brief tale of getting ready for his father's company picnic; Leo was too slow and his father left without him. In recounting the incident, Leo justified his father's departure by pointing out that he needed to get to the picnic on time. When masculine pleasure (going to the picnic as father and son) was anticipated, a sense of duty interfered, and Leo expected the available roles to be either the angry, disappointed father or the lonely, rejected son. Given those choices, and given his close familiarity with the pain of rejection, he orchestrated his pursuit of masculine pleasure in such a way as nearly to guarantee that he would wind up feeling angry and disappointed, so as to avoid what seemed the only alternative, to wit, feeling lonely and rejected. When Leo pursued masculine pleasure at home in the form of sexual gratification, his sense of duty interfered. He wanted compliance from his wife as a marital duty, rather than, say, an act of generosity or of sexual desire, and Mary refused to construe sex as a duty. The memory's complex was fulfilled when he then had to choose between feeling angry and disappointed or lonely and rejected.

In the abstract, it is okay to point this out to the patient, but in the heat of the moment—when he is thinking about initiating sex—the only two characters available are the father and the son of the memory. One of *them* had to change if Leo were to change. Given the power differential between them, and given what I thought I knew about the father's own regret and loneliness that the boy possibly did not know, I thought the father was a better bet than the son to make the first move to relax the pattern. Leo, Mary, and I put our heads together to solve, not their sexual problem, but the father's parenting problem in the memory. We agreed that Leo's father was not sufficiently attentive to how difficult it is for a six-year-old boy to be ready to go someplace at a particular time. We agreed that this problem needed to be solved *before* it got to a choice between duty and relatedness, and that specifically, the father might have given the son more notice appropriate to his age and his schedule.

This intervention within the memory translated to an agreement between Leo and his wife that he would initiate sex by proposing a "date" at least a few hours in advance, to give her time to prepare. I had reminded them that Lenny Bruce once said that the only difference between a man and a woman is that if a woman walks through a plate glass window, ten minutes later she is still not in the mood. Women, we agreed, sometimes need a little notice. Leo's wife felt confident that she could find her interest in him with a few hours head start, especially after I taught her how to choreograph a sexual interlude that would be gratifying for him and, if she was not sexually aroused herself, at least an act of generosity on her part. Conversely, I taught him how to be generous about rubbing her feet and shoulders even when he was not feeling particularly affectionate. Several months later, they found that he was initiating sex less frequently than they had imagined, probably because it no longer seemed like the battlefield for his complex about whether his father loved him.

The system of figures in a memory is like any system of people and is most effectively changed by entering it. Leo's pattern was constricted to two characters, but the figure of the huffy, stressed father was accessible to intervention, because what he really wanted was to include his son at the picnic. This desire made him amenable to advice just as a real father might have been.

ROLE FLEXIBILITY

In general, the healthier the patient, the more likely any given memory will have a basically warm or usually protective figure in it whose shoes the therapist can stand in. Even if a healthy patient's problematic memory has no such figure in it, the health will imply that there are other memories and other contexts in which such figures exist. This translates into a therapy in which, while the therapist is searching for a way into the problematic complex, other patterns with benign figures in them will assist the therapist and patient in maintaining their relationship outside of the problematic complex. The availability of these other patterns makes the complex into a pothole rather than an abyss. In more disturbed patients, one way to think of the challenge of maintaining a therapeutic relationship is that these alternative, benign patterns are not available as way stations on the journey into the difficult patterns.

When the operative system, the relevant pattern, emerges in the therapy relationship, it is called transference by psychoanalytic writers if it is the patient's pattern and countertransference if it is the therapist's. Since both members of the relationship are human beings with memories, expectations, and complexes, most patterns that emerge in therapy are integrations of the complexes of each party (Buirski & Haglund, 2001). Technically, then, it would be highly unlikely for a disturbed therapist to be a positive change agent. The basic requirements of a therapist, besides training in how to think psychologically about contexts relevant to human behavior, are twofold. One, after she inevitably imposes personal complexes on the therapy relationship, she needs to have warm, benign expectations to which she can retreat and from whose vantage point she can examine what she has done. Two, she needs to be secure enough in the dependability of warm, benign patterns to enable her to venture out into frightening and unpleasant patterns: she needs to be able to play any role necessary to enter the problematic pattern of the patient. These requirements of a good therapist can certainly be bolstered by exposing her to warm, benign supervisory relationships, but a basic disturbance should ensure that she will not be able to function adequately as a therapist, because basic disturbance means, almost by definition, that such securely warm and benign patterns are not available to her. The reader may recall from chapter 5 that assessing the presence of such patterns in early memories was the method by which Mayman was able to beat personality inventories in predicting healthy coronary reactivity (Shedler et al., 1993).

Case Example: Skipping the Shirt

A friend of mine was considering psychotherapy after her coworkers complained that her perfectionism was annoying. She was perfectionistic only about her own work, not about theirs, so it was hard to see what business it was of theirs, but she recognized that her perfectionism sometimes was annoying to herself as well. Also, she had been stalked not too long ago, and this was still on her mind. Her earliest memory, reported when I told her I was writing this book, was of not knowing how to put her own shirt on, going outside to a family function on her lawn shirtless, being laughed at, and feeling embarrassed. The memory is a map of what happens when she transitions from the security of home to the outside world, even when the outside world is as homelike as her own front yard and her own family. If she is inept, she will be embarrassed and exposed. She compensates by making sure there is no visible ineptitude before allowing others to see her. Further, while it is natural to be bothered by having been stalked, the *way* she was bothered, and its implications for a solution, may relate to the memory. She felt she had attracted a stalker by not being fully in control of the image she presented to the world.

The memory provides an easy place for a therapist—or, for that matter, for friends—to stand. Change merely requires that she reveal herself and that the audience not laugh at her. Self-revelation is inevitable, so the interpretive process would serve the function of saying, as it were, "I see you," so as to enhance the effects of not laughing. Without interpretation of her revelations, she might conclude that the absence of laughter was the result of her having successfully covered herself up. The position available in the memory is her presumably well-intentioned but not at that moment empathic family. An easy role for the therapist to play means an easy therapy to do.

UNAPPEALING ROLES

Some roles are extremely difficult to play, and many therapies founder on the refusal of the therapist to play them. In an apocryphal story, an intern asked Frieda Fromm-Reichmann what to do if a patient wants to smear feces on you, and she replied, "Wear old clothes." The point of the story is that the therapist must sometimes be heroic in her willingness to play certain roles. When the role the patient requires is too aversive for the therapist, or any therapist, to play, then the therapy goals should move from changing the complex to papering it over with, for example, cognitive strategies, impulse control, and avoidance of troubling situations.

A healthy therapist has a strong enough sense of self and a secure enough embeddedness in a psychology of warmth and support that she can play a large variety of roles offered by patients' dramas. Each of us though, without exception, has certain fissures on the path of treatment, certain roles offered to us that, because of our idiosyncratic patterns, are difficult for us to play with the requisite lack of seriousness. I do not mean to say that therapy is essentially frivolous by renouncing seriousness; I mean that the *play space* (Winnicott, 1971) necessary for therapy requires an essentially *just kidding* attitude if the therapist is to accept certain casting decisions and if the patient is to confront difficult figures rather than treat them as utterly real and then avoid or attack them. The play space of therapy is maintained in pretty much the same way as the play space of theater. Reliability around show times, fees, and locations let the audience concentrate on the content of the play rather than on its setting. The framework of the theatrical production, including for example not being able to see the wings or the rehearsals, also facilitates attention to the content. Anonymity and neutrality in the theater would mean that the actors do not break character, do not wink at the audience, and do not pass judgment on the play, at least not while it is being performed. Both play spaces require the actors to be just kidding, but not to divulge that they are just kidding.

Another parallel between the theater and the therapy space is that in either setting, any departure from a reasonably adequate setup will dominate the audience's experience. It is very difficult to attend to the content of what is on the screen at the movies if any of the expectations regarding the *frame* (Langs, 1978) of the theater are disappointed. Thus, if the air is very hot or very cold, if people are talking in loud voices, and so on, the content of the picture is relatively ignored. Similarly, it is difficult to attend to the goals of therapy—the presumed content of the conversation—if there is a substantial departure from reasonable expectations of privacy or reliability. The patient's metaphorical communication will usually be organized around expressing a reaction to such *frame deviations* (Langs, 1978). By the same token, no theater patron has ever sought the manager after the picture has started to thank her for starting on time, opening the curtain, and having the sound at a good volume. Such a patron is vastly more likely to complain about the house lights not going down when the movie started or about some other frame violation.

While I am on this topic of frame management, I should say that where I disagree with Langs (1978) is on the question of the centrality of technique in good therapy. I find, along with those who investigate and describe *common factors* (Rosenzweig, 1936), that warmth, good intentions, a capacity to build and maintain healthy relationships, genuine curiosity, the courage to be intimate, self-scrutiny, and circumspection are better predictors of good therapy than is good technique.

Certain roles are difficult for each of us. Supposedly, Janet Leigh never took a shower again after filming *Psycho*. If true, it was almost certainly because the experience meshed with certain patterns of her own. Michael Caine once noted that he can murder someone on stage and his wife never treats him like a murderer, but if he kisses an actress on stage, his wife invariably asks him if he was really just acting. In other words, when things are too real, the game is disrupted. When we are needed to play roles that are very similar to problematic roles that appear in our own complexes, things can get too real. I will return to this problem in chapter 13, "Anticipating and Resolving Treatment Impasses," since many impasses arise out of the overlap between the role offered by the patient and that which is toxic to the therapist.

Finding a place to stand within a difficult pattern is most obvious when all the roles are unappealing. Kohut's (1971, 1977) analysis of narcissistic transferences says that there are generally only two roles available, the idol and the garbage dump, and you have to accept one of these to do the therapy. Many disturbed people have even less appealing roles as the only ones available in their problematic complexes.

Case Example: Taut Sheets

A paranoid schizophrenic woman, Lisa, came to see me after one of her numerous hospital discharges. Almost thirty, she was living with her parents, despite having eloped immediately after graduating from high school. She lived with her husband for three years in another state, but when he died from a cocaine overdose, she was hospitalized for the first time. After that first discharge, she returned to her parents' house. She described her father as "intellectually brutal" and her mother as invisible. She had not worked in any capacity since her husband died, had not dated, and had not made any friends. We jointly described her condition as ghostly, with enormous ambivalence about returning to life. Every eight to ten months, she would become convinced that her father had poisoned her husband, and she would be rehospitalized, starting with a new therapist upon discharge.

Lisa's earliest memory was of a perfectly white hospital room with crisply made beds with military corners and sheets stretched so tight that, as the saying goes, you could bounce a coin off them. Nobody was in the memory, and on inquiry, this seemed even to include Lisa. "It's as if I was aware of this room but I'm not actually in it," she said. "But I'm sure it happened," she added. Her next earliest memory was of an extended period in her childhood when she believed her mother was a changeling. A changeling is an impostor child switched by fairies, but Lisa thought the term applied to adults as well. When I asked for a specific occurrence, she had trouble finding one. "Every night she would put me to bed and I would pretend that she was my mother so she wouldn't think I saw through her." "*Was* she your mother?" I asked. "Well, of course. You don't believe in changelings, do you?" Her earliest memory of her father involved him humiliating and berating her for misusing a word in front of guests. She wet her pants and ran from the room, but she was not looking where she was going and ran into the piano. "I knocked myself silly," she said.

Lisa described looking at want ads in the paper and not having the faintest clue which ones to apply for. "I might enjoy police work," she would think, reflecting on how much she has liked certain cop shows on TV. Because she knew enough not to trust her inclinations as to which jobs she might be suited for, she never applied. I suggested that such a mistake as applying for the wrong sort of job might be like misusing a word in front of other people, but she did not see the connection. I tried explaining it to her, but it seemed obvious to me as I did so that she was not listening like a therapy patient, but like a little girl being berated for not understanding. I tried to point *this* out, but her humiliated attitude merely increased. It seemed like everything I said was an indictment. If I tried approaching her as the substitute mother, by commenting on the low level of authenticity in our interchanges, she would pretend to agree with me. If I commented on her pretense, she would pretend to agree with *that*. The roles available to me were her tyrannical father, with whom it was impossible for her to participate in a meaningful conversation, her changeling mother, with whom she would pretend to be engaged, and utter emptiness. I had no place to stand.

Or did I? Around that time in my practice, my patients began accusing me of being perfectionistic about technique. By *accusing*, I do not mean conscious concern. Instead, there were dreams, memories, and free associations that made me realize that I was striving for perfection. I had always said that one of the things I liked most about therapy—and fathering—was that the best therapist who ever lived was not all that much better at it than I was. I meant that therapy is merely an enterprise of human relating, and while it can be done well, it cannot be done terrifically well. My musician friends were haunted by recordings of the greatest performers of all time, people who played flawlessly, brilliantly, and musically all at once. In contrast, the greatest therapists—relationship-based therapists, I mean: even therapists have to contend with the genius of Erickson (Haley, 1973) and Madanes (1981) if they are not basing the treatment on the relationship—were just people trying to form healthy relationships with patients. Somehow, though, I had turned this human enterprise into an engineering marvel. I did not just start and end sessions exactly on time—something I still do—I also began to feel that a session was truly successful only if I did not speak at all or, if I had to speak, if I delivered a well-crafted and comprehensive interpretation of recent events in light of existing complexes. I *never* answered a question; I *never* made small talk; I *never* smiled.

One patient dreamed that he wandered into a chapel and saw me at prayer. He tried to talk to me, but I was so deeply in prayer that I could not hear him. I interpreted this dream as his awareness that I was attending more to a psychoanalytic ideal than to him. Another patient dreamed that he was having dinner with his mentor, anxious about making a good impression. The wine was extremely expensive and reportedly heavenly, but it was served in crystal goblets so fine that they could not be picked up without crushing them. This too I interpreted as an unconscious comment on the preciousness of my technique.

With Lisa, these other patients had prepared me to consider identifying with the taut sheets. I had not even considered the memory interpretable when I first heard it, seeing it instead as an indicator of the extent of her impairment. To recall an event in which she was not present not only reflected on the weakness of her rationality, it also neatly depicted the sense of emptiness associated with psychotic relatedness. Now, however, I considered the memory as a roadmap to that emptiness. Somewhat literally, the setting of a hospital room suggested that it might be particularly relevant to her sense of being a patient, that is, to our relationship. My desperation to find a place to stand led me to consider the emptiness of the room as one figure in the memory's system and the tautness of the sheets as another. Perhaps these figures were as mutually interdependent as the classic narcissistic husband and depressed wife. When Lisa is a patient, clinical perfection disperses her, and when she disperses, clinical perfection ensues. Between us, this seemed reasonable enough: the more psychotic she seemed, the more careful I was. Perhaps my caution was also making her more psychotic.

To intervene, I had to step into the role of the taut sheets (stepping into the role of emptiness was beyond me). I had to accept Lisa's view of me as uninterested in her and only interested in maintaining a pristine office. Once I saw the advantage of this—to facilitate an engagement with her sense of emptiness—I also saw repeated opportunities for playing this role. For example, on a very cold day, after she sat down some water began to condense on her upper lip. Lisa was an extremely prim woman, and such an anomaly was very difficult for her to bear. Beside her lay my Kleenex box, clearly intended for patient use, but there was no way to use it without thereby announcing her presence in my office. I have had many patients who have used a piece of Kleenex and then tucked it away somewhere on their person, rather than dispose of it in the wastebasket also clearly for that purpose. This typically led to a discussion about whether the patient's unappealing products were welcome in my office. With Lisa, after witnessing her mortification for having to use a piece of Kleenex and then tucking it in her glove, I said, "You don't carry a handkerchief," clearly implying that she might not be at all welcome to use my things, and possibly castigating her as well for her unpreparedness. She replied, "I'm sure you wouldn't want to see me with my makeup running." I did not pursue this, but I thought it was the most genuine interchange we had had to date.

I was reminded of a parable that one of my college professors made up about an art museum where the staff constantly had to clean up after the public. Tired of this constant deterioration—the gum on the carpet, the fingerprints on the display cases, and the wearing away of the velvet ropes—the staff opened their own museum where such things never occurred. The secret of their success was that they opened a museum in which there was no art, only display cases, frames, labels, and lighting. The public never came and the staff were very happy. I have often reflected on how much more smoothly a clinic would run if there were no patients, and how much easier education would be without students. With Lisa, I decided to run a therapy that would have been perfect if not for her presence.

Before long, she entered my office for a session and did not take her usual seat, standing behind it instead. We looked at each other for several minutes, me thinking about having no place to stand and her having no place to sit. Finally, I said, "If you want, after you leave today, I'll wipe off the seat with a cloth and fluff it up to put it back the way it was." Perhaps she understood this as an invitation to exist only temporarily, as I intended. At any rate, she sat down and told me about her week. From that day on, while I normally ended sessions "on time," meaning within twenty or thirty seconds either way of the official stopping time, with Lisa I began to end the sessions when the second hand of my clock swept past the twelve, even if she was in the middle of a sentence. She accepted this with her characteristic politeness.

Having established what I considered to be a relationship between unwelcoming tautness on my part and nonexistence on hers, I began to experiment with relaxing my vigilance. I would speak in less than complete sentences, nod my head occasionally when she spoke, and even smile when I greeted her. Perhaps predictably, she interpreted these attempts to humanize our relationship as romantic overtures. Lisa began to speak of our "dates," and made repeated references to the fact that she was a woman and I a man. She would think of something and stop herself from relating it by saying aloud, "A lady does not speak of such things to a gentleman." Instead of us having a transference, the transference had us. I could not think of a way to interpret this turn of events without making it worse, so I reverted to extreme tautness, and she resumed her practice of relating to me the events of the week, largely without commentary. This went on for several years, during which I would ask colleagues if I was doing her any good, and they would remind me that she had not been hospitalized or even been overtly psychotic since the day she met me (except perhaps for our brief period of "dating"). I avoided any discussion with her of what was going on between us, even though I see such discussion as the defining characteristic of good therapy, and instead I restricted myself to summarizing the stories she told me without editorializing. Slowly, minute changes could be observed in her attitude toward her own stories. She would recognize and comment on the way her niece treated her as a crazy aunt who did not need to be taken seriously. She dared to criticize her father's treatment of her mother as a servant.

More years flew by, as Lisa solidified an intelligent perspective on her life. She even introduced some criticisms of her husband, who for years was presented as a kind of saint, a creative genius. We never again spoke of our relationship until our final session, some ten years after the therapy had started. By then, Lisa had developed what I think of as an *as if* adjustment (Deutsch, 1942), still hollow on the inside, but functional on the outside, and deriving a modicum of genuine satisfaction from her external adjustment. She had a few "activity friends," as she called them, meaning they were not really close but they did a lot of things together. She had a clerical job that was simple and undemanding. She had decided to liberate herself entirely from the role of mental patient, and that meant, ultimately, stopping treatment. In our last session, after catching me up on the events of the week, she acknowledged that I had helped her. "From the day my husband died until I started coming here," she said, "no one knew or cared where I was or what I was doing. These appointments have been the place where I was supposed to be on Thursdays at three. Most people never realize what a gift it is to be *expected* somewhere." I agree with her: Even more primal than the need to *be* loved, perhaps, is the need to love others, to be necessary. And as much as the regularity of our sessions made her feel securely that she was an object of my affection, they gave her an opportunity to provide affection as well.

Normally, I pretty much impose a handshake on my patients in the last session. To me, the handshake is like the lunch bell or the end-of-the-workday whistle in those old cartoons where the wolf and the sheepdog are pals when they are not on the clock. The handshake, the rituals around starting and ending sessions, and the rituals around paying the fee are all signals that the game is on or off. Of course, we are not always acting the roles of wolf and sheepdog; we act whatever roles the underlying complex lays out for us. Part, maybe most, of what it means to be seriously disturbed is that these sorts of signals are poorly understood (Bateson et al., 1956). Because of the dating episode when it was unclear to her whether we were just kidding or not, I was not at all sure that Lisa would understand the handshake as I intended it, so I just let her go.

In retrospect, I had trouble finding a way to be with her that did not merely replicate one of her problematic modes of relating, that did not leave her either submissive or false. Her early memory of the crisp bedsheets and the sterile hospital room gave me a place to stand, from which a restorative relationship could develop.

Case Example: Playing in the Mud

Steve's presenting problem was that he had never held a job for more than a few months despite having enough intelligence to graduate from college without ever buckling down and without ever relinquishing his refusal to complete meaningless assignments. He attributed his spotty work history to "authority problems," by which he meant his disrespect for "idiots," a term that encompassed any boss who asked him to do anything that seemed unnecessary to Steve. The rest of his life was going fairly well, especially considering his intermittent employment. In his mid-twenties, he had remained close friends with high school and college chums. He had been in two serious relationships, but the overall status of his economic life was not particularly conducive to settling down.

Steve described his father as rigid, strict, and ridiculing of him under a variety of academic and athletic circumstances. He described his mother as distant, but generally a good mom. He told a story about a time when she was angry with him and he kept laughing at her. Eventually, she began to hit him with a belt, but he would not stop laughing. His point was that she tried her best, but he was incorrigible. These parental images suggested a general problem in authority situations, where to Steve, compliance meant capitulation, forcing him to rebel even when the authority figure was being fairly reasonable. This formulation prepares the therapist for an onslaught of rebellion if and when the therapist begins to impose on the therapy rules and procedures that seem arbitrary to Steve. The therapist would have to be prepared for being cast in the role of an angry, authoritarian parent.

Steve's early memories told a different story. His earliest memories of his mother included her helping him transition from crying to having a good time on his first day of school, and Steve visiting her at the candy store where she worked and getting free chocolates. His earliest memory of his father was of playing superhero outdoors, Steve running across the top of a picnic table and leaping into space where his father caught him and flew him around the yard. His earliest memory of all was as follows: "My parents were working on the house and I was just playing in the mud and dirt. I used to love playing in the mud. They got mad at me because I was all muddy." In contrast to the first three memories, which depict strong and caring parents, the last memory involves conflict.

What differences in the situations occasion the problematic pattern as opposed to the supportive patterns? The candy store memory is much like the problem memory: a parent is working, a child is needy, the child is gratified. In the candy store memory, however, the child's gratification meshes perfectly with the parent's work: she sells chocolates and he wants chocolates. In the problem memory, the child's needs are opposed to the parents' work: the parents are painting or gardening or whatever, and the child plays in the mud. Another difference is that the candy store is clearly a place of work, albeit a workplace with intrinsic gratifications. The yard is a place of play. When the situation clearly calls for work, the pattern that emerges is one that meshes needs and obligations; when the situation calls for play, the pattern that emerges is either the superhero memory in which child and parent are in synch, or else the parent's injection of work makes the child's play into an irritant.

This analysis changes the meaning of the symptom. Is it true that Steve resents all authority that seems arbitrary to him, or just under certain circumstances? Further inquiry into the details of his many resignations provided some support for the idea that he is at his worst when work is injected into play, not when work is pure work. Thus, he quit one job when a boss's dereliction of duty meant that he, Steve, had to give up leisure time at work to pick up his boss's slack. Another resignation stemmed from an incident when he was told to do something during a lunch break, and yet another when he was expected to come in for a shift he had off. His work history did not entirely fit this formulation, but it was close enough in these three instances to indicate a possible pattern.

Regardless of the exact nature of Steve's repeated resignations (and not to be slighted is the idea that none of these jobs were particularly well-suited to him), the early memories suggested that the therapist would not have nearly so much trouble finding a place to stand in addressing Steve's problems as one might expect from the generic description of a man with authority problems. Instead of the overbearing parent he described as his father, the memories provided a role for an industrious, caring, supportive parent. Even the parents who remonstrate with him for being muddy are only annoyed, not overbearing or authoritarian.

Let us try to anticipate the emergence of the problematic pattern in the therapy relationship. It is hard to imagine an authoritarian therapist refusing to explain why, for example, the sessions start and end on time with Steve reacting rebelliously. One hears about therapists who act like that, but I have the impression they are rare. Instead, one imagines the pattern emerging with Steve in the role of the disapproving parent. A helpful and supportive therapist might occasionally take a breather, forcing or systemically cantilevering Steve into a nonregressed posture. For example, the therapist chats about a recent election, the weather, or some news event. The therapist's relaxation might confuse Steve's sense of his role in the moment. Is he now responsible for managing the relationship like an adult, or is he still in the therapist's hands, like a child? Is he working or playing? Thus, the therapeutic crisis will perhaps not derive from Steve's anticipation of intolerance from the therapist, but from Steve's own intolerance.

A direct application of the problematic pattern leaves Steve in the role of the muddy child; a systemic application of the pattern allows for anyone to occupy that role. Thus, his explosive resignations may have been based on the emergence of this road map in a landscape where work and play are confused, not because he resented his parents' authority, but because he perceived a slack or playful boss as confusing work and play: Steve's guidebook in such situations called for anger at the person who was playing, just as his parents were angry at him for playing in the mud in an ambiguous situation.

The systemic view, again, is that a pattern will emerge in the therapy rather than a direct version of the interaction with the patient always in the same role. This view prepares the therapist, who is looking for a place to stand, to play any role in the scenario instead of being on the lookout primarily for moments when the parental role is offered.

Chapter Twelve

Illuminating Presenting Problems

[E]very problem . . . contains and suggests its own solution.

—L. Sullivan, "The tall office building
artistically considered." (1896, p. 403)

The variables that produce early memories have much in common with the variables that produce presenting problems. This statement holds true over a wide variety of theoretical orientations, as described in chapters 3–5 with respect to behaviorism, systems theory, and various psychoanalytic approaches. Interpretation of patients' early memories can highlight these variables' applicability to presenting problems. Even though the same information may be available on the basis of a preexisting guide to the type of problem, in other words, on the basis of theory, using the patient's early memories as a guide enhances the working alliance with the patient around the connection between his inner life and his problems. Also, it enhances the mutuality of the collaboration between the therapist and patient, as the therapist demonstrates that the answer really is in the patient and in their interactions, and not in the therapist's knowledge base. Finally, finding guideposts to a solution in the patient's early memories enhances the patient's investment in the applicability of the road map, as compared to a map to the problem provided by a distant theorist.

Admittedly, *any* narrative involving the patient's childhood and his family could be used to illuminate most problems, because *any* road map is better than none at all. The reason that any map is preferable to no map is that any map can be emended and improved with new information, until an adequate picture of the operative pattern is obtained. Also, any reasonable map of the situation can be an inducement to try *something*, and if that does not work, to

181

try something else, whereas many patients are stuck where they are, trying nothing at all. Finally, any reasonable map allows the therapist and the patient to put their heads together and consider where they are on the map, whereas the absence of a map (or rule book) invites the patient to construe the therapist's moves as things she is doing to him rather than contextualizing them as things she is doing as part of a larger plan (this is discussed further in chapter 13). As noted in chapter 1, "Why Early Memories?," I think that early memories are especially useful for the reasons described there.

Presenting problems, perhaps needless to say, are themselves memories or maps of troubling situations and not the troubling situations themselves. The patient reports as a reason to seek therapy a narrative that is itself responsive to the environment in which it is produced, to the patient's idiosyncratic construction of why things have gone wrong, and to the roles the patient plays. For this reason, we typically treat them as problematic patterns rather than as single instances, and presenting problems are as susceptible to communicative and systemic interpretation as are memories. Such interpretations must be managed delicately, as patients are often attached to the idea that the problem they want help with is the problem they need help with. Using early memories to illuminate presenting problems can help resolve the problem while also addressing the factors that gave rise to them.

CASE EXAMPLE REVISITED: JELL-O OR SYMPATHY

Let's revisit Jean, from chapter 7, where I used her memory of Jell-O and sympathy as an example of a systemic interpretation. Here, I will use her memories to shed light on her presenting problem: her tendency to defer her own needs to those of others. She provided numerous examples, from her willingness to be the designated driver when her friends go out drinking to her cleaning up after her roommates to her letting her boyfriend decide what to do on their evenings together. The therapist could have sent her to a women's group for consciousness-raising, or given her articles and books to read on gender theory, or started a dialogue on how her version of being a woman was incompatible with some of her needs. Any of these moves, however accurate their underlying premises, would run the risk of starting the therapy train, if you will, without her on it.

A systemic understanding of a presenting problem will describe its function, its systemic purpose that the system resists relinquishing. Much of what we need to know about the concept of resistance can be found in the old joke about the man who consults a psychiatrist about his brother, who thinks he is a chicken. His only speech is clucking, he pecks food from the floor, and he sleeps in a nest.

When the psychiatrist learns this has been going on for years, she asks the man why he has come to consult her now, rather than when the problem started. "Well, up until recently," says the man, "we've needed the eggs."

The idea, of course, is that all symptoms, annoying or debilitating as they may be, also serve some purpose. Psychoanalysts and behaviorists tend to agree that symptoms get rewards in a form that is usually weaker than desired but which avoids punishment by being disguised. Systems theorists are more likely to reflect on the fact that if a pattern does not have some kind of protective, self-perpetuating strategy, it will never become a pattern in the first place. The communication theory wing of systems theory, though, tends to see things as the behaviorists and psychoanalysts do. Watzlawick et al. (1967) consider the typical symptom to be analogous to what happens when a passenger on a plane realizes that her neighbor looks boring and talkative: she pretends to be asleep. However, she feels guilty about pretending to be asleep because she was taught not to lie and it is denigrating to the other person. Therefore, she actually falls asleep. They, too, see symptoms as compromises between the patient's needs and what she is willing to communicate to herself and others.

Regardless of how one construes resistance, then, dropping Jean into a ready-made solution is likely to arouse it. Applying her early memories as a road map to the terrain in which the symptoms occur is one way to try to help her navigate the bigger picture, or at least to strategize some way of inducing her to travel along the right road, rather than merely pushing her in the right direction. Pushing typically produces a push back.

Jean's earliest memories were as follows:

> I was in the hospital. I was in a crib-like bed. I was really young, like two or three, having my ear fixed. My parents were there. My brother was there. He is two years older than me, and I remember the nurse asking him if he wanted some Jell-O. I feel like he declined, but I said I would like some. But the nurse said I couldn't have any and took my brother to get some anyway.

> It was Christmas and I walked in and for Christmas I got this kitchen set. I don't remember why I was so excited about it but I was.

> I was playing in my room and I had this big huge bunny rabbit stuffed animal. I decided to color on the walls and hide it with this stuffed animal because I knew I'd be in trouble if I did it. But my mom came in my room and she saw me coloring on the wall before I could hide it and she became very angry at me.

These memories personalize the sex-role issues invoked by her presenting problem. Instead of being seen as a generic woman in a generic patriarchy with a generic tendency to put other people first, Jean can use these memories as a personal guide to her complex and, one hopes, out of it.

The first memory has already been interpreted in chapter 7 as a map to what happens in helping relationships (since it takes place in a hospital). The characters are the idle parents, the professional helper, the needy unsatisfied girl, and the nonneedy satisfied boy. The parents do nothing in this situation, and the professional or educated helper provides only for the boy who does not want provisions. The girl's neediness—her situation as a patient—precludes her getting what she wants, and not getting what she wants keeps her needy. A real-life version of this complex could emerge if the professional, educated part of her were making dispassionate decisions about whose needs to meet: she has found as a matter of logic that the household runs better when she does other people's chores and the romance is smoother when she defers to her boyfriend. One goal that emerges for this system is to empower the parents to make decisions, in other words, to base decisions more on empathy than on efficiency.

The second memory signals how smoothly, even joyously, things go when she is identified with the stereotypical feminine role. She is happy to get a kitchen set for Christmas, and her happiness with this sort of thing produces a sense of bounty in the world around her. The third memory suggests the fate of her expressive urges when she does not hide them behind cute, feminine masks like stuffed animals: such urges are chastised.

All told, it is not simply a matter of politicizing Jean and helping her find a voice in a system that favors boys over girls. It is instead a matter of helping the boy inside her find an active voice that does not need to be hidden behind lace. The boy inside her is nurtured only when he is not needy, when he demurs. The key to helping him may be found in the last memory. It may be that there is a systemic relatedness between her impulse to hide her expressiveness, its destructive overtones, and her mother's reaction. The impulse to hide her expressiveness leads her away from constructive outlets like drawing on paper instead of on walls: if she wanted paper, she would need to ask her mother. The expectation that her expressiveness will be unfed leads her to draw on the walls, and this in turn leads to an angry reaction by her mother. Expectations of anger from her mother lead her to hide her desire for expressiveness. It is not hard to imagine that she bites her tongue until it hurts, and then finally complains to her roommates and her boyfriend in a way that makes them not want to meet her needs.

A number of treatment options present themselves, including consultation at home, couple's therapy with her boyfriend, and family therapy to get her parents to endorse her various expressive needs. In individual therapy, the therapist can help her identify disguised or mild attempts at expressiveness and, by showing curiosity and a welcoming attitude toward these, help her learn that they need not always expect frustration. As in all essentially psychoanalytic therapies, the therapist would need to be anonymous enough so that the conditioning effects did not apply only to that one relationship, but instead could generalize to all ambiguous relationships. Whatever role in the pattern the therapist is cast in, there should be beneficial options available to him. In the role of nurse, the therapist can inquire as to what might make the girl more comfortable and can wait for the boy to express his desires before gratifying them. In the role of parent, the therapist can base his reactions on concern for her expressiveness more than on deference to correctness or concern for trivial aspects of the frame (dismay with the coloring of the walls should not overshadow his concern for her expression). In the role of boy, the therapist can refuse what he does not crave, as for example when the patient inevitably defers to her perceptions of his needs. In the role of the girl, the therapist can demonstrate his equanimity when, as is inevitable, he occasionally expresses himself more than is called for by the needs of the therapy.

Case Example: Permission to Walk

A twenty-three-year-old white man, Tom, realized there was something wrong after he graduated from a university with a degree in a literature and he was still waiting tables in his New England college town. He did not even have enough ambition to *apply* for a higher status job, he said. His parents were middle-class professionals, and his younger brother was away at school. His mother had been in a wheelchair since he was eight years old because of an automobile accident, but she still worked in an office. He reported emotionally moving, and fairly predictable, reactions to her disability. He did not see any connection between her condition and his lack of ambition, until he was asked about his earliest memories.

Tom's earliest memory was of looking at an aquarium with his dad. "I just remember looking at the brightly colored fish." The feeling tone of the memory, he reported, was pleasant. His next earliest memory was watching his brother play with his food. This was an auditory memory of his brother's gleeful laughter and the family's enjoyment of him. When asked about his earliest memory of his mother, Tom remembered something from an even earlier age: "I was first learning to walk, and I thought I wasn't allowed to walk. I thought I wasn't allowed to stand. So when my mom came in the room, I sat down immediately."

In pursuing a developmental accomplishment, my interpretation goes, Tom has a sense that success would somehow displease his mother, and he deals with this concern by avoiding success. Situations devoid of any sense of accomplishment (looking at the aquarium, his brother playing with food), in contrast, can be pleasant and even joyous. The early memory is a map that shows the relationship between his lack of ambition and his mother's disability. He is so quick to spare her whatever it is that he thinks he is sparing her that he does not even know for sure what he is protecting her from. His subdued approach to life is accidentally reinforced by the positive experiences he expects to find and does find when he is not trying to achieve anything. His relationships at the restaurant were comradely and even familial, making it a pleasure to work there. Tom lets the pleasure of these relationships keep him underemployed, as he imagines that this kind of relatedness is available only when there is no ambition in sight.

As in most cases, several treatment options are available. A family therapist might help Tom and his mother explore their mutual expectations and fears if he were to function independently. A strategic therapist might have Tom promise not to tell his mother if he applies for a better job, that is, a job that suited him on more levels than waiting tables did. An individual therapist might help him dispel the sense that he is supposed to have a better job, although this strategy would make more sense if his current job truly suited him and he was haranguing himself for not having a perfect job.

The early memory, used as a guide, seems clearly to suggest that a better job than waiting tables would be more like learning to walk than like striving after perfection. A therapist could help make a better job more palatable to Tom by comparing this hypothetical new job with one that was even more independent, even more gratifying, and even higher status. In other words, the therapist might help Tom construe a job he found challenging and productive to be like sitting down so as not to threaten his mother, because this job was still not as challenging and productive as it might be.

Other interventions are suggested by the memory. For example, Tom could be encouraged to call his mother daily, which might serve to prove to him that he was still under her sway, even if he applied for gratifying work. In a relationship-based therapy, Tom and the therapist could identify the moments when he disqualifies himself. It would not be too surprising to hear him balk at offering an insight for fear of stepping on the therapist's turf, for example. This might teach him to distinguish what worked with his mother from what is required by others. Tom's therapist might also look for moments when the pattern expressed itself with the roles reversed, when the therapist felt she needed to disqualify *her*self to make Tom comfortable. For example, she might fear that a glimmer of enjoyment of her own work would be construed as smirking at her good fortune, and she might instead stifle herself in this respect. Then, in the role of the boy in the memory, she could try expressing a bit of that satisfaction, prepared to discuss its impact on Tom however he might react.

The memory of pretending to be unable to walk shed light on his presenting complaint, which centered on his work life.

Case Example: Plucking the Beard

Kevin was a nineteen-year-old black college student at a major university when I was working at the school's counseling center. He had recently been arrested for exposing himself to a series of women in the stairwell of the university library. He had no prior record, appeared contrite, and did not otherwise menace his victims. The judge continued the trial with an understanding that the charges would be dropped if he made an earnest effort in therapy. Also, the judge was sympathetic with Kevin's situation. Kevin had been recruited, as a star high school athlete, for the college's acclaimed basketball team, but after two months of concerted effort, he had not made the team.

After clarifying who my client was—Kevin, not the court and not the attorney—and the limits of confidentiality—the judge wanted only a statement of effort, not specific details—I formed an impression of him as not all that disturbed and sought details of his crimes. According to Kevin, he had not been sexually aroused during these incidents, and he was unable to say how it occurred to him to expose himself. He would stand in the stairwell, and if one or two women passed by, he would pull out his penis, saying nothing. If there were a man present, or too large a group of women, he would just walk past them. All the incidents were over the course of two weeks, shortly after he was cut from the team.

Kevin reported that he had never been a good student, cruising instead on his basketball prowess. High school was a long party of hoops, drinking, and unemotional sexual liaisons. His mother was a solid figure in his life, the center of the family. She worked in a clerical job. Kevin said he was one of the very few guys among his friends whose father lived at home with the family. He said his father got up early every morning, put on his uniform, went to work in public transportation, came home at night, ate dinner, watched television, and went to bed. Kevin described his father's entire life as a "devotion," the fulfillment of a promise to Kevin's grandmother that he would not be the kind of man (like his father, no doubt) who got in trouble with the law, botched his responsibilities, and shamed his mother.

Kevin's early memories were relatively warm, specific, and secure. His earliest memory of his father, though, was of watching his father plucking hairs from his chin with a tweezers in front of the bathroom mirror. "The ones he missed shaving?" I asked. "No," said Kevin. "Instead of shaving." In Kevin's memory, his father plucked his entire beard periodically instead of shaving. The behavior suggests a psychological conflict between grooming and virility. The actual memory is even more specific: when men are self-involved (looking in the mirror), one must choose between responsibility and virility, between being manly in the sense of being a breadwinner (well groomed, but feminized, and living on the straight and narrow) and manly in the sense of being aggressively free of constraint (bearded and wild).

The memory helped Kevin understand the relationship between his failure to make the basketball team and his showing his penis to strangers. In fact, months later, he told me that the actual term the players used for what he was on the basketball court was "pussy," not because he was cowardly, but merely because his shot could be blocked. Flashing, though ultimately humiliating of himself, in the moment at least made him feel that women were the "pussies." He was also desperately resisting the (to him) effeminate and all-too-civilized course of his father's life implied by giving up sports and trying to get a college degree. Exhibitionism was like tagging a building with a gang insignia.

The memory also suggests some solutions. The mirror's self-involvement depicts the extent to which his father went through this struggle alone, and Kevin too was now going through it alone. He had not even begun to sort out which of his friends liked him and which liked being around a basketball player. He certainly had never met a woman he let behind the curtain of his athletic stardom. The memory also invites the father and son to have some sort of relationship besides observation. Indeed, the classic solution to this masculine dilemma is for the boy to identify with the father, to see the father as virile within the home. Identification makes dutiful men feel admired, and it makes sons feel they have someone to admire. The memory suggests that the father could have involved the son in masculine pursuits, rather than force him to witness the father's renunciation of them.

Kevin accepted suggestions from me that he pursue mutually enjoyable activities with his father, but he had managed to keep his arrest a secret from his parents, and he was adamant about not involving them in therapy. That left us with individual work. For better or worse, this was before anyone considered sex offending to be a field requiring specialized expertise, and before almost anyone considered white people to be of questionable competence in treating black people without specialized consultation. Thus, we were two young men (this was a long time ago) trying to sort out their masculinity, complicated by my being white and Kevin's being black, by my being dominantly expert in the path left for him to pursue (education) and Kevin's being dominantly expert in a path closed to both of us (my fastball peaked when I was ten years old, and I never had a jump shot), and by my being the therapist and Kevin's being the patient.

We resorted to the most basic of psychoanalytic principles: we talked about this stuff. Was I lording it over him when I used words he didn't know? Who paid me to talk to him and how much was it? Was it intrinsically degrading for a black man to seek help from a white man? Could I survive a fair fight with him? Do only sissies care about women? Do only loose women like sex? The more we talked, the less difference it seemed to make that I was highly educated, white, and paid to be there, and the more the conversation itself seemed to matter. Eventually, we used his memory of his father to catch each other trying to sustain the relationship by denying our virility. For example, Kevin commented once that physical prowess was not of any consequence in a middle-class existence and I told him he was plucking his beard; he asked me once why I thought he resisted trying his hardest at school, and when I answered, "I'm not really sure," he told me I was plucking *my* beard.

One of us introduced into our conversation the movie *Jaws*, which Kevin had seen numerous times. I construed the movie as the tale of what happens when men get together: a dangerous shark emerges, and the men must decide whether they are going to control the shark or whether the shark is going to control them. Some intellectualize about the shark, some take it on directly and are destroyed by it, some honor its power and remain conscious and resourceful in limiting its damage. The friendship and respect that develops between two of the men leads to a relationship without a shark. Kevin eventually felt that we had achieved that sort of grudging respect for each other, despite our differences—he identified with Roy Scheider's New York cop and saw me as the intellectual Richard Dreyfuss character.

When the school year ended, so did we. Kevin had squeaked through with passing grades. He decided that the major university was not for him, partly because the course work was difficult, but mainly because not being on the basketball team overshadowed everything else for him. He felt he had done well enough to leave with dignity, transferring to a smaller school where he had a good chance of making the basketball team.

The memory of watching his father pluck his beard illuminated some of the variables underlying Kevin's exhibitionism.

Case Example: Music on the Radio

John, a white accountant in his early thirties, reported that he suffered from chronic anxiety punctuated by periodic panic attacks. The anxiety was hard to pin down, as it consisted of fairly constant feelings of nervousness and a sense of dread. The panic attacks occurred every few weeks, but he had never discerned a pattern. Over the years, a combination of antianxiety medication and square breathing had helped him control the panic attacks, and he had not had a full-blown episode for over a year. The last one seemed to be in response to thoughts he had been having about applying for a similar but better-paid position in another firm. John's previous therapist, who introduced him to the psychiatrist prescribing the medication, thought that he was self-defeating, and that John pulled the rug out from under himself by becoming extremely anxious whenever he contemplated succeeding at something. When John decided to quit therapy because he felt it was not going anywhere, the therapist told him that he was pulling the rug out from under the therapy as a self-defeating gesture.

John's earliest memory was of "driving back from a day at Niagara Falls with my parents. This was before they were divorced. I was around four. The song, 'Good Day Sunshine' was playing on the radio, and I remember thinking that was funny because it was really dark and gloomy out." In this memory, John is traveling from the honeymoon capital of the world with people who will soon be divorced; the radio is telling him it is a sunny day, but he can see for himself that a storm is brewing. Whom is he to believe? His parents or his own lying eyes?

If good news is not to be trusted, how is he ever to feel secure? His parents told him before, during, and after the divorce that they loved him, but these were the same people who seemed to tell him, if not verbally then by their actions, that the family would last in perpetuity. His therapist had annexed a theory of anxiety as self-defeating and had imposed it on John's experience of the world, even though John tried to tell the therapist that it did not fit. His therapist had recapitulated the memory rather than change its pattern, in that both the therapist and the parents in the memory are trying to convince John to ignore his own sense of things.

Systemically, the pattern that emerged was of lying parents and a confused, insecure child when times were supposed to be good. Significantly, John was as often in the lying parent role as in the insecure child role. He was no better at communicating believably to himself than his parents were. He would tell himself that everything was going to be all right, that he deserved the higher pay of a different job, and that his wife loved him, but he never managed to do it any more believably than his parents did. "I like a look of agony," wrote Emily Dickinson, "because I know it's true." When John was having a panic attack, his world would seem to fall apart, but at least he knew he was getting the straight dope.

The early memory provided a different roadmap for understanding John's anxiety from the self-defeating template his previous therapist had used. Importantly, it was a roadmap derived from John, not from a textbook. Instead of a therapy about John's need to undermine himself, it would be a therapy about his inability to reassure himself. The therapist's job would be, when in the child's role, to show John how to manage uncertainty about statements. This was likely to happen when John related incidents or reactions that the therapist could not possibly verify. At these moments, the therapist would show John that ambiguity need not be met with either paralysis or blithe certainty; it could be met with reasonable yet changeable confidence and tentative but not too tentative decision making. The therapist's job would be, when in the parents' role, to welcome John's suspicions and his perceptions of inconsistencies rather than require him to ignore them. By showing a good-natured humility when caught in an inconsistency, the therapist could change authoritative statements from being a source of silent doubt to being an opportunity for friendly exploration.

Chapter Thirteen

Anticipating and Resolving Treatment Impasses

To Doctor Empirick
When men a dangerous disease did 'scape
Of old they gave a cock to Aesculape;
Let me give two, that doubly am got free
From my disease's danger and from thee.

—B. Jonson: *To Doctor Empirick*

METACOMMUNICATION

Communication theorists (Bateson, 1972; Watzlawick et al., 1967) offer an intriguing interpretation of psychological treatment. Setting aside for the moment the purpose of symptoms and how they develop, these writers conducted and observed psychotherapy sessions and concluded that the therapist teaches the patient how to metacommunicate about issues that are currently communicated via symptomatology. *Metacommunication* means communication about communication. Therapists teach patients how to talk about their symptoms and thus teach them how to talk about the issues that the symptoms communicate. This translates conceptually into the ability to take a time-out and talk about what is going on. It is a familiar concept, whether expressed as Socrates' *examined life*, ego psychologists' *conflict-free ego sphere*, or Skinner's (1957) inquisitive, nonpunitive verbal community. The *working alliance* was originally considered to be a relationship between the patient's *observing ego* and the analyst (Bordin, 1979). Early memories, and the systemic approach to complexes underlying my interpretation of them, can help us understand when the observing ego is available and when it is not.

Everyone has complexes, as discussed in chapter 7. These are disadvantageous (i.e., neurotic) patterns of expectation that govern behavior (Jung, 1926). The defining characteristic of a complex, as opposed to a mere pattern, is the absence of a figure in the pattern analogous to an observing ego. In other words, if the problematic pattern has a figure in it capable of metacommunication, it would not likely become much of a problem. Conversely, if any pattern lacks a figure in it that can check its usefulness in a given situation, it is likely to become problematic. Being in a complex is analogous to using a map, being incapable of considering that the map is outdated, and following it blindly no matter what roadblocks, dead ends, and one-way streets reality throws in the path.

Ideally, the primary communicative obstacles to successful treatment are the necessary ones posed by the patient's outmoded roadmaps, and not ones imposed by the therapist. These obstacles are necessary under the presumption that the problematic pattern is going to be hard to talk about, and it must arise in the therapy relationship to be changed therein (the analysis of transference in psychoanalytic terms). Other sources of communicative obstacles create treatment impasses, rather than treatment opportunities. Some of these, including the therapist's complexes, telling lies, and avoiding what is going on in the room, are addressed in this chapter, and early memories are used as guides to clearing up these problems.

An important type of communicative obstacle occurs when the subject matter of the patient's symptoms or the subject matter that arises in therapy cannot be metacommunicated about because it puts the *therapist* in a complex. If the *therapist's* observing ego is not available, then a productive conversation about the patient and about the therapy cannot occur. If we think of a personality disorder as the equivalent of virtually always being in a complex, then it is obvious that a personality-disordered therapist is only rarely likely to be helpful in conducting metacommunicative sessions. Instead, the personality-disordered therapist, or the therapist in a complex, will provide just another relationship where it is dangerous for the patient to be honest, and defensive maneuvers and symptoms will flourish. Since all therapists are human beings, we all are capable of being put in a complex, and we need to learn ways of accessing our own observing egos when this happens. Practically, when the therapist is put in a complex, it usually means that the place to stand offered by the patient's operative complex is too aversive for the therapist for personal reasons. The offered role has too much personal meaning for the therapist to play it with the necessary "just kidding" attitude.

The patient's early memories can be used to depict role relationships the therapist will have to play, the better to prepare us for those roles, and the better to remind us that the role we will find ourselves in will only be a role. The following example illustrates the use of a memory to help resolve a treatment impasse that stemmed from the need to play an unappealing role.

Case Example: Dressing for the Zoo

Ted, a gay man in his mid-twenties, came to see me for help with his achievement motivation, also noting that his love life was unsatisfying for lack of a durable relationship. He had completed college with excellent grades, took the LSAT and scored very high, but never applied to law school. He was making a decent living selling cars, but he felt his intellectual life was stagnating. He had not read a good book in over a year. One childhood memory of his father struck me as most relevant among a number of other memories that suggested a generally healthy young man. In this memory, his father was to take him to the local zoo. Ted, age six, was ready to go, wearing shorts and flip-flops. His father scowled at his attire and told him to change. Ted had the impression that the shorts, which were quite short, and the flip-flops were too girlish, recalling that his father had once criticized the flip-flops because one cannot run fast in them. Back in his room, Ted thought it would be funny to dress as masculine as possible, which in his mind meant like his father's work attire. He put on his one pair of long pants that were not jeans, tucked in a buttoned shirt, and wore his one pair of shoes that were not sneakers. He slicked his hair with water, and combed it with a crisp part. Instead of comedy, though, his effect was unexpected. "Now you look *good*," said his Dad, and off they went.

This memory stood for the proposition that his father was always good to him, but never really knew him. More specifically, the memory suggested that in masculine landscapes, Ted felt accepted only when he faked stereotypical masculine traits. And when he mocked these traits, he felt utterly invisible. The father who wanted a masculine boy cultivated a faker, and the faker cultivated a father who did not need to see him as he really was. A typical frustration was Ted's skill at skating, which led his father to sign him up for hockey. Throughout his childhood, he skated and shot well enough to make one hockey team after another, but he rarely got on the ice, as it was obvious that he would sacrifice scoring to avoid being checked or checking opposing players. His coach called him the team pacifist. He tried playing goalie for a while, but he was not good at it. His father frowned at Ted's interest in figure skating. So Ted looked like a hockey player but was not one; he felt like a figure skater but ignored the feeling to please his father. Ted linked this conflict to his weak ambition, noting that law school represented to him a hockey uniform. Selling cars was like wearing shorts and flip-flops. What, I wondered aloud, would be like figure skating? What would be self-expressive, energetic, and personally suitable? This conversation was a very difficult one for Ted to engage in productively, as his thinking about his career was dominated by the image of his father, which seemed to say that it must either be law school (come to the zoo with me) or you are on your own. Therapy could be a place to explore and resolve the difficulty Ted experienced in trying to think productively about his life.

I had by then been doing therapy long enough to have played numerous challenging roles, including especially the role of the abusive parent. Many patients who have been excessively punished need us to contain an authoritarian image, to play the role gracefully. Most of us relinquish that role at first, not liking to be seen as authoritarian, but with supervision and attention to the patient's needs, we usually learn that it is better for the therapist to be seen as autocratic than to disperse the image and keep it out of the room. Thus, I was not at all wary of playing the role of Ted's father, who was not abusive, not even mean. I did not foresee a problem. Closer attention to the memory might have helped prepare me though. It seems in retrospect that a time would have to come when one of us would expose his girlishness and the other would disapprove.

Therapy progressed smoothly for several months, as Ted explored his vocational interests, his father's anticipated reactions to them, and his lack of interest in casual sex. One hurdle was cleared when he told me about his father's reaction when he came out to his parents. His mother was disappointed, embarrassed about having to tell her relatives, worried that she would not have grandchildren, but not condemning. His father was much calmer and superficially more accepting. He said, "I guess I always knew," a statement that Ted experienced as a dismissal, that Ted was never a real boy and now never would be. I managed not to take sides on this story. Instead, I brought his attention to the situational issues, asking him how typical the response had been for his father. Essentially, I invited him to empathize with the father who was finding out his son was gay, just as he had immediately empathized with his mother. Ted thought that sometimes he took his father at his worst and let that define their relationship, and I wondered aloud if his father might not do the same with Ted. After the phrase "real boy" came up numerous times, I asked Ted if he recalled how Pinocchio became a real boy. He did not remember, and I demurred, so Ted rented the movie and cried copious tears, he said, when he discovered that Pinocchio became a real boy by saving his father from the whale.

Another hurdle was cleared when a stranger, a man, whistled at him while he was crossing the street. Ted was upset that the fellow could tell he was gay. Instead of pointing out that the guy might just whistle at everyone, and might do so for a lot of reasons, I let him mull it over on his own terms. Specifically,

I would have guessed that the fellow was mocking him for taking pride in his body, as one might whistle at a bodybuilder. Ted was slim, tucked in his shirts, and wore pants that fit. The overall impression was not overtly gay so much as that of a man who looked good, knew it, and liked to advertise it. That certainly comports more with stereotypical femininity; men may tend to advertise power more than looks. It seems obvious, in light of the memory, that Ted's ability to mask his sexual orientation was important to him, or more accurately, what was important to him was to feel that its revelation was up to him. I said this to him, and we discussed it, but the discussion was fairly abstract given that we had not found the pattern in the room yet.

Then, Ted told me he had started a real relationship. They dated, and did not have sex until they both had begun to feel the possibility of commitment. Almost incidentally, Ted mentioned after a month or two that his partner, Steve, was in his forties, a professional man, a homeowner. I was filled with disapproval and tried to express it mildly, utterly unaware that I was no longer doing therapy. I thought it was my place to tell him that he should find someone his own age and that he was subordinating his chances for vocational and even domestic maturity by pursuing this relationship. I am going to draw a curtain at this stage over my personal complexes, but I will acknowledge what might be called an essentially Oedipal horror at the idea of fatherly men hunting for significantly younger mates: I prefer a bright line between the generations. I was disgusted in graduate school by the professors (male and female both) who slept with students. Unaware of what was really going on between us, I had become the father telling him he was too girlish for choosing a man whose established situation appealed to him.

Naturally, Ted was upset by my behavior, but for whatever reason he did not fire me. Perhaps my judgmental response freed him from the anxiety of having to face alternative ways of being with me, now that he had found familiar turf in the therapy. Perhaps he saw my judgments as a problem in the context of a larger, overall beneficial relationship. He predictably responded in the terms of the memory in which he pretended to be as manly as his father was: he pretended to be on equal footing with Steve, pretended to be a man, and thereby pretended to be on equal footing with me.

He complained about my attitude, but I was not deterred. I was so committed to hearing only metaphors of good or bad therapy for my own guidance that I had trouble deciphering his direct complaints. It has been said that a patient will speak symbolically and make the symbols increasingly clear until the therapist is finally hit over the head with them. With Ted and me, it was just the opposite. He started out hitting me over the head, and had to retreat into symbolic speech before I could finally hear him. He told me he and Steve had ordered a pizza, and when the delivery man arrived, they could not get the screen door open to get their food. Ted had to go out the back door and around the house to pay the guy. This finally hit home; I felt there was a screen door between us, a barrier we could talk through but which prevented the delivery of nurturance.

Because it took me so long to get what I had done wrong, I apologized a bit too profusely. I went slightly beyond taking responsibility for injecting into the therapy a somewhat arbitrary view of Ted's relationship with Steve. I said that he had given me an opportunity to see him in short pants, that is, as a child with respect to Steve, and I had denounced rather than welcomed him. This seems like an acknowledgment of what was specifically wrong with what I did in terms of the memory. But I was too upset with myself when I said it, and my distress awakened a caretaking response in Ted. Now he was disguising his girlishness not to defend himself from me, but to make me feel better, to preserve our relationship, to go metaphorically to the zoo with me.

After we discussed this twist, I pointed out how he had come out to me, not as gay, but as someone interested in an older man. I was disappointed, as his parents had been, that his love life was not what I would have designed for him. As with his mother, and lately with his father, he was able to interpret my reaction as misplaced but ultimately driven by concern for him. The rest of our therapy was spent on articulating the way in which masculinity is a performance, but a dreadful performance in which any hint of it being a performance is met with anger and intimidation. I thought then and still think the reason so many hypermasculine men hate gay men is because gay men make it clear that masculinity is a performance. Gay men are like magicians who tell the audience how the tricks are done, and other magicians are bound to resent them, especially the magicians who actually believe that their own their tricks use magic. As Dorothy Parker said of Hollywood back when leading men were tough guys: scratch an actor and find an actress.

Ted and I talked of masculinity for several more months, especially of how it played out between the two of us. He assumed that I was straight and explored whether that made me more of a man than he was. He knew I was an educated professional, and this too raised the question of manliness. We both explored how we performed our roles of men while we were together. Toward the end of the therapy, he admitted the "awful truth" about himself: he was actually interested in law after all, and he decided to apply to law school.

Ted's early memory of dressing for the zoo put the issues of masculinity and performance in front of us, where we could use them for guidance to negotiate the potential potholes and roadblocks in the relationship we were trying to maintain between us as two men.

LYING ON THE COUCH

Surely, patients lie to us regularly, though we may rarely catch them at it. It is of course the height of silliness to lie to one's own therapist, whose job it is to take information supplied by the patient and to use it for the patient's benefit. When patients tell a lie, they are deceiving the person they are paying to use information on their behalf and creating a communicative impasse. It is like hiring an interior decorator and not admitting which colors one likes. In spite of the silliness, though, it must happen all the time, as an analysis of the behavior will reveal.

Lying is verbal behavior designed to avoid an aversive response from the audience, or to garner an otherwise unlikely reward, at the expense of an accurate representation of some present or past occasion. We usually distinguish lying from other forms of inaccuracy (ignorance, unconscious motivation, misplaced faith in a third party's report, for example) by reserving the term *lying* for situations where the speaker knows she is misrepresenting some situation. In this context, *knows* means that the speaker has learned to observe herself and can see the difference between what is (or what was) and what she is saying. The best liars believe their lies, which is precisely analogous to Watzlawick et al.'s (1967) description of a symptom: a communicative misrepresentation authenticated by the subject's belief. Pretending to get angry to intimidate others is a lie; genuinely feeling angry because this posture has been reinforced by its intimidation of others is a symptom of narcissism. Symptoms—misrepresentations that the patient believes are true—are grist for the therapeutic mill; lies are a source of unnecessary impasses.

A lie occurs when, despite the payments and the alliance and the trust, the expectation of immediate punishment outweighs the advantages of keeping the therapist informed. Recall that punishment does not mean disciplinary action; it means any aversive stimulus. In therapy, the most common punisher is disapproval by the therapist, and patients lie to avoid it. They may also lie to get the reward of approval, but many therapists avoid this by never approving of patients. These therapists have learned that approval may be a powerful reinforcer, but its use makes neutrality sound like disapproval. In other words, the therapist who expresses approval when the patient reports something good or when the patient behaves usefully in the session soon finds herself inadvertently communicating disapproval whenever she withholds approval. This happens not only because the silence of neutrality sounds withholding after a series of approving statements; it happens also because the expression of approval makes the patient view the therapist as someone who is evaluating him. Once approval is injected into a therapy, the patient is bound to seek it, primarily by lying to avoid disapproval or by lying to obtain the reward directly.

The danger in therapy is always that it will become a farce, with the therapist complimenting the patient and the patient complimenting the therapist and no other change occurring.

Since none of us are capable of being perfectly neutral, we always inject approval and even disapproval into the therapy relationship. Once neutrality becomes established as the ideal stance by the therapist, our own departures from it become aversive reminders that we are all too human. Good supervision helps us notice these departures and connotes them as interpretable moments rather than as signs that we are imperfect. Good technique requires us to metacommunicate with patients about our injection of approval or disapproval and its effect on the patient, but therapeutic privilege makes it easier just to blame the patient as an approval-seeker or a liar.

Occasionally, a patient will lie not because we have turned the relationship into an approval-seeking situation, but because of a history of punishment for revealing certain kinds of information. A patient with a history of being scorned for expressing anger may simply lie when he is angry at his therapist. The therapist's job is to make the relationship as welcoming as possible so that the patient feels free to express previously punished thoughts, wishes, and emotions. The soothing and nonjudgmental environment of the therapy extinguishes their fearful associations and detoxifies their negative effects. The therapist accomplishes this partly by interpreting very slight expressions of anger to demonstrate to the patient that such expressions will not be punished. When a therapist says, "Last week I expressed an opinion about your mother and this week you came late to the session to express your anger and distrust at me for being opinionated," she is really trying to communicate her availability for looking at her own contributions to impasses and at the same time trying to show the patient that expressions of anger will be treated as communications rather than as punishable disruptions.

Lying itself usually has a punishment history. Most people grow up in communicative contexts where adults are paying enough attention to know when a child is lying and also to punish these lies (one hopes with mild reprimand rather than the rod). One frequent result of the punishment of lying is that children learn not to think about the kinds of things that, if considered, would make them want to lie. In other words, the punishment of lying leads to repression. Therapists who make a virtue of honesty must be careful not to punish lies, lest they accidentally foster repression.

The effects of punishment include responses detectable by polygraph, which forms its theoretical basis for use as a lie detector. Unfortunately, in practice, polygraphs are used in situations where there are such pervasive expectations of punishment that it cannot isolate those associated with lying. A fascinating bit of polygraph history is that after developing a primitive version based on blood pressure, psychologist William Moulton Marston went on to create Wonder Woman and her magic lasso, which could make anyone tell the truth. An appeals court rejected the admissibility of evidence from Marston's lie detector, creating the Frye standard for admissibility, which said that scientific evidence was inadmissible if the methodology was not "generally accepted" by the relevant scientific community. As ego psychologists were learning at about the same time that Marston was relegating the magic lasso to fantasy, there is no way to leap over the garden wall and get at the underlying truth. The shape and texture of the wall, though, often contains a lot of useful information about what is behind it.

Case Example: Hiding an Accident

I caught Maria, a divorced mother of two, in a lie. She was a realtor who had buried her Puerto Rican identity in a successful effort to make her customers comfortable. After her husband left her for another woman, she began to question whether she had buried so much of herself that it had cost her the marriage. He had said, "I don't know you anymore," and she wondered how she had become a white woman, which to Maria meant tasteful, understated business suits, a midsize high-end but not luxury sedan, a house in an upscale, professional neighborhood, and more concern for her children's grades and college prospects than for their zest for living. Her parents called her children their Americanos, trying to introduce Puerto Rican cuisine over their preferences for burgers, pizza, and peanut butter.

Maria's early memories were all positive. She recalled trailing her mother around the kitchen, helping her make dinner for a large family gathering, needing some attention and supervision but feeling indispensable at the time. She remembered her father teaching her to ride a bike. Her unhappiest memory from early childhood involved the death of the neighbor's dog when it was hit by a car. I let myself believe that this business of subordinating her identity was not related to her character, but stemmed from the pursuit of financial success. It never occurred to me that a woman who would bury her identity would also bury the sources of burial as a coping strategy, which with hindsight seems obvious. Also, for reasons of my own, I wanted to believe we were working on an economic/political problem. I wanted to treat her for being oppressed by middle-class America, not for being oppressed by her family.

The therapy went well for many months. Maria used the sessions to detail her decisions to hide herself, and to articulate what was hidden, while reporting constant progress on introducing Puerto Rican elements back into her home life, most notably the instruction of her children in Spanish, but also music, clothing, and food. She was still strictly Ann Taylor at work.

A close friend of Maria's had gotten divorced about five years before Maria did. Her close friend's ex, a Latino named Felipe, had expressed some interest in getting together with Maria, in terms that she described as unclear regarding his intentions. In a session that took place on my own wedding anniversary, she discussed with me at length the pros and cons of meeting him for coffee. I was distinctly aware of the coincidence, since my wife and I had met while she was dating a friend of mine. A few weeks later, Maria reported that she and Felipe had met for coffee, and a few weeks after that, she reported that they were romantically involved. Maria's relationship with Felipe became another marker in her latinization, and she had only positive things to say about it. Her friend, Felipe's ex, reportedly was fine with their seeing each other.

Several months later, Maria mentioned in passing that Felipe was taking her to a fashionable restaurant the following night for their six-month anniversary. This was exactly six months after Maria first told me that he had suggested a chat, hardly an occasion for an anniversary. It was obvious, assuming this really was the six-month anniversary of something noteworthy, that six months ago something had occurred between them that she had not mentioned to me at that time for several weeks. I tried not to sound too accusatory when I told her that she had first said his name to me exactly six months earlier. Maria denied it at first, trying to distract my attention by changing the subject, making up some nonsense about why they were celebrating this week, and then finally admitting that the first time she mentioned him to me as having suggested a chat, they had actually slept together the night before. Maria said she had wanted me to think of her as someone who would be careful and temperate in choosing a mate, and as someone who would not get involved with a friend's ex without giving the issues serious consideration. She had lied to me for weeks about the pace of their relationship. She recalled her relief when she had felt that their fictional relationship had advanced to the point when she could gracefully introduce their romance, so she could stop lying to me.

I could not think of any particular mistake that helped turn our relationship into a lie, into what we later called an "Anglo therapy" instead of the needed "Latino therapy." I had of course made the general mistake of not recognizing how artificial our work had been. Maria recognized, though, that the personality (rather than political and economic) factors that had driven her to disguise herself at work had driven her to disguise herself with me. She spontaneously told me two early memories, previously unmentioned, that guided us through the impasse of our very polite therapy.

In the first memory, Maria had an "accident," messing her pants at about age four while playing with friends in the front yard. She was embarrassed, so she snuck into the house, slipped into the bathroom, cleaned herself up, and threw the soiled underpants into the trash. In the second memory, Maria recalled the only time her father ever lost his temper with her. He had told her not to play with a certain girl under any circumstances. The girl had come by the house and told Maria she knew where they could find some snakes, and the two walked off to a nearby creek. When her father found her, he pulled his belt from his pants in a rage, and struck her with it several times, then marched her back home, half dragging her.

The first memory suggests that when she is in a social scene (playing in the front yard), her "parents" (the part of her that could be monitoring her physical needs) are unaware of her physical needs and cannot manage them judiciously. Once her physical needs become undeniable (the accident), her parents remain unaware of them. There is not an effective feedback loop between her needs and the part of the system charged with meeting them. The pattern played out in therapy when she impulsively had sex with Felipe and tried to clean up the mess—the bodily function that she expected to meet disapproval—all by herself without cluing me in to what happened. Like the accident in the memory, it was not a horrible mess, but keeping it from me hindered my ability to develop a welcoming relationship with her physical needs. The same pattern was operating when I did not look closely at her personal psychological investment in becoming a white woman. By keeping her psychological rather than political reasons for hiding her Puerto Rican traits out of my awareness, I helped set the stage for mishandling them.

I am suggesting that the underlying psychology that I should have noticed but did not was like Maria's need to go to the bathroom in the memory: noticeable but inconvenient and not submitted to parental scrutiny for decision making. My politically motivated refusal to consider such issues was like surreptitiously cleaning myself up. In the memory, the parents cannot be expected to act differently as a form of intervention, since they have no basis for knowing that something is wrong. Prior to the mess's occurrence, however, the parents could have communicated more willingness to treat messes warmly and acceptingly. The character of the girl could decide, in the memory's own terms, to seek parental assistance after her underlying issues become undeniable. As the therapist, there was not much for me to do except to make the environment welcoming. However, as someone dimly aware of my own political desires, I could have submitted these to supervisory scrutiny, which would have awakened me, I think, to how superficial our relationship had remained.

The second memory suggests that there is one peculiar set of circumstances that will enrage her father, but it is hard to tell what those circumstances are, so the possibility of rage seems indiscriminant. One imagines with hindsight that the girl in the memory had some history of abusing other children, and that Maria's father reacted out of fear, not just anger at being disobeyed. But on the memory's own terms, this knowledge is not available, and the girl in the memory might not be able to distinguish the circumstances of the beating from having an accident in her pants. Seeing the differences between the two situations might lead her to seek help (parental input) with fairly normal regressions. One thing we therapists can be pretty good at, when we are not exercising the therapeutic privilege of blaming everything on the patient, is to investigate our lamentable conduct and help the patient recognize its distinguishing features, compared to parents who tend to exercise the privilege associated with their power, and thereby make children generally rather than specifically fearful of punishment.

The second memory suggests that when she associates with known bad company, the parental part of her becomes enraged. Psychologically, what is "known bad company"? It is a part of the system that causes harm and is gratified by the harm it causes. These kinds of impulses are best socialized by recognizing them in children, mildly restraining them, and providing pro-social outlets for them. A girl who wants to hurt her little brother can be taught to compete with him on terms that, while not nearly as gratifying as tossing him down the stairs, are at least mildly satisfying by producing victory. Pro-social alternatives cannot be introduced if the parents' attitude toward the impulse is one of utter rejection. Maria apparently retained a sense that at least one bundle of impulses, represented by a little girl who finds snakes, was unintegrated into her family's portrait of her. In this memory, snakes can be seen as vaguely dangerous but fascinating natural creatures

One concern in therapy is always that order and maturity will expel the creaturely and vital. Usually, though, the patient's abject suffering can be counted on to insist on inclusion of the bodily, the ugly, and the sinful. With Maria, an unfortunate coalition emerged between us against authenticity and vitality; for me these became forbidden psychological reasons for her adjustment and for her they became a dangerous allegiance to the bad girl and her snakes. Neither of us dared take the first step toward welcoming the creaturely and vital. Like Maria's adjustment to the States, her adjustment to therapy left vitality behind; I was turning her, as her expectations of the States had turned her, into a shell of a woman, a symbol of politics rather than a woman with a history.

In the second memory, the onus is on the figure of the father. Rather than issuing orders to a little girl bound to forget them, he should include the bad girl into the purview of his influence. Of course, I am not talking about what fathers should do with actual bad girls from other families; I am talking about what the father figure in the system of the memory can do. In the terms of the memory, he can feel a bit of relief that nothing bad has happened yet, and then help both girls hunt for snakes. All I needed to do, probably, was to have kept an attitude that there was more here than meets the eye, rather than to exclude Maria's psychology because it made us both uncomfortable and because I wanted the therapy to be about politics and ethnic identity.

Stepping into the father's role, I suggested that she had perceived me as capable of getting angry over her hiding things, and the more potential she sensed for me to get angry, the more it made her want to hide things. "Do you want to hear about my first night with Felipe?" she asked, a trap if ever I have heard one. *No* means do not play with the bad girl; *yes* means that *I* want to play with the bad girl. "If it's relevant," I said. Maria paused, mulling this over. She looked at me mischievously and said, "What if I took off all my clothes and tried to seduce you?" Sure, our relationship was superficial and excluded a lot of important things, but I had still spent almost ten months with her, and I felt we had developed a good *real* relationship even if the therapeutic relationship had danced around the scary stuff. The fact was, I trusted her. So I just rolled my eyes at her, communicating (I think) that we both knew nothing even close to that could happen between us. I think the process of rolling my eyes, rather than issuing a formal, verbal response, also communicated a lack of caution about our relationship, and therefore an invitation to be more spontaneous and genuine.

The "bad girl" became a central figure in the therapy, as Maria came to see how vitality had been given a bad name, a Puerto Rican name, in her psychology. "Fitting in" socially was, as she had always known, a pressure to act white, but what we were considering together was how acting white and acting good had become conflated for her.

What terrible things did Maria's bad girl crave? Like an actor practicing improvisation who at first associates freedom-from-script with sex and scatology, Maria had a few weeks of therapy filled with the apparent freedom of discussing sex and defecation. The only part of this verbal diarrhea worth mentioning was her admission that she had never had an orgasm with a partner, and precious few on her own. I gave her typical psychoanalytic advice: I disguised it as an interpretation. "If pursuing orgasms is as natural and exciting and sinful as hunting for snakes, it would be difficult for you to expect creative and industrious effort from a sex partner, for fear that he would become enraged." In other words, give Felipe his marching orders.

After the initial wave of sex and scatology, we began to identify what in her current life she was really hiding from the parents of her imagination. These things, as perhaps expected, were the day-to-day ugly thoughts and feelings that most people either repress or ignore. For example, an overweight client was unsure about seeing a house, and finally decided just to "hop in" for a quick look. Maria felt her body tense up, she said. I remained silent for a truly prolonged period while we just looked at each other. Finally, she acknowledged that she had ridiculed the client in her mind for thinking she was capable of hopping anywhere. She was ashamed as a Christian and as a feminist for thinking such a thing. Here, though, was an opportunity for the father of the memory to have a different response to Maria's association with badness, as I interpreted her shame as a beating one administers to oneself.

Another example of the complex emerging between us occurred when Maria balked at the whole idea of therapy. She felt I was inducing her into a sinful state and excusing it with a lot of psychological jargon. She thought the therapy was turning into a breeding ground of bad thoughts and twisted fantasies. "You like getting people all messy, don't you?" she hissed at me. Even though she was threatening an abrupt termination and even though she was speaking so angrily, I felt as I did when my children would get mad at me, more curious and apologetic than truly concerned about the future of the relationship. Again, I trusted her. In light of my sense that our basic relationship was still intact, though, I just spelled out what I thought was going on. I said, "I guess I'm getting a small taste of what that belt felt like, now that I'm with the bad girl and enjoying her company." After discussing what had happened between us, using the memory as a template, I did do some alliance building by pointing out that what makes children good citizens is inclusion of their naughty impulses into the adults' purview, not exclusion of them. A harsh attitude does not lead to growth, it just leads to good behavior in front of others and bad behavior when there are no parents around. Intellectually, Maria agreed with this, solidifying our alliance around the work we were doing.

A few months later, we terminated. Maria had learned to tolerate herself better, if not entirely to appreciate her creatureliness. Her *children*'s impulsivity was another matter, however, and she reported a new era of freedom and enjoyment in celebrating their needs and wishes.

USING EARLY MEMORIES,
NOT JUST TALKING ABOUT THEM

Another major type of communicative obstacle in treatment occurs when the patient or the therapist only pretends to metacommunicate. Under the perceived threat of upsetting consequences, a person will avoid behaviors that produce those consequences; she will even avoid situations associated with them, the better to avoid the behaviors that could produce them. If the same person is then persuaded to engage in the same behaviors she has been avoiding, she can solve the dilemma by faking them. She looks like she is doing what the new situation requires while avoiding what the old situation has punished.

This conflict that produces faked behavior is central to psychopathology and central to its treatment. One sees it clearly in abused children who are placed in foster care. These children—many of them, anyway—have learned to avoid intimacy because their experiences with intimacy have been unpleasant. In foster care, or in new adoptive homes, they are encouraged to participate in intimate, familial interactions. They can get the approval of their new parents while avoiding the expectation of injury learned from their old parents by pretending to be personally close and emotionally connected in the new family. By *pretending*, I do not mean conscious deception; I mean doing what is asked in what looks like the manner that was asked but that still avoids the closeness that precedes devastation.

Adoptive parents are hardly to be blamed for not recognizing that the kiss goodnight accompanied by a smile is not the same as the kiss goodnight accompanied by a smile, since the two behaviors differ only in the contingencies that produce the smile. Ideally, the smile is not learned; it is a respondent that accompanies the pleasure associated with the kiss. These children, in contrast, learn to smile as an operant: When they do not smile, the parents issue mild rebukes ("Aren't you happy?"), and when they do, the parents reward their smiles with pleasantness. Because fake behaviors are so easily produced, it is extremely difficult for adoptive parents to evoke the genuine, scary behaviors associated with intimacy to show the child that these behaviors will produce good results in the new family. Eventually, after many months or even years, adoptive parents often do detect the difference, not in the kiss goodnight itself, but in the absence of other behaviors that the faking led them to expect, such as cheerful glances and spontaneous hugs. They love their children more than their children love them.

Similarly, in therapy, we try to evoke in our patients their previously punished behaviors associated with intimacy, love, and industry. Our practical purpose, in behavioral terms, is to demonstrate that these behaviors can be fruitful where once they were pointless or punished. In other words, we want the signals of intimacy that occasion avoidant behaviors to mean an opportunity for gratification instead of a sign of danger; we want the conditioned aversive stimuli associated with personal closeness and self-expression to extinguish as markers of trouble. However, it is so much easier for patients to pretend to engage in these behaviors than to do so genuinely, we expect the pretense will occur. We tell them to say whatever comes to mind, holding nothing back, but we know they will not.

Even more problematic is the fact that it is easier for *us* to fake therapy than to do it. Because the therapist has so much more power than the patient does, it is natural to exploit that differential by blaming the patient for whatever missteps occur along the way. Virtually every session presents the therapist with a choice: (a) I will not talk about what is going on in the room because its implications diminish my power and self-regard; (b) I will talk about what is going on in the room because I realize that our interactions provide the leverage necessary for change, but I will focus on the patient's psychology rather than put myself under scrutiny; or (c) I will talk about what is going on in the room and take responsibility for cocreating whatever happens between us.

There are several costs and benefits to the last, preferred option. Among benefits, the patient gets to experience an intimacy in which the power differential is not used at her expense, allowing her to change her expectations of power differentials. By discussing her life with a therapist who takes responsibility for his own psychology and his contributions to problems, she is inclined to take responsibility for her own contributions to situations, rather than to defend herself. Otherwise, the therapist's press for change is met by countervailing forces. The therapist models a way of relating to other people that allows for connection and intimacy rather than a way of relating that evokes interpersonal caution.

Among costs, the therapist who takes responsibility for his contribution to the therapy interaction feels disempowered, not in control of the therapy, not in control of the clinic or other environment in which the therapy unfolds, and not in control of his unconscious motivations. The therapist is shamed by the larger therapy establishment for blurring the distinction between doctor and patient. His livelihood is threatened when he questions the utility of diagnosing the patient and the wisdom of constructing the treatment plan around the insurance benefits. Most importantly, he has no more inclination to explore his inner world or to express his ugliness in the imperfect environment he has created than the patient does. This last drawback comes into play with special force at the outset of psychotherapy training, when the therapist is trying to learn how to make a setting both comfortable enough and vigorous enough that a person in this setting would divulge secrets. Beginners need support, and often are told, in effect, "She is resisting you," rather than, "Would *you* be utterly honest with you? What might you do differently to enhance her potential for honesty?" Such challenging questions immediately, of course, implicate the supervisor's ability to create the kind of intimate and honest space with the therapist that the therapist is trying to create with the patient. The next step is for the supervisor to ask herself and the therapist, "What can *I* do differently to make you feel like being scrupulously honest while you are with me?" Such a question requires renunciation of supervisory privilege, the power to blame supervision problems on the therapist.

One place where only pretending to metacommunicate is rampant is in groups of therapists—conventions, case conferences, and training programs. Otherwise intelligent people get together and act as if it is humiliating to have a psychology. Since the ability to metacommunicate is interpreted as a sign of health, therapists are careful to look like they are circumspect about everything. A psychoanalytically oriented student, Bill, told me he was anxious about his upcoming clinical competency oral examination. Only half-jesting, I told him there was only one skill needed to pass: regardless of what comments were made about his case presentation, he had to be able to scratch his chin thoughtfully, nod appreciatively at the commenter's sagacity, and say, "That's interesting. I'll have to think about that."

"Let's practice," I said. "I'm your examination chairperson. 'Bill, it's obvious that you don't care a hoot about the patient. You are conducting this session to convince everyone that you are not in love with your umbrella.'"

Bill scratched his chin thoughtfully, nodded at my sagacity, and said, "That's interesting. I'll have to think about that."

"You'll do fine," I said.

When a person is in a complex, or when a person has a personality disorder, everything that happens is incorporated into it, because the only available roadmap dominates the landscape's ability to communicate that the map is outmoded. Speaking to a person in a complex leads to the speech either being ignored (as speech by the audience is ignored by the actors) or being incorporated into the complex (as unscripted speech by actors is integrated into the play). Since therapists are constantly talking therapy to patients, patients in a complex while in the therapy room will incorporate the therapy talk into the complex. The therapists may say, in effect, let's talk about what just happened, and the patient will hear it as a dominance move, for example, and respond accordingly. It is hard to tell the difference between the collaborative patient's "Yes, let's talk" and the submissive patient's "Yes, let's talk." It is even harder, of course, for the patient to distinguish the collaborative therapist's "Talk to me" from the domineering therapist's "Talk to me." Confirmation bias—hearing what one wishes and expects to hear—tends to make the therapist mistake agreeability for health and the patient mistake forcefulness for dominance. Both errors, of course, are the therapist's responsibility. The therapist is responsible for not mistaking the patient's fear for cooperation, and the therapist is responsible for taking the patient's confirmation biases into account when speaking.

Obviously, if the therapist loses his temper or has sexual contact with a patient, he has failed to metacommunicate, to distinguish between play and reality. Less obviously, therapists who look like they are doing therapy— metacommunicating, interpreting what is happening in the room, managing the relationship—often are not. Instead, they may only be participating in a relationship that looks enough like therapy that nobody gets suspicious (although the patient can usually be counted on to respond cautiously about revealing herself when the therapist is only pretending).

What, then, is the difference between doing therapy and pretending to do therapy? It is a difference that I had hoped to imply in the title of this book, "using early memories" rather than just talking about them. Just talking about things keeps them out of the room, out of the conditioning effects of the therapy. Allowing the pattern in question to emerge in the therapy relationship puts the therapist in a position to change the pattern rather than merely to offer advice on how to handle it. I think the expression of patterns in early memories is distinctively well suited to this purpose.

Chapter Fourteen

Deadly Therapy

Everybody is talking about the weather but nobody does anything about it.

—Mark Twain

The difference between a therapy that engages a problematic pattern and a therapy that merely discusses it is analogous to theater director Peter Brook's (1968) distinction between good theater and "deadly theater." His description of deadly theater is so relevant to psychotherapy, in my opinion, that I think it is worth reviewing here. It sheds light on the most pervasive kind of impasse in therapy, that of avoiding rather than entering the patient's complexes. Here, I am following Goodwin's (2001) example that examined the parallels between Brook's deadly theater and the deadly classroom.

Theater is deadly, according to Brook, when it does not really engage the audience. The *really* is because audiences do not always want to be engaged, and often we enjoy a play or movie more when it leaves us alone emotionally, and engages us only superficially. Brook gives the example of the theatergoer who wants to become more "cultured" and prefers his Sophocles not to be played *for* the audience but to be shown *to* the audience as originally done (as if anyone can say how Oedipus was originally performed: usually this is code for stodginess). He also mentions the literature professor who prefers a remote Shakespeare or a distant Verdi, allowing him not to be bothered by the production, allowing him to recite the lines along with actors (preferably sotto voce), or to watch for and smirk at any departures from the text or the score. Melodrama and sitcoms are deadly theater; at best, they can be entertaining distractions, but they are never designed to change us.

Deadly therapy, then, is therapy that is occasionally interesting when the topic of conversation is interesting, but it is not about changing the patient.

Indeed, many therapists specifically say that therapy is not about changing patients. They say it is about exploring issues, or laying out options, or giving choices. These therapists are like actors who say that it is not their responsibility to tell a story in a way that is comprehensible to the audience.

Brook notes that actors may be trying to find a way to engage the audience, but such efforts are often seen as intrusions on the audience's space. Fighting this tendency is the perennial call to play tragedy as it is written. Brook notes that *as it is written* is not much of a guide. Aside from all that is not and can not be written, the responsiveness between a particular audience and a particular cast on a specific night cannot be anticipated. Brook notes the inferiority of an actor trying to portray pride independently of an audience, compared with one of his stage directions in which he asked the actress playing Isabella in *Measure for Measure* not to kneel before Angelo until the audience couldn't take any more. The analogy is a therapy that defines and recommends interventions independent of the patient's immediate sensibility. Such manualized treatments may teach patients how to hide their symptoms, but they are unlikely to change response tendencies, except for the most stereotypical of symptoms, that is, except for symptom presentations that imply the same underlying patterns for most patients (Westen, Novotny, & Thompson-Brenner, 2004). For example, Alcoholics Anonymous was designed for a certain kind of drinker—one who, in short, drinks to express his pride, anger, and masculinity by exerting dominion over the bottle (W., 1953). It is hardly a surprise that its effectiveness is diminished when applied to all drinkers, for example via court order.

Brook notes the effect of time limitations on deadliness. When economic realities force plays to go up with only three weeks' rehearsal, there is little the company can do besides memorize their lines and block their places on stage. Actors, lighting designers, playwright, and director cannot experiment to see what works, with *what works* being operationally defined as what the director, sitting in the seats, responds to as the surrogate audience. Similarly, time limitations in therapy can often impede the therapist's chances for learning how to work with a particular patient. Compare the role of the supervisor, by the way, with the role of the director in rehearsal. The deadly supervisor teaches the therapist how to follow the script, the treatment plan, the manual; the lively supervisor identifies with the patient and provides explicit feedback, versus the actual patient's metaphorical feedback, to the therapist about what works. Brook notes that having plenty of time is no good if it is not put to good use, and by the same token, having plenty of time to enter and change a patient's complexes will do no good if the therapist uses the time to avoid this kind of engagement.

Brook notes that "good theater depends on a good audience" (p. 21), adding, though, that it is very difficult for an audience to transform itself into a good audience once it is in the theater. His point is that a responsive, attentive, enthusiastic audience will cultivate an engaged and communicative performance. The same might be said of responsive, attentive, and enthusiastic patients: the rich get richer. What can therapists do to help patients be good patients? Brook says that an audience's responsiveness can be maximized by making artistic decisions with a specific play, theater, era, and audience in mind. Transporting productions to other countries is especially likely to produce deadliness. What works in London may not work in New York, and the director in rehearsal who acts as a surrogate for the typical Londoner cannot at the same time act as a surrogate for the typical New Yorker. Business that works on a particular stage cannot be exported to a different theater, and business not designed for a particular stage is deadly in the sense of being nonresponsive to its environment. In therapy, interventions that are not designed for a specific patient at a specific moment in a specific therapy are deadly. At a time when many of my interpretations had turned into canned speeches because I was imitating rather than doing psychoanalytic therapy, one patient told me that she dreamed she was clothes shopping and could not find anything that fit because all the dresses were "off the rack," where she needed something tailor-made because of the shape of her body. "Off the rack" became my watchwords for generic deadliness.

Another thing the company can do to maximize the audience's responsiveness is to make sure that the goal of technique is to heighten the audience's interest in the subject matter of the play. Two great sources of deadliness in theater are using technique to replace the subject matter and presenting subject matter without relying on technique at all. With the former, the goal might be said to be to heighten the audience's admiration for the novelty or creativity of the troupe. With the latter, the goal might be described as the presentation of the subject matter *as written*, which confirms the audience's expectations but does not produce discussion or interest. Yes, that can produce interest in Shakespeare or Verdi, but it does not produce interest in Edmund or Gilda. Lively therapists also use technique to heighten interest in the subject matter, by making it manifest in the room, but they do not use technique so noticeably as to make the treatment solely or primarily about the mechanics of the therapy.

In general, then, a lively therapist is content-driven enough to ensure that the conditioning effects of the therapy relate to the patient's problems, and technique-driven enough to ensure that the conditioning effects in the room generalize to other situations. The lively therapist's behavior is both specific to the moment and generic enough to transfer learning to life situations. Lively theater presents plays whose subject matter is, if not universally applicable, at least resonant with many people, but presents it in a manner that engages a specific audience.

Bullough (1912–1913) conceived of ideal theatergoers as somewhere between what he called under-distancers and over-distancers. Under-distancers relate the subject matter to themselves, but do so before understanding it in its own context. He mentions the apocryphal example of the man who shouted out during a production of *Julius Caesar*, warning Caesar of the impending plot on his life. Over-distancers understand the meaning of the play, but do not apply it to themselves. A friend of mine, a musician, enjoyed a production of *Amadeus*, but afterwards was surprised to hear my concern that it might have raised questions for him about his own career, even after I had discussed how pedestrian my own professional efforts seemed in light of Mozart's gifts.

Deadly theater may keep audiences from understanding the subject matter or it may not engage them enough to apply it to themselves. Deadly therapies are conducted by under-distancers and over-distancers; any one of us can be either at a given moment. The under-distancing therapist talks about what is going on in the room or converts the patient's material into a topic of conversation whose purpose is to make the therapy exciting, but the meaning of the material on its own terms is not understood. The patient and therapist are friendly (or, sometimes, are enemies), but there is no greater purpose in the relationship than in any other social connection. The over-distancing therapist conducts an intellectual analysis of the patient, and even of the transference, but does not really enter it. The patient learns to intellectualize about her problems, even learns to constrain her symptoms, but the underlying patterns remain the same.

Intersubjectivity's (Stolorow et al., 1987; Buirski and Haglund, 2001; Buirski, 2005) emphasis on "two-mind" versus "one-mind" psychology may be seen as an attempt to enliven psychotherapy. Deadly theater divides the contributions of audience and company; it may be construed as a "one-mind" approach to theater in which the company puts on the play and the audience perceives it. Lively theater might be construed as "two-mind" theater in which, with the director's help, the audience and company cocreate the theatrical event.

Behaviorism's distinction between rule-governed and contingency-shaped behavior (Skinner, 1953) is also relevant. Rule-governed behavior adheres to contingencies not experienced directly but described by words: "Don't touch the stove." Contingency-shaped behavior is directly learned in relation to the environment: The child touches the stove, it hurts, and the child does not touch it again under those conditions. The two forms of learning are not mutually exclusive; following rules becomes contingency-shaped when the rules work and direct contingencies often produce rules to facilitate later application of what was learned. Still, rule-governed behavior reinforces obedience to authority along with whatever behaviors are guided by good rules, and contingency-shaped behavior reinforces attention to the environment along with whatever behaviors are shaped by contingencies. This divergence is analogous to the distinction between the rigid parental respect in Confucianism and the immediate awareness and suspicion of rules in Taoism (Graham, 1981). In the interpersonal realm, rule-governed behavior decreases intimacy, even though there are obvious advantages if we can benefit from the knowledge of those who have gone before us and have experienced various situations. I think that attending to the supervisor or to books deadens therapy, though supervisors and books have much to teach, and attending to the patient as the relevant source of information about the efficacy of interventions enlivens therapy. Good supervisors offer suggestions (rules of conduct) but remind the therapist that the ultimate arbiter of their utility will be the effect of the suggested conduct on the patient.

My thesis is that early memories are especially well suited to the task of making therapy livelier. As sources of implicit rules of conduct, their use benefits from their being derived from the patient rather than from the therapist, the supervisor, or textbooks. Their intrinsic systems provide avenues for the therapist to enter the patient's problematic patterns, while the fact that they constitute the opening of the patient's autobiography helps ensure that they will be applicable to the patient's life and that the benefits of developing the autobiography will accrue. Psychosocial history, in general, is harder to enter than an early memory because it does not represent specific patterns in specific contexts. Immediate material from the sessions or events from the week can bring the therapy very much into the room but do not always seem clearly, as subject matter, to relate to the patient's character or identity. Early memories, like good literature and good theater, are specific enough to be understood as subject matter on their own terms and personally meaningful enough to be applicable to the patient's life and to the therapy dyad.

References

Ablon, J. S., & Jones, E. E. (1999). Psychotherapy process in the National Institute of Mental Health Treatment of Depression Collaborative Research Program. *Journal of Consulting and Clinical Psychology, 67*, 64–75.

Adler, A. (1931/1937). *What life should mean to you.* (Alan Porter, Ed.). Boston: Little, Brown, and Company.

APA Working Group on Investigation of Memories of Childhood Abuse. (1998). Final conclusions of the American Psychological Association Working Group on Investigation of Memories of Childhood Abuse. *Psychological Bulletin, 4*(4), 933–940.

Asimov, I. (1969). *Asimov's guide to The Bible: Volume Two, The New Testament.* New York: Random House.

Baer, R. (2003). Mindfulness training as a clinical intervention: A conceptual and empirical review. *Clinical Psychology: Science and Practice, 10*, 125–143.

Barkley, R. (1998). *Attention-deficit hyperactivity disorder: A handbook for diagnosis and treatment.* New York: Guilford.

Basso, K. H. (1996). *Wisdom sits in places: Landscape and language among the Western Apache.* Albuquerque: University of New Mexico Press.

Bateson, G. (1972). *Steps to an ecology of mind.* Chicago: University of Chicago Press.

———. (1979). *Mind and nature.* New York: Dutton.

Bateson, G., Jackson, D., Haley, J., & Weakland, J. (1956). Toward a theory of schizophrenia. In G. Bateson (1972), *Steps to an ecology of mind.* Chicago: University of Chicago Press.

Bettelheim, B. (1943). Individual and mass behavior in extreme situations. *Journal of Abnormal and Social Psychology, 38*, 417–452.

———. (1982). *Freud and man's soul.* New York: Knopf.

Boal, A. (1979). *Theatre of the Oppressed.* New York: Urizen Books.

Bordin, E. (1979). The generalizability of the psychoanalytic concept of the working alliance. *Psychotherapy: Theory, Research, and Practice, 16*(3), 252–260.

Brook, P. (1968). *The empty space*. New York: Atheneum.

Bruhn, A. (1985). Using early memories as a projective technique: The cognitive perceptual method. *Journal of Personality Assessment, 49*(6), 587–597.

———. (1990). *Earliest childhood memories. Volume 1: Theory and application to clinical practice*. New York: Praeger.

———. (3/19/05). http://www.arbruhn.com.

Buirski, P. (2005). *Practicing intersubjectively*. Lanham, MD: Aronson.

Buirski, P., and Haglund, P. (2001). *Making sense together: The intersubjective approach to psychotherapy*. New York: Aronson.

Bullough, E. (1912–1913). Psychical distance as a factor in art and an aesthetic principle. *British Journal of Psychology, 5*, 87–118.

Campbell, T. W. (1998). *Smoke and mirrors: The devastating effect of false sexual abuse claims*. New York: Plenum.

Chess, S. (1951). Utilization of childhood memories in psychoanalytic theory. *Journal of Child Psychiatry, 2*, 187–193.

Chiesa, M. (1994). *Radical behaviorism: The philosophy and the science*. Sarasota, FL: Authors Cooperative.

Commission on Children at Risk (2003). *Hardwired to connect: The new scientific case for authoritative communities*. New York: Institute for American Values.

Conquergood, D. (1998). Beyond the text: Toward a performative cultural politics. In S. J. Dailey (Ed.), *The Future of Performance Studies: Visions and Revisions*. Annandale, VA: National Communication Association.

Corey, F. C. (1998). The personal against the master narrative. In S. J. Dailey (Ed.), *The Future of Performance Studies: Visions and Revisions*. Annandale, VA: National Communication Association.

Cousineau, T. M., & Shedler, J. (in press). Predicting physical health: Implicit mental health measures versus self-report scales. *Journal of Nervous and Mental Disease*.

Darwin, C. (1859). *On the origin of species by means of natural selection*. London: John Murray.

———. (1871). *The descent of man, and selection in relation to sex*. London: John Murray.

Dawkins, R. (1976). *The selfish gene*. Oxford: Oxford University Press.

———. (1996). *Climbing mount improbable*. New York: Norton.

Deutsch, H. (1942). Some forms of emotional disturbance and their relation to schizophrenia. *Psychoanalytic Quarterly, 11*, 301–321.

Eliot, G. (1871/1994). *Middlemarch*. London: Penguin Books.

Exner, J. (2003). *The Rorschach: A comprehensive system*, 4th ed. New York: Wiley.

Feyerabend, P. (1975). *Against method*. London: New Left Books.

Fowler, C., & Hilsenroth, M. J. (1995). Early memories: An exploration of theoretically derived queries and their clinical utility. *Bulletin of the Menninger Clinic, 59*(1), 79–98.

Frank, J. D. (1971). Therapeutic factors in psychotherapy. *American Journal of Psychotherapy, 25*, 350–361.

Freud, S. (1898/1962). The mechanism of forgetfulness. In J. Strachey (Ed. and Trans.), *The standard edition of the complete psychological works of Sigmund Freud* (Vol. 3, 287–297). London: Hogarth Press.

———. (1899/1962). Screen memories. In J. Strachey (Ed. and Trans.), *The standard edition of the complete psychological works of Sigmund Freud* (Vol. 3, 300–322). London: Hogarth Press.

———. (1900/1953). The interpretation of dreams. In J. Strachey (Ed. and Trans.), *The standard edition of the complete psychological works of Sigmund Freud* (Vol. 4, Vol. 5, 339–630). London: Hogarth Press.

———. (1901/1960). Childhood memories and screen memories. In *The psychopathology of everyday life*. In J. Strachey (Ed. and Trans.), *The standard edition of the complete psychological works of Sigmund Freud* (Vol. 6, 43–52). London: Hogarth Press.

———. (1910/1957). Leonardo da Vinci and a memory of his childhood. In J. Strachey (Ed. and Trans.), *The standard edition of the complete psychological works of Sigmund Freud* (Vol. 11, 57–137). London: Hogarth Press.

———. (1911–1915/1958). Papers on technique. In J. Strachey (Ed. and Trans.), *The standard edition of the complete psychological works of Sigmund Freud* (Vol. 12, 85–171). London: Hogarth Press.

———. (1914/1958). Remembering, repeating, and working-through (further recommendations on the technique of psycho-analysis II). In J. Strachey (Ed. and Trans.), *The standard edition of the complete psychological works of Sigmund Freud* (Vol. 12, 145–156). London: Hogarth Press.

———. (1915/1958). Repression. In J. Strachey (Ed. and Trans.), *The standard edition of the complete psychological works of Sigmund Freud* (Vol. 14, 146–158). London: Hogarth Press.

———. (1917a/1955). A childhood recollection from *Dichtung und Wahrheit*. In J. Strachey (Ed. and Trans.), *The standard edition of the complete psychological works of Sigmund Freud* (Vol. 17, 147–156). London: Hogarth Press.

———. (1917b/1963). Analytic therapy. In *Introductory lectures on psycho-analysis*. In J. Strachey (Ed. and Trans.), *The standard edition of the complete psychological works of Sigmund Freud* (Vol. 16, 448–463). London: Hogarth Press.

———. (1917c/1963). The development of the libido and the sexual organizations. In *Introductory lectures on psycho-analysis*. In J. Strachey (Ed. and Trans.), *The standard edition of the complete psychological works of Sigmund Freud* (Vol. 16, 320–338). London: Hogarth Press.

Gilligan, C. (1982). *In a different voice*. Cambridge, MA: Harvard University Press.

———. (2002). *The birth of pleasure*. New York: Knopf.

Goethe, J. W. (1808/1985). *Faust: Part 1* (Peter Salm, Trans.). New York: Bantam Books.

Goffman, E. (1959). *The presentation of self in everyday life*. New York: Doubleday.

Goodwin, J. (2001). Challenging and transforming deadly spaces of authority: steps towards a responsible and responsive educational body. Borderlands: Remapping Zones of Cultural Practice and Representation. University of Massachusetts Amherst. March 31, 2001.

——. (2005). Applied theatre in corrections: Community, identity, learning and transformation in the facilitated, collaborative processes of performative, artistic praxis. (Unpublished doctoral dissertation, University of Massachusetts, Amherst, 2005.)

Graham, A. C. (1981). *Chuang-tzu: The inner chapters* (Ed. and Trans.). London: George Allen & Unwin.

Grencavage, L. M., & Norcross, J. C. (1990). Where are the commonalities among the therapeutic common factors? *Professional Psychology: Research and Practice, 21*(5), 372–378.

Haley, J. (1973). *Uncommon therapy: The psychiatric techniques of Milton H. Erickson*. New York: Norton.

Haney, C., Banks, W. C., & Zimbardo, P. G. (1973). *Study of prisoners and guards in a simulated prison* (Naval Research Reviews 9 (1–17)). Washington, DC: Office of Naval Research.

Hayes, S., Follette, V., & Linehan, M. (Eds.) (2004). *Mindfulness and acceptance: Expanding the cognitive-behavioral tradition*. New York: Guilford.

Hillman, G. (2001). *Journey of Discouragement and Hope: An Introduction to Arts and Corrections* [Web page]. Community Arts Network. Retrieved April 10, 2005, from the World Wide Web: http://www.communityarts.net/readingroom/ archivefiles/2001/12/a_journey_of_di.php.

Hirn, Y. (1900/1960). *The origins of art*. Excerpted in M. Rader (Ed.), *A modern book of esthetics*, 72–76. New York: Holt, Rinehart, & Winston.

Horney, K. (1950). *Neurosis and human growth*. New York: Norton.

Johnstone, K. (1981). *Impro: Improvisation and the theatre*. New York: Routledge.

Jones, E. E. (2000). *Therapeutic action*. New York: Aronson.

Jørgensen, C. R. (2004). Active ingredients in individual psychotherapy: Searching for common factors. *Psychoanalytic Psychology, 21*(4), 516–540.

Jung, C. (1926). A review of the complex theory. In *Collected Works*, Vol. 8, 92–104. New York: Bolligen-Pantheon.

——. (1928). Two essays in analytical psychology. In *Collected Works*, Vol. 9. New York: Bolligen-Pantheon.

Karson, M. (1980). Is aesthetic judgment impaired by neuroticism? *Journal of Personality Assessment, 44*, 499–506.

——. (2001). *Patterns of child abuse: How dysfunctional transactions are replicated in individuals, families, and the child welfare system*. New York: Haworth.

——. (2005). Ten things I learned about report writing in law school (and the eighth grade). *The Clinical Psychologist*, 4–11.

Karson, M., & Dougher, M. (1980). *Is psychoanalytic technique the natural consequence of behavior theory?* Unpublished manuscript.

Karson, M., Karson, S., & O'Dell, J. (1997). *16PF interpretation in clinical practice: A guide to the Fifth Edition*. Champaign, IL: Institute for Personality and Ability Testing.

Karson, M., & Kline, C. (4/4/04). Two interpretations of Jim Wood's specimen Rorschach protocol. *WebPsychEmpiricist*. http://wpe.info/papers_table.html.

Kelly, G. A. (1955). *The psychology of personal constructs*. New York: Dutton.

Kernberg, O. (1975). *Borderline conditions and pathological narcissism*. New York: Aronson.

———. (1984). *Severe personality disorders*. New Haven: Yale University Press.

Kohut, H. (1971). *The analysis of the self*. New York: International Universities Press.

———. (1977). *The restoration of the self*. New York: International Universities Press.

Kris, E. (1956a). The personal myth. *Journal of the American Psychoanalytic Association, 4*, 653–681.

———. (1956b). The recovery of childhood memories in psychoanalysis. *Psychoanalytic Study of the Child, 11*, 54–88.

Krohn, A., & Mayman, M. (1974). Object representations in dreams and projective tests. *Bulletin of the Menninger Clinic, 38*, 445–466.

Langellier, K. M. (1998). Voiceless bodies, bodiless voices: the future of personal narrative performance. In S. J. Dailey (Ed.), *The Future of Performance Studies*. Annandale, VA: National Communication Association.

Langs, R. J. (1959). A pilot study of aspects of the earliest memory. *A.M.A. Archives of Neurology and Psychiatry, 81*, 709.

———. (1965a). Earliest memories and personality: A predictive study. *Archives of General Psychiatry, 12*, 379–390.

———. (1965b). First memories and characterologic diagnosis. *Journal of Nervous and Mental Disease, 141*, 318–320.

———. (1967). Stability of earliest memories under LSD-25 and placebo. *Journal of Nervous and Mental Disease, 144*, 171–184.

———. (1978). *The listening process*. New York: Aronson.

Langs, R. J., Rothenberg, M. B., Fishman, J. R., & Reiser, M. F. (1960). A method for clinical and theoretical study of the earliest memory. *Archives of General Psychiatry, 7*, 523–534.

Laudan, L. (1981). *Science and hypothesis*. Dordrecht, Holland: D. Reidel.

Linehan, M. (1993). *Cognitive-behavioral treatment of borderline personality disorder*. New York: Guilford.

Loftus, E. (1979). *Eyewitness testimony*. Cambridge, MA: Harvard University Press.

Loftus, E., & Ketcham, K. (1994). *The myth of repressed memory: False memories and allegations of sexual abuse*. New York: St. Martin's Griffin.

Madanes, C. (1981). *Strategic family therapy*. San Francisco: Jossey-Bass.

Madison, J. (1788/1945). The particular structure of the new government and the distribution of power among its parts. In A. Hamilton, J. Madison, and J. Jay, *The Federalist* or *The new constitution*, No. 47, 321–329. New York: The Heritage Press.

Mahler, M., Pine, F., & Bergman, A. (1975). *The psychological birth of the human infant: Symbiosis and individuation*. New York: Basic Books.

Maslow, A. (1962). *Toward a psychology of being*. New York: Van Nostrand.

Masterson, J. F. (1981). *The narcissistic and borderline disorders*. New York: Brunner-Routledge.

Mayman, M. (1968). Early memories and character structure. *Journal of Projective Techniques and Personality Assessment, 32*, 303–316.

Mayman, M., & Faris, M. (1960). Early memories as expressions of relationship paradigms. *American Journal of Orthopsychiatry, 30*, 507–520.

McLean v. Arkansas Bd. of Ed., 529 F. Supp. 1255 (E.D. of Ark., 1982).

McWilliams, N. (1999). *Psychoanalytic case formulation*. New York: Guilford.

Meichenbaum, D., & Turk, D. C. (1987). *Facilitating treatment adherence: A practitioner's guidebook*. New York: Plenum.

Murfee, E. (1995). *Eloquent evidence: Arts at the core of learning*. Washington: The President's Committee on the Arts and Humanities.

Nietzsche, F. (1879/1962). Introduction. In *Philosophy in the tragic age of the Greeks* (Marianne Cowan, Trans.). Washington: Regnery.

———. (1886/1966). *Beyond good and evil*. New York: Vintage Books.

———. (1891/1977). *Thus spake Zarathustra*. In W. Kaufmann (Ed. and Trans.), *The portable Nietzsche*. New York: Penguin Books.

Nigg, J. T., Lohr, N. E., Westen, D., Gold, L. J., & Silk, K. R. (1992). Malevolent object representations in borderline personality disorder and major depression. *Journal of Abnormal Psychology, 101*(1), 61–67.

Ogden, T. (1981). *Projective identification and psychotherapeutic technique*. New York: Aronson.

Park-Fuller, L. (2000). Performing absence: the staged personal narrative as testimony. *Text and Performance Quarterly, 20*(1), 20–42.

Rank, O. (1936). *Will therapy and truth and reality*. New York: Knopf.

Rom, P. (1965). Goethe's earliest recollection. *Journal of Individual Psychology, 21*, 189–193.

Rosenzweig, S. (1936). Some implicit common factors in diverse methods of psychotherapy. *American Journal of Orthopsychiatry, 6*, 412–415.

Santayana, G. (1910). Introduction. In *Spinoza's Ethics and De Intellectus Emendatione* (Andrew Boyle, Trans.). New York: E. P. Dutton & Co.

Schachter, D. (2001). *The seven sins of memory: How the mind forgets and remembers*. Boston: Houghton Mifflin.

Selvini-Palazzoli, M., Boscolo, L., Cecchin, G., & Prata, G. (1980). Hypothesizing—Circularity—Neutrality: Three guidelines for the conductor of the session. *Family Process, 19*, 3–13.

Shapiro, S., & Shapiro, S. (2002). Silent voices, bodies of knowledge: Towards a critical pedagogy of the body. In S. Shapiro & S. Shapiro (Eds.), *Body movements: Pedagogy, politics and social change*. Cresskill, NJ: Hampton Press.

Shedler, J., Mayman, M., & Manis, M. (1993). The *illusion* of mental health. *American Psychologist, 48*, 1117–1131.

Skinner, B. F. (1953). *Science and human behavior*. New York: Free Press.

———. (1957). *Verbal behavior*. New York: Appleton-Century-Crofts.

———. (1971). *Beyond freedom and dignity*. New York: Knopf.

———. (1974). *About behaviorism*. New York: Random House.

———. (1985). Cognitive science and behaviorism. *British Journal of Psychology, 76*, 291–301.

———. (1987). What religion means to me. *Free Inquiry, 7*(2), 12–13.

Stolorow, R. D., Brandchaft, B., & Atwood, G. E. (1987). *Psychoanalytic treatment: An intersubjective approach*. Hillsdale, NJ: Analytic Press.

Stuart, R. B. (2004). Twelve practical suggestions for achieving multicultural competence. *Professional Psychology: Research and Practice*, *5*(1), 3–9.

Sullivan, L. H. (1896). The tall office building artistically considered. *Lippincott's Magazine*, *57* (March), 403–409.

Tolstoy, L. (1869/1957). Epilogue, Part 2. In *War and Peace* (Rosemary Edmonds, Trans.). London: Penguin.

U.S. v. Carroll Towing Co., 159 F.2d. 169 (2nd Cir., 1947).

Van Erven, E. (2001). *Community theatre: global perspectives*. London, New York: Routledge.

W., B. (1953). *Twelve steps and twelve traditions*. New York: Alcoholics Anonymous Publishing.

Wali, A., Severson, R., & Mario, L. (2002). *The Informal Arts: Finding Cohesion, Capacity And Other Cultural Benefits In Unexpected Places Executive Summary Of Final Report*. Chicago: The Chicago Center for Arts Policy at Columbia College.

Watzlawick, P., Bavelas, J. B., & Jackson, D. (1967). *Pragmatics of human communication*. New York: Norton.

Watzlawick, P., Weakland, J., & Fisch, R. (1974). *Change: Principles of problem formation and problem resolution*. New York: Norton.

Weiss, J. (1993). *How psychotherapy works*. New York: Guilford Press.

Westen, D., Novotny, C., & Thompson-Brenner, H. (2004). The empirical status of empirically supported psychotherapies: Assumptions, findings, and reporting in controlled clinical trials. *Psychological Bulletin*, *130*(4), 631–663.

Whitehead, A. N. & Russell, B. (1910). *Principia Mathematica*. Cambridge: Cambridge University Press.

Wilson, E. O. (1998). *Consilience: The unity of knowledge*. New York: Knopf.

Winnicott, D. W. (1971). *Playing and reality*. London: Tavistock.

Wood, M. (2003). *Shakespeare*. New York: Basic Books.

Index

About the Author

Michael Karson teaches in the Graduate School of Professional Psychology at the University of Denver. Prior to that he practiced psychotherapy and consulted in the child welfare system for twenty-five years in Massachusetts. He is the author of *Patterns of Child Abuse: How Dysfunctional Transactions are Replicated in Individuals, Families and the Child Welfare System*, and he is senior author of *16PF Interpretation in Clinical Practice: A Guide to the Fifth Edition*. He is also an attorney.